DATE DUE			

Migration, Kinship, and Community:

Tradition and Transition in a Spanish Village

Migration, Kinship, and Community:

Tradition and Transition
in a Spanish Village

Stanley H. Brandes
Michigan State University

Academic Press

New York   San Francisco   London

A Subsidiary of Harcourt Brace Jovanovich, Publishers

ACADEMIC PRESS, INC.
111 Fifth Avenue, New York, New York 10003

United Kingdom Edition published by
ACADEMIC PRESS, INC. (LONDON) LTD.
24/28 Oval Road, London NW1

Library of Congress Cataloging in Publication Data

Brandes, Stanley H
      Migration, kinship, and community : tradition and
transition in a Spanish village.

      (Studies in social discontinuity)
      Bibliography: p.
      Includes index.
      1.   Becedas, Spain—Social conditions.   2.   Becedas,
Spain—Rural conditions.   3.   Migration, Internal—Cas-
tile.   I.   Title.   II.   Series.
HN590.B39B73 1975   301.32′6′0946359   74-27775
ISBN 0–12–125750–9

61584

To George McClelland Foster

STUDIES IN SOCIAL DISCONTINUITY

Under the Consulting Editorship of:

CHARLES TILLY
University of Michigan

EDWARD SHORTER
University of Toronto

Contents

Preface

Más vale lo malo conocido que lo bueno por conocer—"Bad things, already familiar, are preferable to good things, still unknown." This Castilian saying underscores the much reputed traditionalism of rural Spain, the tendency of her people to adhere to time-tested ways, to resist outside influences and temptations, to stick narrowly within the psychological and geographic confines of the *patria chica*, the small local unit, be it village or town, in which one is born, marries and dies.

However true this national portrait may have been in the past, it can no longer be said to apply. For the Spanish countryside today is undergoing an upheaval of unparalleled magnitude and rapidity. With increasing speed, advanced agricultural machinery is being introduced, small dispersed land parcels are being consolidated, and huge tracts of dry, barely productive fields are becoming rich and fertile through modern irrigation projects. Concomitant to these changes is an astounding migration of peoples. In marginal mountain villages, where the terrain prevents the transformation of outmoded agricultural techniques, men who can migrate to the cities or to foreign countries are doing so in growing numbers. The same pattern can be found in more productive regions, where machinery has created an enormous excess labor market.

The result of this tremendous migration has been the rapid depopulation of the countryside. Almost weekly, one can read in Spanish provincial newspapers about how isolation and loneliness have impelled the few remaining inhabitants of a settlement to leave, thus creating a virtual ghost town. For all but a few fortunate areas, migration has, at the very least, sharply reduced the numbers of young men and women of childbearing age in the small communities. No matter what its magnitude, the rural exodus is presently affecting Spaniards of all regions and social strata.

The purpose of this volume is to assess the nature and impact of depopulation on a small peasant village in southwestern Castile, called Becedas. Located in one of the highest permanently populated regions in the Iberian peninsula, Becedas' agricultural situation has become increasingly marginal over the past two decades. The mountainous, broken terrain which surrounds the village makes large-scale land consolidation and mechanization virtually impossible. Nearby villages, with a more favorable and gently rolling topography, benefit from vigorous governmental programs designed to modernize agricultural production methods. Yet Becedas must reconcile herself to the continued use of a centuries-old technology, a technology that places villagers in a steadily less advantageous market position.

It is this technological stagnation, above all, which sets Becedas apart from many other European peasant communities represented in the social scientific literature. For although Becedas has experienced enormous economic and cultural changes over the past generation, these changes have not been generated by technological transformations. Rather, they have occurred despite the marked persistence of ancient modes of production. Becedas' story, in part, is that of a village trying to modernize by transcending and circumventing the impediments caused by an outmoded technology.

If any single, overriding factor may be isolated to account for the recent changes, it is emigration. More than anything else, the high rate of migration out of the community has been responsible for vastly altered land tenure arrangements, standards of living, marriage patterns, and, in fact, a whole array of new village conditions, attitudes, and culture patterns. Traditional life is still largely observable in Becedas, and it is important, for the ethnographic record, to describe and analyze it fully. Yet even when considering the most time-honored features of village culture, we must turn persistently to emigration for an understanding of contemporary patterns. Though hardly two decades old, the exodus has everywhere left its mark.

If emigration has created significant socioeconomic alterations, does this also mean that Becedas, as an ongoing peasant community, is doomed to oblivion? The extant literature would lead us to believe that it does.

Even the titles of major synthesizing volumes, such as *The Vanishing Peasant* (Mendras 1970), *Peasants No More* (Lopreato 1967), and *The European Peasantry: The Final Phase* (Franklin 1969), emphasize the disappearance of peasant life on the continent. And this view is confirmed by numerous case studies, which confront us with a restricted range of probable alternatives for the future of rural Europeans: (1) impoverished isolation, (2) proletarianization as agricultural laborers, or (3) total integration within urban national culture, society, and economy. Are prosperity, economic development, and modernization antithetical to the survival of an autonomous peasantry, as these alternatives indicate? It is to this question that the present work is, in large measure, directed.

My thesis, in brief, is that, in Becedas, the traditional mechanisms of community integration and identity have survived and even become extended in the face of acute economic and cultural change. Throughout the mountainous regions of Europe, massive emigration and technological stagnation usually portend either the increasing marginalization and demise of small peasant communities, or their rapid transformation into tourist centers or incipient bedroom communities to nearby industrial plants. In Becedas, however, the same ecological conditions have created a village of independent proprietors living in prosperous circumstances and sharing as never before in the cultural benefits of their developing society. Moreover, these changes have not resulted in social disintegration and atomization, as we have been led to suspect. To the contrary, the viability of the community as an ongoing, discrete entity, with its own identity, cohesiveness, and sense of integrity, has remained relatively secure. The new economic adaptations and cultural patterns brought on by emigration are becoming incorporated within and phrased through a familiar structural framework. Thus, while it can no longer be claimed that Becedas is today a classic peasant community, the village is still very much a part-society, in Kroeber's (1948) and Foster's (1953) sense of the term.

All over the peasant world—in Asia, Latin America, the Middle East, portions of Sub-Saharan Africa—rural peoples are subject to the same transformations that have occurred and are still occurring in Europe. Within the relatively small European continent there exists an extraordinary degree of cultural and ecological diversity. Far from eliciting a uniform response, industrialization and modernization have stimulated a variety of rural adaptations. To the extent that socioeconomic conditions in Europe mirror conditions elsewhere, the European experience foreshadows what we may expect to happen in other parts of the world. Hopefully, the present analysis will point the way to a heretofore relatively unrecognized route in the modernization and economic development of traditional peasant peoples.

Acknowledgments

Throughout every stage of the present study, I benefited enormously from the assistance and encouragement of friends and colleagues. Professors Richard Herr, Susan T. Freeman, and Carmelo Lisón Tolosana gave freely of their time and advice throughout the early months of fieldwork, and helped me establish myself as an independent researcher in Spain. Officials of the Consejo Superior de Investigaciones Científicas in Madrid, and of the Casa de la Cultura and Ministerio de Hacienda in Avila, assisted me fully in the use of their libraries and documentary collections. Ignacio Bengoechea and Delfín Ibáñez Niño, both of the Confederación Hidrográfica del Duero in Valladolid, saved me hours of labor by providing me with a copy of their outline village map, and José Luis García of the University of Salamanca helped with the collection of migration data. To May N. Diaz and Stanley Chojnacki I owe thanks for comments on portions of an earlier draft of the manuscript.

Two people deserve a special word of gratitude: first, George Foster, whose love of fieldwork, respect for informants, and care in data analysis have served as a constant source of inspiration to me; and second, my wife Judy, without whose supreme enthusiasm, adaptability, and sensitivity to surroundings this study might never have taken place. Both these people have been intimately involved in every aspect of my research.

Most of all, I must offer heartfelt thanks to the people of Becedas, who form the subject of this study. They willingly and good-naturedly tolerated our little invasion of their world, and openly gave of their knowledge. No fieldworker could ever hope for a more hospitable research environment, or a more accepting and sympathetic people, than that found in Becedas. In recognition of the villagers' own desires, as expressed to me in 1972, I herein abandon the community pseudonym Navanogal, which I have to this point employed in publications. I can only wish that this volume will impart to the people of Becedas some small measure of the very great recognition they deserve.

My family and I resided in Becedas during two separate periods, the initial stay from April 1969 to June 1970, and a two-month revisit during the summer of 1972. The preparation, research, and write-up of the study were supported by grants from the National Institute of General Medical Services (Training Grant GM-1224), Wenner-Gren Foundation for Anthropological Research, and Michigan State University All-University Research Fund. To all these agencies I am indebted for providing me the opportunity to engage in the work I love best.

Migration, Kinship, and Community:

Tradition and Transition
in a Spanish Village

Plate 1 Amador Trapero plowing an orchard.

I

Migration and Peasant Society

PEASANTS AND THE PEASANT COMMUNITY

To most laymen, as indeed to many social scientists, the term "peasant" often evokes a noticeable degree of discomfort, particularly when used in reference to European peoples or to peoples of European ancestry. Commonly, peasants are associated with the distant past, or with extremely poor, economically undeveloped parts of the modern-day world. They are, of course, also an essential ingredient of fairy tales and romantic sagas and, on this ground, are thought to be the proper subject matter of folklorists and literary experts. More often than not, when people learn that students of contemporary Western culture also focus on peasants, they greet the knowledge with a mixture of curiosity, disbelief, and mild amusement. Only among a relatively limited but growing group of scholars is such parlance immediately accepted and understood.

It is not difficult to comprehend why the term frequently produces a confused reaction. For, to most Americans, the word "peasant" is value-laden and simultaneously brings to mind a mixture of negative and positive personality attributes. On the one hand, in the English lan-

1

guage as in many others, the term is clearly derogatory and may be used effectively as an insult. To say someone is a peasant is to call him a rural bumpkin and to paint a hopeless caricature of folksy naiveté. The word, in this sense, connotes stubbornness, die-hard conservatism, and lack of sophistication. Even academics, who have devoted their work to the study of traditional rural culture, have unwittingly perpetrated this negative image by defining the peasantry according to its presumably blind, uncritical adherence to fixed customs (Mahr 1945)—as if we modern Americans were guided entirely by rational motives and objective considerations.

At the same time, the word "peasant" conjures images of a bucolic ideal in which purity and harmony reign supreme, undisturbed by the corruption, anonymity, and personal animosities of modern urban existence. In this more positive sense, the peasantry is viewed as a poor but essentially contented group of people who dress in antiquated fashion and adhere to quaint and colorful customs and beliefs. This notion, as the famous ethnohistorian Julio Caro Baroja (1963) has pointed out, has been a deeply ingrained feature of Western philosophical and popular thought since antiquity. It became an important component of nineteenth-century Romanticism and is, even today, embodied in a whole school of folkloric studies devoted to ferreting out and describing in minute detail the unique festivals, songs, tales, proverbs—the whole dying heritage—of rural communities, which are viewed as repositories of the moribund spirit (*Zeitgeist*) and wisdom of the past. Here, we are confronted with an image of peasant, not as uncouth backward farmer, but rather as personification of the rural ideal and of what we ourselves might have been were it not for the contamination of urban, industrial life.

In fact, a casual drive through the contemporary European countryside does not necessarily clarify whatever sterotypic image of peasants we may have had. For the sharp juxtaposition of traditional and modern elements is as likely to jar and confuse the observer as to illuminate. From the highway—always depending, of course, on the region—we may observe the distinctive checkerboard pattern of small fields. Off in the distance is a tightly compact settlement of seemingly ancient houses, closely clustered in topsy-turvy fashion, with the whole dominated by a tall belfry. So far, our peasant stereotype is confirmed. Directly ahead, however, is a man in modern urban costume driving a large tractor and wearing an expensive wristwatch. Our picture is also disturbed by numerous television antennas jutting from the village rooftops, and by a maze of telephone wires polluting the landscape. In Brittany, we may stop to buy gas from an old woman wearing the traditional long black dress and high white coiffe. Along the Cantabrian range of northern Spain, the same service might be provided by a miniskirted lass in tri-heeled wooden shoes. These are, to be sure, just superficial manifestations of rural life, but they serve to illustrate the ambiguous and transitional nature of the European countryside, and the difficulty that confronts us if we attempt to categorize.

Fortunately, these kinds of stereotypes and impressions have not impeded social scientists of various disciplines and theoretical persuasions from trying to define peasantry and distinguish peasant communities from other rural types. In setting forth criteria for the definition of peasantry, scholars have tended to fall into two separate camps: those who emphasize the relationship between the small rural community and the outside world, and those who stress the social and economic organization of the community itself. These approaches are by no means mutually exclusive, for the internal structure of any group is largely a product of the way it is tied to the wider socioeconomic milieu. Yet, for analytical purposes, it is convenient and justifiable to differentiate between the two schools of thought, always keeping in mind that they provide complementary rather than contradictory portraits.

The definition of peasants as having a special relationship to the outside world may be traced to the work of the anthropologists Alfred Kroeber and George Foster. In 1948, speaking specifically of European countrymen, Kroeber wrote: "Peasants are definitely rural—yet live in relation to market towns; they form a class segment of a larger population which usually contains also urban centers, sometimes metropolitan capitals. They constitute part-societies with part cultures" (Kroeber 1948: 284). Foster's (1953) contribution, coming a half-decade later, was to seize this definition and apply it to a whole category of rural people found in all of the world's major civilizations, past and present. The kernel of both their arguments was that peasant communities were indeed "part-societies with part cultures." Without describing in detail the many debates aroused by this catchy though amorphous formula, let us now obtain an overview of the various dimensions of the Kroeber–Foster definition—political, economic, cultural, and social—as they have emerged in the social science literature.

The political dimension emphasizes peasant incorporation within a large centralized legal and authority system. To Eric Wolf, at any rate, it is the administrative and political ties of countrymen to a state which is the critical defining feature of a peasantry.

> Not the city, but the state is the decisive criterion of civilization and it is the appearance of the state which marks the threshold of transition between food cultivators in general and peasants. Thus, it is only when a cultivator is integrated into a society with a state—that is, when the cultivator becomes subject

to the demands and sanctions of power–holders outside his social stratum—that
we can appropriately speak of a peasantry. [Wolf 1966: 11][1]

Peasant communities, by extension, are low-level political–administrative
units whose internal affairs are regulated by laws and requirements imposed from above. In its relations with the state, the peasant community
is almost always said to be subordinate and impotent.[2]

The economic dimension of the Kroeber–Foster formula stresses the
nature of peasant exchange, particularly the absence of self-sufficiency.
Saul and Woods' recent conceptualization embodies this idea. Peasants,
they say, are "those whose ultimate security and subsistence lies in their
having certain rights in land . . . but who are involved, through rights
and obligations, in a wider economic system which includes the participation of non-peasants" (1971: 105). Peasants are integrated into
their respective national economies, relying on the products and services
that cities provide, and disposing of their surplus produce, usually also to
urban centers, in return for the cash necessary to make purchases. Often
too, peasants need cash as "funds of rent" (Wolf 1966: 10), periodic
charges paid to political powerholders who claim ultimate ownership over
the land.

The cultural aspect of peasant relations with the outside world has
always been one of its most critical distinguishing features. Since Foster's
(1953) early work, scholars have recognized that peasants maintain local
cultural traditions that are only varients of the larger culture in which
they are found. It has become common to adopt Redfield's (1956) terminology and distinguish two separate but interdependent levels of culture in preindustrial civilizations: the Great Tradition, including the
codified, written tenets and laws, which are closely adhered to by the
urban elite and which form the substratum of beliefs and practices of all
people within the wider society; and the Little Tradition, the local-level
beliefs and practices which derive ultimately from the Great Tradition
but which are not accepted much beyond the single community in which
they are found. Within each peasant community exist elements of both
these traditions. To this extent, every peasant community shares a common heritage with hundreds of other similar communities, but at the
same time is virtually unique; in other words, each peasant village is a
part-culture.

As Foster (1953, 1967) Marriott (1969), and others have pointed
out, there is a constant interchange between the Great and Little Tra-

---

[1] Recently, Foster has accepted Wolf's modification of his original definition, noting,
however, that powerholders are normally concentrated in cities (Foster, 1967:4).

[2] George Dalton (1974) has just published a brief, though convincing, critique of
this view.

ditions. Elements of the Little Tradition, such as local deities or regional folk songs or savings, may occasionally become "universalized," as it is said (Marriott 1969); that is, they are adopted by and incorporated in the Great Tradition. Much more commonly, however, elements of the Great Tradition, which almost always originate within the vibrant and stimulating atmosphere of large cities (Redfield and Singer 1954), diffuse downward and become "parochialized," simplified and transformed into unique elements at the local level. Peasant villages thus become little cultural enclaves, with customs and defining features of their own. Even to the most casual observer, however, they are recognizable as belonging to one larger culture, be it Spanish, Chinese, or Mexican, rather than to another.

Turning finally to the social dimension of peasantry, how may we understand the notion that peasants constitute "part-societies"? In the simplest sense, this means that peasants form just one stratum—almost always the lowest—within a large, complex, more or less hierarchically organized nation state. But in a more important way, to say that peasants constitute a part-society is to recognize the highly localistic bonds and identities of these rural peoples. To be sure, the peasant community is administratively, economically, and culturally tied to a much larger national system. But at the same time, it is this community within which most of a peasant's day-to-day activity takes place and among which the vast bulk of his social network is to be found. To a peasant, it is the village as a whole which sets standards of conduct and applies sanctions for their maintenance. It is the village, too, which provides a peasant with a feeling of security and identification in any relations he may have with the outside world. For this reason, each peasant village is its own tiny country within a larger country, or one of numerous little similar social systems within a bigger one.

This brings us to the second major perspective on peasantries, that which emphasizes the structural relationships within peasant communities themselves. Social scientific notions on the nature of the rural community must be traced at least as far as the late nineteenth century, to the works of Maine (1861), Tönnies (1963), and Durkheim (1964). Though none of these men spoke explicitly of "peasant" communities, in the sense that we understand them today, their ideas about the characteristics of small rural settlements have filtered into contemporary peasant studies, and exert a lasting influence on the way we perceive the internal organization of peasant villages throughout the world. In subsequent chapters, we shall be examining their specific concepts in detail. Here, it is sufficient to discuss the modern social scientific idea of community, always keeping in mind it has had a long and deeply ingrained history. Again, the picture is a composite of many disparate theories.

Scholars have been guided by three overriding notions about the internal structure of peasant communities, all of them emphasizing village unity and identity. First, it is said that these communities are small-scale entities in which all the members live in long association and come to know each other well. For Shanin (1971: 244), "the characteristics of the peasant village—its members being born into a single community, undergoing similar life experiences and necessarily involved in close, personal interaction—make for the highly traditional and conformist culture peculiar to the rural community. . . . The village is the peasant's world."

The small size of peasant communities and the intensity of ties within them have led people to call them "face-to-face" societies, not in the sense that everyone is constantly in everyone else's presence, but rather in that there is a fund of common knowledge about all community members. As Bailey (1971: 4–5) puts it, everyone in the community is invested with a reputation, the sum of common opinions which others hold about him. Because peasants of a single village know that they will have to live out their lives in one another's presence, and because their affairs are potentially or actually bound so closely with those of the others in the community, they are extremely sensitive about their reputations. In such an atmosphere, gossip flourishes, and it is through gossip, joking, ostracism, and other informal mechanisms of social control that the community keeps its members in line. To be sure, peasants are bound to the legal–administrative network of their respective nations. But each peasant community is also a law-enforcement agency unto itself, in that it sets its own behavioral rules and makes sure they are adhered to. In this sense, each community draws a boundary between itself and others and imparts to its members a feeling of distinctiveness vis-à-vis the outside world. One's reputation is nowhere so important as within one's own community, nor is anyone but a community member likely to concern himself with it.

Community identity and cohesion is also a product of a second critical characteristic of peasant settlements: their relative economic, social, and cultural homogeneity. Economically, as Frankenberg (1966: 287) has said, "most inhabitants in the [rural community] tend to be engaged in one common activity—agriculture." Community members not only share the same basis of subsistence, thereby creating a common way of confronting similar problems, but also organize labor along the same lines. Franklin (1969: 15–20) and Shanin (1971: 238–245) state the dominant opinion when they point to the importance of the family farm among peasantry. Within the peasant community, each household typically forms the basic unit of production and consumption, and carries out virtually the same activities as all other households. The tasks of each family are those of every other. Peasant labor organization thus creates a situation within each village which Durkheim (1964) would refer to as "mechanical solidarity," or social cohesion brought about through the mutual sympathies of people who share similar life circumstances.[3]

Socially, there are several respects in which the peasant community is homogeneous. Status differences may be minimal, particularly to the extent that everyone within the peasant village has more or less the same economic problems and social situation. Redfield (1947: 297) put it nicely when he said,

> The members of the [peasant] society have a strong sense of belonging together. The group which an outsider might recognize as composed of similar persons different from members of different groups is also the group of people who see their own resemblances and feel correspondingly united. Communicating intimately with one another, each has a strong claim on the sympathies of the others. Moreover, against such knowledge as they have of societies other than their own, they emphasize their own mutual likeness and value themselves as compared with others. They say of themselves "we" as against those who are "they."

In many parts of the peasant world, the sense of local distinctiveness held by each community vis-à-vis others has functioned to reduce status distinctions within the community itself.

It is often said, too, that peasant communities are homogeneous in that the basic organizational cell for all individuals is the family or kinship group. Whatever the dominant household or descent type, the community is composed of an aggregate of equivalent small units, thereby structuring social relationships along the same lines for all individuals. Equally significant, family ties for peasants are generally viewed as being strong and involving a host of mutual rights, obligations, and loyalties. And because the individual's life is so intimately bound to that of his family or kinsmen, so too is his reputation. A person is judged as much by the opinions that others hold of his family as by those they have of him.

Community homogeneity, finally, has a cultural dimension as well. People within the same village generally share the same values and have the same notions of what constitutes good and bad behavior, correct and improper ways of going about things. A community, as Bailey (1971: 4–9), has pointed out, is a moral entity, and it is the common set of moral standards held by members of a peasant village which, above all, acts to weld them together and serves to differentiate them from others. It is this set of standards, too, which allows peasants to feel that they understand

---

[3] It should be noted that, even though this economic definition has been discussed in the context of agricultural enterprises, farming is not the only occupation characteristic of peasants. As Foster (1967:6) has stated, "It is not *what* peasants produce that is significant; it is *how* and *to whom* they dispose of their produce that counts." All the economic criteria for identifying a peasantry may suit a community of potters or fishermen as well as they do an agricultural populace. Farmers form the most numerous, but certainly not the only, occupational type among world peasantry.

and can control the behavior of fellow community members. To this extent, they are more trusting and feel more comfortable in the presence of fellow villagers than with outsiders.

We come at last to the third internal organizational characteristic of peasant communities: the predominance of what Wolf (1966) has termed "multistranded" relationships. All interpersonal ties are invested with a variety of meanings. Thus, the household is not only a social group but also a production unit, and so closely bound are economic and domestic relationships that household members themselves can make no distinction between them. Similarly, community membership involves not only a common residential base, but also participation in shared ritual activity. In other words, interpersonal bonds within the peasant village involve multiple and overlapping roles, and people relate to one another simultaneously on several levels—economic, religious, and political, as well as social. This feature of interpersonal relationships is said to intensify village bonds and create a close cohesive network within the peasant community.

Thus far, we have presented a static portrait of peasants. We have tried to show, first, that peasants are defined primarily by their relationship to the outside world, and, second, that peasant communities have been considered to possess certain organizational features that give them an internal unity and distinguish them truly as part-societies. As mentioned, the discussion is a distillation—and a highly oversimplified one—of ideas that have developed about peasantry and the peasant community over the course of several generations. There is probably no single scholar who would subscribe to all the characteristics and definitional criteria set forth. Yet, when taken as a whole, these notions do represent analytical strands that have dominated contemporary peasant studies.

When we turn to the question of change in the countryside, we must take into account both community relations with the outside world and organizational features within the community itself, for most scholars have attributed changes within the peasant community primarily to alterations in the external ties of peasants. Let us now examine some prevalent ideas about how rural communities lose their critical sense of unity and distinctiveness, thereby becoming nonpeasant.

THE DISAPPEARANCE OF PEASANT COMMUNITIES

Having set forth both the criteria for the identification of peasants and the organizational features of peasant communities themselves, we may now ask why some rural cultivators are peasants and others modern farmers. Why, for example, does it disturb us to refer to a cultivator in Iowa as a peasant, while we are perfectly willing to use this appellation when speaking of a person with the same occupation in India, Egypt, or southern Europe? What is the threshold that separates peasants from modern farmers, and how can we identify when a community becomes nonpeasant in character? When, in short, can we proclaim the disappearance of the peasantry? The answers to these questions are in part implicit in the preceding discussion, though our purpose will be best served by drawing them out and placing them in relief. For the time being, we shall be concerned primarily with diagnostic criteria, rather than with the causal factors that bring about peasant demise.

It is possible to discern three overridingly important symptoms of the end of peasantry, which may be encountered time and again in the social scientific literature. (1) loss of cultural distinctiveness, (2) reorientation of economic identities and priorities, and (3) atomization and realignment of community social relationships. All of these changes in some way involve a restructuring of community ties to the outside world. In all cases, bonds to the larger society are altered to the point where the community cohesion and distinctiveness, which are the hallmarks of the peasant part-society, are no longer evident. As Halpern (1967: 124) says, "a fundamental impact of the rural revolution is the decline in the autonomy of the village community. It is no longer a world apart even in a limited way but an integral unit within the modern state."

Let us first examine the loss of cultural distinctiveness by the peasant community. The Little Tradition is a product of what anthropologists call *culture lag*, that is, the emulation of cultural styles of previous (usually urban) generations. Foster (1967: 11) describes this process as follows:

> Throughout history, they [the peasantry] have replenished and augmented their cultural forms by imitating customs and behavior of other members of their wider society. But since peasants comprehend imperfectly what they see in cities, the urban-inspired elements they acquire are reworked, simplified, and trimmed down so they can be accommodated to the less complex village existence. And because this process is slow, by the time urban elements are successfully incorporated into village culture, urban life has changed and progressed; thus, peasants are always doomed to be old fashioned. No matter how hard they have tried, what they have believed to be the last word has almost invariably reflected the city forms of earlier generations.

Almost always, it is this time component, the extremely slow process by which elements from the urban elite diffuse downward and outward to the peasantry, that creates the discrepancy between the Great and Little Traditions and provides the opportunity for, and conditions favorable to, regional differentiation. In fact, even adjacent villages within the same region interpret and accommodate to the same urban forms in slightly different ways, and these differences, in the local context, become magnified to the point where they create identifying boundaries between communities.

It is clear that this situation is different from that which prevails in contemporary rural America. A variety of conditions on this continent have assured that the modern urban ideas, products, and services are available to citizens in virtually every corner of the nation. Farmers in rural Iowa can buy the same supermarket produce, watch the same television programs, hear the same news broadcasts, and read the same fashion-setting magazines as do the urbanites of Milwaukee or Chicago. The population density of rural Iowa is lower than that in the city, but the life style and cultural repertoire is basically equivalent in the two types of settings.

To the extent that rural–urban cultural distinctions are becoming similarly eliminated in developing societies, so too we are witnessing the eclipse of peasant communities. From Latin America, Asia, the Middle East, southern Europe—in fact, from all over the peasant world—we receive steady reports of the blurring of rural–urban differences and the leveling of national cultures. This not only means that the identifying cultural symbols that differentiate one rural community from another become lost, thus reducing the distinctiveness of peasant settlements; it also spells the breakdown of cultural homogeneity within each community, by introducing virtually the same wide range of opinions, ideas, and world views that is found in urban areas. In these ways, communities become at once less discrete and more atomized than they were traditionally.

Similarly, changing economic relationships and identities also have been taken as indicative of the end of peasantry. This is true in two senses. First, in the modern setting, economic relationships become increasingly divorced from social ties, or, as Wolf (1966) would say, multistranded bonds become single-stranded. This is essentially the process that Max Weber (1958: 367) had in mind when, in 1906, he wrote:

> The old [peasant] economic order asked: How can I give, on this piece of land, work and sustenance to the greatest possible number of men? [Modern] capitalism asks: From this given piece of land how can I produce as many crops as possible for the market with as few men as possible?

The emphasis of this view, subsequently adopted and made popular by Chayanov (1966, Wolf 1966: 14–15), is that peasant economies are labor-intensive, seeking to find productive work for all available hands, while modern farming economies are capital-intensive, placing a precise monetary value on man-hours of labor and calculating this cost against profits. Thus, with the peasant household, "whether it be technical or economic, every decision concerning the farm also concerns the family, and vice-versa, since one cannot be separated from the other" (Mendras 1970: 81).

In the modern farming household, on the other hand, the head of the family is an occupational specialist and, to this extent, operates like the urban merchant, artisan, or doctor, apart from any regard for the labor commitment of his family. In other words, to the household head, agriculture becomes an occupation rather than an all-encompassing way of life.

Over and above the household level, too, there is a differentiation of economic from social roles, such that friendship, neighborship, and community membership do not necessarily imply economic obligations, as they generally do among traditional peasantry. In fact, it is said, there is a disintegration of extrafamilial relationships as they become extraneous to economic activities: "The system of inter-family economic, social and cultural relations is considerably weaker in such villages and gives way to relations over and beyond local bonds" (Galeski 1971: 125). The general impression is that the overlapping of economic and social roles operates as a glue that creates a tightly knit interpersonal network within the peasant community. Once these roles become separated, the glue disintegrates and intracommunity relations become at once less intense and more atomized.

This brings us to the second and related economic indicator of peasant decline: the breakdown in traditional cooperative forms of labor. Both Erasmus (1956) and Foster (1973: 60–61) have pointed to the importance of reciprocal economic labor exchanges in peasant societies throughout the world, and to the fact that these exchanges arise not only out of economic necessity, but also out of the need to validate and reinforce social relationships. They trace the decline of economic cooperation to the cultivator's acquisition of a modern rationalistic mentality, in which the desire for monetary profit conflicts with, and overtakes, the need to meet the economic obligations to a wide variety of kinsmen, friends, and other community fellows. "When he finds it is cheaper to hire a few hardworking peons instead of paying for food and drink for a larger number of fiesta-minded friends [who have gathered to help him with his work], he is ready to let this aspect of tradition slip into the past" (Foster 1972: 61). The substitution of commercialized individualistic work patterns for traditional cooperation thus also promotes breakdown of the close interpersonal network within the peasant community.

These economic developments all bear on our final indicator of the postpeasantry, that of social atomization. In the simplest sense, this means that the cultivator's network of interpersonal relationships is no longer tightly bounded within community limits, nor, as we have seen, is it based on intensive multistranded ties within his village. Largely for this reason, the postpeasant's identity no longer automatically emanates from his membership in a particular community. Rather, he happens to live in a certain village simply because it is occupationally the most convenient locale.

On a deeper level, however, social atomization results from the disappearance of the community as a discernible, unified moral and legal entity. Bailey (1971) considers moral unity, as expressed in common ideas about what is good and bad, proper and improper, to be the most critical defining feature of community. As previously discussed, the cultural homogeneity of the traditional peasant community does provide moral unity, in that its members hold a common set of standards for behavior, which comprise the basis for evaluation of all individuals. Once a community becomes heterogeneous, with individuals or groups possessing different sets of values, the common basis for judgment is eroded, and people no longer measure their behavior with reference to what others around them think. Informal sanctions (such as gossip, joking, or ostracism) are, under these conditions, relatively ineffective means for the community as a whole to assert control. Formal, anonymous legal mechanisms, imposed by agents from outside the community, come to predominate, and what was previously a peasant community becomes, insofar as the quality of interpersonal relationships is concerned, merely like a small city. In the new context, a person's reputation no longer helps to define community boundaries, for each individual comes to have many separate reputations, each particular to the variety of groups with whom he is tied socially and economically. And because these groups are not coterminus with the residential community itself, the importance of that community per se for each individual is considerably diminished.

All of the foregoing changes—cultural, economic, and social—are separated here for analytical convenience, though they are generally viewed as part of the same unified process of development, all stemming from the same causes and operating mutually to reinforce one another. So influenced are we by the notion that economic changes within rural communities are accompanied by social atomization and the loss of community identity and cohesion, that we hardly question the matter any more.

Do these changes really reflect one highly integrated developmental process? Does the acceptance of urban culture imply the loss of comcunity identity? Does economic adaptation necessarily yield community atomization and the separation of economic from social life? In short, are rural communities becoming less discrete and cohesive along with their increasing economic and cultural incorporation within the wider society? To examine these questions, we shall be focusing on a single small village in southwestern Castile, a village that has experienced a considerable degree of economic and cultural change as a result of massive migration. Let us first explore the relevance of migration to the question of the viability of peasant communities, as it has been portrayed in social scientific literature.

MIGRATION AND THE FUTURE OF THE PEASANT COMMUNITY

As we have seen, there have evolved different emphases in the definition of peasants and peasant communities, some focusing on the interrelationships of rural people with the outside world, and others concentrating on organizational features within the rural communities themselves. In either case, the migration of large numbers of people from these settlements to industrial centers in the home country or abroad may have a significant impact on the quality of economic, social, and cultural life in the countryside. Migration may, for example, denude a community of necessary farmhands, thus impelling cultivators to consolidate small, dispersed land parcels and to purchase tractors and other farm machinery for their efficient exploitation. This spells the transformation from a labor-intensive to a capital-intensive system of production. Migration, too, may produce an alteration in the peasant's economic self-identity. When a man witnesses many of his own neighbors and kinsmen resettling in the city and adopting new occupations, he begins to measure himself against them and think of himself as a farmer rather than as the head of a household farming enterprise. In other words, his economic role as head of the farm becomes increasingly divorced from his social role as head of the family, and he is that much further along the road to modernity.

Socially a reorientation takes place as well. Migration creates an expansion of each peasant's interpersonal network, such that ties with non-villagers are not only added to those with villagers themselves, but also may take precedence over intracommunity bonds. Should this occur, one's reputation among outsiders eventually becomes more important than one's reputation among fellow villagers, and the informal mechanisms of social control, operative in traditional times, become obsolete. The economic circumstances brought on by migration might also impel a restructuring of class relationships within each community. Mechanization and land consolidation often stimulate the development of a class system, consisting of large landholders and landless laborers, where none existed before. Under these conditions, the farmers with a slight financial edge are the ones who can best afford to modernize their enterprises, thus creating impossible competition for the less advantaged smallholders, who sell their parcels and are reduced to wage labor. A basically egalitarian social structure thus becomes hierarchical.

Perhaps above all, migration provides the conditions necessary for the disappearance of unique regional and local cultural traditions. Migrants become channels of communication, or "brokers," as Wolf (1956) would say, transmitting new customs, ideas, and fashions from the city to the countryside. They themselves become objects of prestige and models for emulation. And, through remittances and gifts, they provide postpeasants the means for maintaining an increasingly urban life style. As the eminent Spanish sociologist, Victor Pérez-Díaz (1971: 39), has put it:

> Emigration, in the course of the process of change, is oriented towards the suppression of their [the peasantry's] conditions of existence. The principal condition of existence is the contrast between the countryside and the city. And the process underway, which emigration symbolizes, works toward the reduction of this contrast, toward relative homogenization. This process of homogenization signifies that global society is unified under an urban, industrial model, through the expansion of this model in the rural orbit, and through the reduction of the unique conditions of rural life. . . . The integration and cultural unification of society under this model signifies a change of historical epochs, a change in the history of relationships between the countryside and the city. [my translation]

Migration, in other words, is one of the great forces operating today to dissolve the age-old part-society–part-culture relationship between rural peoples and their wider regional and national entities.

By way of caution, we should keep in mind that migration has not, and in many cases still does not, have this effect alone. For there are numerous instances in which migration may be viewed as part of the traditional social order and, indeed, as necessary for the maintenance of that order. Hence, it is useful to distinguish between two types of migration, differentiated on the basis of their relatively conservative or progressive roles. The first we may term *institutional migration*, that which is inherent in, and the supporter of, traditional socioeconomic relationships. This is found most conspicuously among peasantries in which impartible inheritance and the stem family prevail. The rural Irish (Arensberg and Kimball 1968), Japanese (Embree 1939), and Basques (Douglass 1969), for example, have had to maintain a delicate man–land ratio, which has precluded the division of farmsteads among heirs. One child inherits the farmstead, marries, and lives on with the aging parents. The siblings marry heirs to other farmsteads, live on singly with the heir, or migrate. Here, migration is a built-in economic safety valve for the perpetuation of the established order. Even where partible inheritance occurs, subdivision of parcels may become excessive for the maintenance of all heirs and their families, as has occurred, for example, in Galicia in northwest Spain (Gómez–Tabanera *et al.* 1967). Migration in these cases may become a regular and institutionalized solution to land pressure, operating little, if at all, to alter basic structural relationships within the society.

The second type of migration we might call *transformational migra-*

tion, because it is closely linked to profound changes in the economy and social structure of a people. Throughout history, there have been numerous examples of such transformational migration, among them the process of sedentarization by which previously nomadic groups gradually settle in agriculturally oriented towns and villages, and the large-scale involuntary transport of slaves from one setting to a completely different one. In the contemporary world, the most prevalent type of transformational migration is urbanization, the enormous exodus of people from the countryside to the city, which is ordinarily considered a necessary part of economic development. Typically, there is a substantial growth in the secondary and tertiary sectors of the economy, which usually have their locus in the city, and a consequent rise in the need for labor. At the same time, agriculture and other primary pursuits become increasingly mechanized and efficient, enabling rural people to produce more than before with fewer hands. The final result is an abrupt shift in the nation's population distribution, with urban areas expanding at the expense of the rural. This is, to be sure, a highly oversimplified sketch of an extremely complex process. It is presented here merely as representative of a type of migration that is closely bound to a wider process of socioeconomic change, a change that is perhaps as important to the future of the world as was the Neolithic revolution seven or eight millenia ago.

It is this type of transformational migration that is presently occurring in Spain and deeply affecting both urban and rural people. Certainly, as Kenny (1972: 124–125) points out, rural migration has been a persistent feature of Hispanic life over the past several centuries. But migration rates have never been so high as they have been since the late nineteenth century, when Spaniards began to move in large numbers to the Americas and to the countries of northern Europe (Del Campo Urbano 1972: 103–120).

Though the bulk of Spanish migration until 1950 was directed to foreign lands (González–Rothvoss 1953), this movement has been complemented over the past two decades by a massive migration of people within Spain itself. A cursory examination of the figures is enough to reveal the enormity of the recent internal migration. Throughout the years from 1901 to 1950, the number of migrants within Spain (as measured by movement from one province to another) varied annually from 95,000 to 117,000. During the decade 1951–1960, however, the annual number of internal migrants averaged over 229,500, about doubling the figures of previous decades. Since 1961, not a year has passed during which there have been fewer than 347,000 internal migrants; and in the period 1962–1970 alone, over 3½ million Spaniards, representing more than a tenth of the total population, made a significant change of residence within the country (Del Campo Urbano 1972: 134–135).

Though these figures gauge the movement between provinces, it is clear that the more significant dimension of this population change is the migration from rural to urban areas. As demonstrated in a number of recent studies (Benítez 1967; García Fernández 1964; Martínez 1966; Siguán 1966), the rural exodus has characterized all of Spain during the past two decades. During the first half of this century, from 1900 to 1950, the proportion of the Spanish population active in agriculture dropped from 70% to 50%. Though these figures are of undoubted significance, it is striking that during the 13 subsequent years, from 1950 to 1963, the proportion dropped fully 10% more (Flores 1969: 129). At the same time, there has been an enormous growth of Spanish cities. The largest cities, those with more than 100,000 population, are the ones that have experienced the most rapid and dramatic expansion, such that the proportion of Spaniards living in these urban centers increased from 9% in 1900 to 28% in 1960 (Díez Nicholás, 1972: 193). Even smaller cities, those above 10,000 population, have experienced significant growth, all at the expense of the rural areas (Díez Nicholás 1972: 155–169).

It is hardly surprising that the urbanization process has been matched by an astounding industrial growth. In fact, the highest rates of internal migration in this century have occurred in the years since 1950, as well as in the decade 1920–1930, that is, during the periods of greatest Spanish industrialization (Díez Nicholás 1972: 171). To take just one indicator of this economic growth, the years 1950 to 1965 witnessed a fivefold increase in steel production, from 681,000 to 3,515,000 tons. Over the same period, electrical energy production rose from 7 to 31 billion killowatt hours. Growth is visible in other industrial areas as well, all of which have developed rapidly since 1960 (Pérez–Díaz 1969: 31). To these figures must be added the enormous recent rise in tourism, one of Spain's most profitable industries. In 1971, for example, over 26 million foreigners visited the country, an overwhelming figure when we consider that Spain's total population at the time was under 34 million (Instituto Nacional 1972: 33, 355).

No wonder, then, that the country's largest industrial centers—Madrid, Barcelona, and Bilbao—and its heavily touristed coastal regions are growing at faster rates than the rest of the nation (Díez Nicholás 1972: 192–196). It is only in the context of this booming Spanish economy that rural depopulation, and especially the rise in internal migration, may be understood. For it is this economic development that has provided the unskilled and semiskilled jobs by which former peasants generally earn their living when moving to the city or to centers of tourism.

The astounding economic development and internal migration that has recently taken place in Spain cannot but help affect people of all regions and social strata. Certainly, the small Castilian peasant communities of

Iberia's heartland can be no less disturbed by these changes than the rest. Traditionally, peasant villages in Old Castile, such as the one analyzed in this book, have been archtypical "closed corporate communities," in Wolf's (1955, 1957) sense of the term. They have been corporate in that they have held large quantities of land and other resources in common and have organized themselves for the allocation of rights over these resources. They have sharply limited participation by outsiders in community economic affairs, thereby effectively restricting their membership to those who have been born or married into the village. High rates of community endogamy, constant participation in an elaborate round of community processions and other religious events, as well as a tendency to restrict the flow of outside goods and ideas into the community, all have operated to isolate and insulate it against outside incursions and development. It is largely because of these village characteristics that Caro Baroja (1957) has referred to the "sociocentrism," or inward-looking and self-contained nature, of the Castilian *pueblo*. Despite the *pueblo*'s undeniably important relationships with the outside, it was, in terms of the daily life of its inhabitants, a little world unto itself.

As Wolf (1957) points out, even though the closed corporate community has been a tenacious and widespread form of peasant existence, it cannot resist being broken down under certain socioeconomic conditions. In particular, Wolf states that high rates of community migration and the requirements of a national market system, which demands economic specialization, operate to transform the closed community into an "open" peasant community. Economic individualism and the dissolution of community barriers against outside commodities and ideas tend to undermine the sense of village identity and cohesion that prevails under traditional circumstances.

Is this development inevitable, as so much of the literature suggests? In subsequent chapters, we shall be examining the answer to this question in detail by looking at recent developments in the Old Castilian community of Becedas. Becedas has experienced a high rate of out-migration over the past two decades. During that time, too, it has become increasingly involved in the world market, and its farmers have had to specialize to a greater degree than ever before. The people of Becedas are also more prosperous than ever, and share as never before in the cultural benefits of their developing society. By all expectations, these changes should have resulted in the social atomization and disintegration of the community. Instead, however, the viability of the community as an ongoing, cohesive entity, providing its members a sense of integrity and identity, has remained secure and, perhaps, even become strengthened. Before examining why, let us first obtain an overview of Becedas and its environment.

Plate 2   Antonio Trapero collecting firewood in the Becedas *sierra*.

II

An Overview of Village and Region

BECEDAS AND HER NEIGHBORS

To understand Becedas fully, it is necessary to place the village in time and space, to explore briefly the geographical, economic, and political forces which have helped to shape her present way of life. Among the most crucial of these forces has been the village's physical setting. Situated in one of the highest permanently populated regions of Spain, and endowed with some of the most dramatic vistas, Becedas experiences topographical and climatic conditions which defy most stereotypic portraits of sun-parched, barren Castile. Let us first examine the Sierra de Béjar, within whose limits Becedas lies.

The Sierra de Béjar is located directly west of Madrid, approximately at the juncture of three provinces—Avila, Salamanca, and Cáceres. It forms part of a long chain of mountain ranges that divides Spain in half horizontally, such that the chain has been appropriately termed the "vertebral column of the Iberian peninsula" (Fuente Arrimadas 1925, I: 19). The highest peaks are found in the imposing and somewhat forbidding Sierra de Gredos, where some of Spain's finest fishing and hunting territory is located. The Sierra de Béjar may be seen as a northwestern extension of the Gredos, though it is considerably smaller in area and tamer in aspect than its famous sister. It rises abruptly out of the Leonés–Castilian plain, forming a natural barrier between this region and Extremadura to the south.

The terrain in the Béjar range is rugged in comparison with the softly undulating tableland to the north or south. Approaching the Sierra from either direction, one is struck by the hilly, rocky countryside, carved into small, clearly demarcated plots and, in places, neatly arranged into cultivated terraces. Regardless of the time of year, one also immediately notes the cooler temperature in the Sierra.

Within the Béjar range, there exists considerable climatic and topographical variation. The mountain slopes with a southern exposure are warmer and drier than those facing the north, which are lush and verdant from being fed year-round by melting snows. Because of these differences, villages only a few kilometers from one another are likely to have distinct bases of subsistence, some reliant on dry cereal farming and hog raising, others dependent on irrigated orchards and semitranshumant cattle herding. Consequently, inhabitants of neighboring communities often follow differing modes of life, with separate agricultural calendars, marketing mechanisms, and divisions of labor.

The numerous small villages which dot the Sierra de Béjar at 2 to 5 kilometer intervals do share one common physical feature, however. To a greater or lesser extent, they all suffer from intense cold in winter and are refreshed by relatively cool weather in the summer. Sierra villages are located at over 1000 meters altitude and are surrounded by peaks reaching twice that height. Most of the peaks are snow-covered at least 9 months of the year, and on some the traces of winter snowfall never disappear. Frost and snow are concentrated in the period from December through February, though we experienced a heavy snowstorm in May, and this is not an infrequent occurrence. Even during July, when villagers can temporarily suspend setting out *braseros*, brasiers of hot coals universally used for heating, there is generally an indoor chill. In torrid summer Castile, however, this is usually considered an asset and is the main reason that the region is filled with visitors during July and August.

There are a number of sayings in the Sierra concerning the weather, particularly the cold. One such saying advises that:

> *Hasta el 40 de Mayo*   Until May 40
> *No te quites el sayo.*   Don't remove your heavy garment.

Which means, of course, that the days for dressing lightly never arrive in the Sierra. It is also said that:

Hay que fastidiarse con los Serranillos,	You can't help being annoyed with those of the Sierra
Que al frío le llaman fresquecillo.	For they consider the cold a mere chill.

The weather is never taken for granted. It is a constant topic of conversation and concern and, as we shall see, is one of the most important factors affecting the people's life style.

Located 206 kilometers by road from Madrid at an altitude of 1097 meters, Becedas and its orchards and meadows rest in a narrow valley, the Valle Hondo, running east to west. Bordering the valley on the north is the almost perpetually snowcapped Peña Negra ("Black Rock"), rising to an altitude of 2135 meters and looming large over the nucleated settlement at its base. It is from the snows of this mount that Becedas derives its abundant water supply. The lower slopes of Peña Negra are always green, and here some of the best orchards and largest, most productive woodlands and meadows of the village terminus[1] are found. Here also, located 2 kilometers by dirt road above the village, is a modest estate of three large homes, known collectively as La Rasilla, owned and used as a summer residence by a wealthy banking family from nearby Salamanca.

Bordering Beceda's valley to the south is a row of three sharply protruding hills, the *"Picos"* of Gilbuena, Carrascal, and Neila, as they are popularly known, which vary in height between 1300 and 1400 meters and are drier, craggier, and more severe looking than the Peña Negra. The oaks which cover these hills provide firewood for the villagers, and the acorns and low-lying scrub there are suitable for limited sheep and goat grazing. Toward the base of the Pico de Neila, completely separated from the nuclear settlement, the village cemetery is located. Miguel de Unamuno, who spent seven summer vacations in Becedas, had the following impression of this small range:

> The rocky hills which I looked upon from Becedas—which is at the foot of a high mount—appeared to me like ruins fallen from heaven, upon which green flocks, clusters of acorn and oak trees, swarmed. And around those peaks of Neila and Gilbuena was a robust and smiling countryside. At that hour of the day the landscape lost substance, appearing like a mere blanket over space. Or

---

[1] The word "terminus" is from the Spanish *término*, meaning that territory which is under the authority of an *Ayuntamiento*, or town government.

rather that it was a painting, but more a fresco than an oil, and in any case without varnishing, in which you see the material and its weave, the fabric on which
the picture had been painted. [Unamuno 1968: 236; my translation]

Unamuno was obviously impressed favorably by the territory, and there is
no doubt that it offers welcome relief from the usual stark austerity of
Castile.

As a peasant village, Becedas has always had an important relationship
with the villages and towns in the surrounding region (see Map 1). Most
of the villagers' outside contacts are contained within the area between
Béjar, 17 kilometers to the west, and El Barco de Avila, 13 kilometers to the
east. These two towns are connected by a narrow, winding provincial highway. A bus, popularly called the *correo*, or "mail," because it is the source
of postal service to the village, travels back and forth between Béjar and
El Barco, stopping in Becedas four times daily (except Sunday, when there
is no bus service): 8:30 A.M. and 3:30 P.M. on its westward route, 11:00
A.M. and 7:30 P.M. on its eastward route. The infrequency of bus service
is a serious limitation to villagers, the large majority of whom have no
quick, reliable means of transportation to these cities.

Although now included within the southwestern limits of the province
of Avila, Becedas has always been tied primarily to the town of Béjar
(population about 16,000), the center of a well-known textile industry, in
the province of Salamanca. Traditionally, the Dukes of Béjar were lords
of a large part of the surrounding Sierra, and Becedas, which was under
their jurisdiction, today shares a general architectural and cultural style,
including manner of dress and speech, with all the villages which had this
common centuries-old political bond. Further, Béjar has always operated
as an important religious and economic center for Becedas. For generations, villagers have held Béjar's patron saint, the Virgen del Castañar
("Virgin of the Chestnut Grove," named for the site of her appearance),
in special veneration and, until recently, made an important annual pil-
grimage walking barefooted to her shrine. As an economic center, Béjar's
Thursday and Saturday markets serve as a limited outlet for some
Becedas produce, and in the past served as the primary outlet. Villagers
now, as formerly, travel to Béjar to purchase manufactured items which
are unavailable or overly expensive in Becedas. Further, villagers are turning increasingly to Béjar medical practitioners for solutions to their health
and dental problems, and young people from the village visit the town on
festival occasions for entertainment and diversion. Some go there daily for
secondary education. For Becedas, Béjar has fulfilled a variety of significant
urban functions.

A second important urban contact has been provided by El Barco de

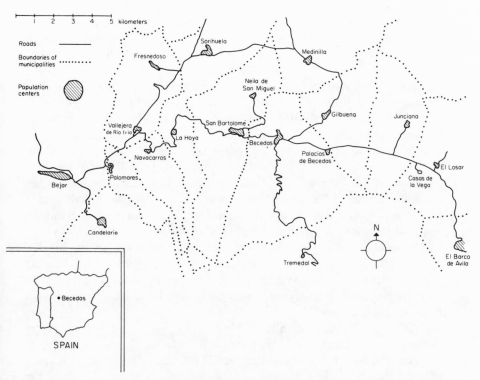

Map 1 Becedas and region.

Avila (population about 3000), which is really no more than a large village with city trappings. El Barco is head of the *partido judicial*, the low-level political and judicial district to which Becedas belongs and is immediately responsible. Here are kept Becedas' official land records, and here too Becedas court cases are brought to trial. Some villagers frequent the small but lively Monday market at El Barco, but they are particularly drawn to the town's several annual cattle fairs. El Barco is more important as a regional center than its size would indicate: Geographically it is the gateway to the Gredos mountains, historically it was a seat of the powerful Dukes of Alba, and economically it is the lifeline upon which numerous tiny hamlets which cluster around it depend. The town was undoubtedly of past strategic importance, for within its limits and immediate vicinity are several Roman bridges and the large Medieval castle of Valdecorneja, perched high on a hill overlooking the Tormes River.

Becedas is one of 11 villages strung along the 30-kilometer highway that runs between El Barco and Béjar. Of all these communities, Becedas is the largest and, almost for this reason alone, the one least affected by the emigration characteristic of the entire region. The people of Becedas often refer to their village as capital of all the surrounding communities, not only for its size, but also for its economic importance. Becedas provides a good many food and manufactured products unavailable in the other communities. Housewives from the four or five villages within walking distance of Becedas go there regularly for shopping. Farmers in the surrounding region bring grain to Becedas' mills for grinding and agricultural implements to its carpenters for repair. Further, Becedas' professional personnel serve the neighboring communities. The doctor makes housecalls in Palacios and Gilbuena, the priest says Mass at Palacios and Neila, and the veterinarian goes out to three or four nearby villages for meat inspection and animal care. Civil Guards resident in Becedas are responsible for order in nine of the surrounding communities. Because Becedas has a higher population and more stores, cafes, and summer visitors than the other villages, it is also said to have more *ambiente* (loosely, "action"), a highly valued quality in which the villagers take great pride. Finally, Becedas residents are generally more prosperous than those of neighboring communities and have a correspondingly higher standard for living. For all these special features, Becedas may accurately be called a "capital," on however small a scale.

Politically, Becedas actually is the administrative–legal head of its *municipio* ("municipality"). The *municipio* of Becedas is comprised of two communities, Becedas and Palacios de Becedas, a geographically independent nuclear settlement, lying 2½ kilometers east of Becedas along the provincial highway. Palacios, with less than half the population of Becedas, is officially classified as an *anejo*, or "annex." The two villages are united under one governing body, the *Ayuntamiento*, which has its offices in Becedas. The *Ayuntamiento* is comprised of a mayor (*alcalde*), appointed by the provincial governor for an indefinite term; 6 council members, elected by the household heads to 6-year terms, which are staggered so that half the council is replaced every 3 years; and a justice of the peace, recommended by the village mayor and officially appointed by a high judiciary court in Piedrahita. All of these offices are known as *cargos honoríficos y gratuítos*, "unpaid and honorific posts," for none of them is monetarily compensated. In addition, the *Ayuntamiento* has a secretary and an *aguacil* (in standard Spanish, *alguacil*, or "bailiff") who hold fulltime, paid positions, the appointments to which are based on State civil service examinations. These officials have their offices in a building which is called simply the *ayuntamiento* ("town hall").

A branch of the nationwide, State-sponsored syndicalist union shares with the *Ayuntamiento* the formal power of governing and organizing the municipio. The *Hermandad* ("Brotherhood"), as this local body is popularly known, is not a traditional governmental organ, having been introduced into the village around 1950, when the entire syndicalist system was implemented throughout Spain. Its ruling board consists of eight officers and a president, chosen by a vote of the board. The sole paid official of the *Hermandad* is a secretary, appointed by the board for an indefinite term. The board itself is elected by a vote of all household heads, but candidates are always named from above by the provincial syndicalist body in Avila. Until 1970, voting for all board members took place every 6 years. Presently there are 8-year terms, with half the board being chosen every 4 years.

It is primarily through these two political bodies, the *Ayuntamiento* and the *Hermandad*, that Palacios de Becedas is formally linked to its larger sister. The bond is asymmetric, with all power belonging to the village of Becedas proper. Of the six *Ayuntamiento* council members, only one is from Palacios. Although this official is popularly thought of as mayor of Palacios, he is in reality subordinate to Becedas' mayor. Palacios has no official members on the governing board of the *Hermandad*. In the 1960s, Palaciegos complained about this situation, so elections were held to choose unofficial representatives from the annex village. Now, there are two such representatives, but they have no vote and, hence, no power over *Hermandad* decisions. Perhaps most important, officials of both the *Ayuntamiento* and the *Hermandad* (excepting only the Palaciego "mayor" and the *Ayuntamiento* secretary, a recent appointee from another Abulense village) are natives and residents of Becedas and, therefore, have emotional loyalties to their own village in the case of disputes with Palacios.

These formal political ties between Becedas and its annex belie the fact that they are really two separate communities. Becedas and Palacios each has its own church in which Mass is celebrated daily. The patron saint of Becedas is Santa Teresa, with an August feast date; that of Palacios is San Juan Bautista in June. There is and has been virtually no intermarriage between the two communities and, for this reason, the surnames found in each are clearly distinguishable. Economically, there are also differences. Palacios relies more heavily on herding than does Becedas, while Becedas residents engage in cooperative work forms to a much greater extent than do the Palaciegos. Above all, the people of Becedas identify with only one or the other community. A Palaciego would never tell an outsider that he is from Becedas. And if a Becedas villager should mention that his community is comprised of two units, it is only to emphasize that he comes from the larger, more influential, and, by implication, superior part of the whole. He would never consider marrying into Palacios, whose inhabitants are rather indelicately called *algo guarro*, "piggish," for their allegedly dirty personal and domestic habits. Finally, since the two communities are geographically distinct, their respective members rarely interact with one another on a daily basis. Becedas and Palacios thus form separate units of gossip and social control. As religious, economic, and social entities, the two villages are essentially distinct.

THE VILLAGE PAST

Becedas' history, like that of so many Spanish villages, is largely obscure. It is known, however, that as a border settlement located near the meeting-point of three separate provinces—Salamanca, Avila, and Caceres—the village's affiliation with larger political and religious units has always been in flux. After the eleventh century reconquest of the Gredos–Béjar region from the Moors, Becedas was dominated by Béjar, under whose influence and control it remained for over six centuries. Not until the general re-organization of the Spanish province in 1833 did the village assume its present political bond to Avila. Ecclesiastically, Becedas was, from the Middle Ages, controlled by the Bishopric of Plasencia in the province of Caceres, whose border lies only 20 kilometers to the south. Not until the 1960s, with a readjustment of ecclesiastic boundaries, was this long as-sociation broken and Avila's clerical jurisdiction imposed. Thus, the vil-lage's formal political and religious ties presently lie with the province of Avila; however, culturally and historically, the village remains a part of Béjar and the surrounding Sierra.[2]

There exist several documents that provide interesting, though re-stricted, portraits of Becedas at particular points in time from the sixteenth through the nineteenth centuries. Santa Teresa de Jesús, the great Spanish mystic and reformer of the Carmelite order, visited the village in 1539, and writes about this experience in her well-known autobiography (Teresa de Avila 1957). She had been sent to Becedas at the age of 23, seeking relief from the pain of a mysterious illness. Becedas, she writes, "had a great reputation for the curing of other diseases, and . . . they said that mine could be cured too. I stayed in that town for almost a year, and for three months of it suffered the greatest tortures from the remedies they applied to me, which were so drastic that I do not know how I endured them" (1957: 34–35). The saint provides a colorful description of her relationship with the village priest, a man "of very good birth and understanding, who had also some learning, but only a little." (1957: 40). She took it upon

---

[2] In spite of Becedas' proximity to Extremadura to the south, the harsh mountains separating the village from this region have greatly obstructed crosscultural influence. Becedas is basically a Leonés—Castilian community.

herself to extricate this cleric from his 7-year-long affair with a female villager:

> I learned . . . about his wretched state and saw that the poor man was not entirely to blame. For the miserable woman had laid spells on him by means of a copper image, which she had begged him, for love of her, to wear round his neck, and no one had had enough influence to make him take it off. . . . When I knew these circumstances I began to show him greater love. . . . Usually I used to talk to him about God, and this must have done him good, though I believe that his affection for me did more. For, to please me, he finally gave me the copper image, which I immediately got someone to throw in the river. Once this was gone he became like one awakening from a long sleep. . . . In the end he entirely gave up seeing the woman, and could never thank God enough for having granted him light. [1957: 41–42]

After a short period of intense torture, caused largely by the "daily purges" and "strong medicines" given her in Becedas, Teresa finally left the village, never to return (1957 : 43). It is appealing to think that generations of Becedas villagers, by making her their patroness, have tried to compensate her for this miserable treatment. Actually, most villagers today know only that Santa Teresa lived a short while in their community. The precise epoch and circumstances of her visit are unknown, except among the few relatively well-read resident professionals in the village.

Surprisingly complete data about Becedas in the eighteenth century are available from the *Catastro* of the Marqués de la Ensenada, who directed a detailed, nationwide property survey in 1751 and 1752. At that time, the village was already *de senorío*, a lordship, belonging to the Duke of Béjar, who received annual dues from the inhabitants. The community contained 591 residents, organized into 160 households, considerably less than the 805 individuals living in 235 households today. The settled village area must have been smaller than at present, for it had only 194 houses, less than two-thirds the 361 now extant. Commercially, the village seems to have been less than lively, for it lacked taverns, inns, stores, bakeries, markets, and fairs. However, the inhabitants practiced a wide variety of occupations. Aside from the vast majority, who are identified as agriculturalists of one kind or another, there existed a public scribe, a school teacher, a "surgeon," a blacksmith, a material cutter, 4 millers, 5 linen weavers, 11 weavers of wool, and various other specialists.

The *Catastro* further mentions that the land was at least in part *regadío*, or irrigated terrain, containing "fruit trees of all species and walnut trees." Among the harvested fruit were the *pera de donguindo*, a type of pear still grown in Becedas, and apples, presently one of the village's main sources of revenue. Over most of the land, there was a regular system of crop rotation, flax and wheat being planted on alternate years. On the poorest terrain, rye was planted every 3 years, the land lying fallow the other two.

It is noteworthy that today's most important sown crops, the potato and the navy bean, are not at all mentioned in the *Catastro*. Evidently, they have not yet been introduced into Becedas from the New World.

In the Becedas of 1751, there was considerable transhumance. More than three-fourths of the village sheep and one-third of the village cows and goats spent time in pasturelands away from home. This pattern is not surprising, since Becedas lay directly in the path of one of the great *cañadas*, or "sheep walks," controlled by the powerful sheepowners guild, the *Mesta* (Klein 1920: 19). Transhumant flocks from as far away as Logroño and Palencia came along the Segoviana, as this *cañada* was known, past Becedas to Béjar. At Béjar the Segoviana fused with another major artery, which originated in León, and continued south through a mountain pass to the fertile winter pastures in Extremadura.[3]

All the above-mentioned evidence—the presence of village textile workers, flax production, and sheep raising—points to the existence of a small-scale cloth industry in Becedas during the eighteenth century. In this connection, it is interesting that two of the most common eighteenth-century surnames in Becedas, Trapero and Ovejero, reflect the villagers' economic activities at that time. Trapero is, of course, a derivative of the word *trapo*, meaning "cloth" or "rag," so that a *trapero* would be a dealer in or producer of such goods. Similarly, the word *ovejero* refers to a person who has some direct connection with *ovejas*, "sheep." It is tempting to hypothesize that in Becedas the sheepraisers (*ovejeros*) provided wool for the clothmakers (*traperos*), though no such exact correlation between name and occupation can be claimed on the basis of the *Catastro* alone. These two surnames, like many of the others listed in 1751, remain among the most common ones in modern Becedas.

The record for Becedas in the nineteenth century is based on a number of important geographies of the day, which reveal significant economic changes in the village, including the growth of the textile industry. The Miñano geographical dictionary of 1826 mentions the existence of "many cloth looms" and a store where "cloths and flannels of all colors" could be purchased. Flax was still a principal crop at that time, though potatoes had also been introduced (Miñano 1826–1829, II: 32). Several decades later, Mellado reported the presence of "many cloth and linen looms" and a "sieve factory." The main crops at that time were rye, wheat, flax, and potatoes, with the latter now being produced in considerable quantity (Mellado 1845: 152). The Madoz geographical dictionary of 1849 lists the

---

[3] The Dukes of Béjar were among the most powerful Mesta members. Their flock of 25,000 sheep was only smaller than that of the Escorial, with 40,000, and the monastery of Santa María del Paular, with 30,000 (Klein 1920: 59).

existence in Becedas of exactly "12 coarse-cloth looms, 19 flour mills, 3 cloth mills, and 8 linen looms." The best land was still being used for flax and wheat, though by this time "all kinds of greens" were also being grown. Two food stores had already been established, and there was irregular mail service to the village from both Béjar and El Barco (Madoz 1849–1850: 99). On the whole, then, there is a sketchy, but nonetheless definite, picture of a flourishing economy in Becedas during the nineteenth century. New crops were being sown, and there was an expanded textile industry. The existence of numerous flour mills suggests either increased production of grain in Becedas itself, or, more likely, a growing population and thriving milling business serving villages throughout the surrounding countryside.

As we shall see in Chapter 4, grain production declined sharply during the first half of the twentieth century, in favor of increasing specialization of fruit and potato crops. With the widespread introduction of inexpensive factory-produced cloth on the Spanish market during the early decades of this century, flax (and hence linen) production was also reduced to virtually nothing. These economic developments seem to have been independent of population size, which remained relatively constant in Becedas throughout this period.

Other than a changing economy, the main factor influencing life in Becedas during the first half of this century was, of course, the Civil War. Villagers are understandably reluctant to discuss this unfortunate episode in their history, and stories are often muddled and conflicting. It is certain, however, that, at the outbreak of the war in 1936, the governing body in Becedas was Republican. Within a matter of months, the Franco rebels established complete control over the entire Sierra de Béjar. In Becedas, leading Republicans, officially denounced by a pro-Franco faction within the village, were secretly taken to another part of Avila and executed. Though this event split the community deeply, the village was at least spared violent conflict throughout the war years. Today, people bitterly remember the community divisiveness, but most major participants in the political struggle are dead, and their children, now the young adults of Becedas, are in no way associated with the tragedy.

More than of political disunity, the people today speak about the severe economic depression brought on by the Civil War. Rationing and a disrupted market forced villagers to do without many of the basic foodstuffs to which they were accustomed. For a while, they were reduced to a diet consisting almost entirely of garlic, potatoes, and coarse bread. Only by keeping this extreme deprivation in mind can we fully understand the attitude of the people of Becedas toward their present economic situation.

THE VILLAGE TODAY

Today Becedas is an archetypical nucleated settlement, its buildings clustered closely together into long, narrow streets. Looking at the village from a distance, Unamuno was reminded by its shape of "an enormous red turtle—from the color of its roofs—with a horn, which was the church-tower" (1968: 237). The settlement is built on a north–south incline, the main streets running up and down the hillside, now branching off from one another, now uniting into small plazas (see Map 2). In physical layout, Becedas well represents the typical Spanish town, which expanded and grew gradually throughout the centuries, without conforming to any preconceived design (Foster 1960: 34–49).

Becedas gives the impression of being a densely populated settlement. Houses and barns form an uninterrupted line down both sides of the streets. Adding to this general appearance are wide balconies, which extend outward from the second story of the residences. Only the few squares and small *huertos*, tiny orchards, provide visual relief. Actually, the village is not nearly as densely populated as the arrangement of buildings would indicate. Of the 361 houses in Becedas, only 233, or 65%, are permanently occupied. Eighty houses, or 22% of the total, are vacant or used merely as storage space, and 43 houses, or 13%, are only temporarily occupied during all or part of the summer months.

Along the east side of the village flows the Arroyo Becedillas, popularly known as La Garganta ("The Gorge"). La Garganta is a wide, rushing stream which is fed year-round by the melting snows of Peña Negra and which, far from Becedas, empties into the River Tormes. It is the pride of the villagers, and the source of the abundant water supply with which they irrigate their fields and maintain their households. Villagers are well aware that such a continual flow of water is rare in Castile and often compare their own favorable position with that of the *pueblos míseres*, "downtrodden villages," which are virtually barren of water in the summertime. As one informant put it, water from La Garganta is *"la alegría que tenemos"*—"our joy."

Near the upper end of the village, La Garganta's stream is diverted into several *regaderas*, or irrigation channels, which run both through the village streets above ground and under the streets into centrally located fountains. The above-ground *regaderas* are indispensible to village life. They are used for obtaining cooking water, for washing clothes and dishes, and for disposing of garbage and other wastes. Although the water in these streams flows swiftly, villagers realize that it often becomes polluted from overuse. For this reason, everyone draws drinking water from the fountains,

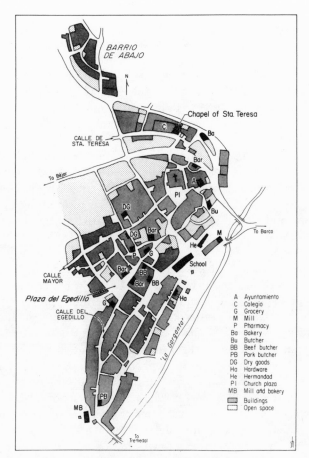

Map 2   Becedas: The village.

whose water remains relatively pure because of its underground flow. People who live at the upper end of the village consider themselves lucky to receive "clean water," as they put it, and women living further down often complain of the barrage of excrement, tin cans, detergent suds, and wads of old torn cloth that clog the *regaderas* and make washing difficult.

It is largely because of its relatively impure water supply that the lower end of the village, known as the Barrio de Abajo, or "Quarter Below," is considered an unpleasant living location. This *barrio*, the only named section of town, is the relatively small quarter lying north of the provincial highway and contains many of the oldest, poorest houses of the village. Because it is inconveniently located far from the present village center, a number of families in the past decade have moved out of it into more

desirable sectors, so that it is now largely composed of barns and uninhabited residences. Only one street in the *barrio*, the Calle de Santa
Teresa, shows any signs of vitality. Here, where the saint is said to have
lodged, a number of houses have been completely rebuilt and modernized.

Also located along this street are the Chapel and Colegio of Santa
Teresa, a private school operated by a community of eight Franciscan
nuns. Funds for the founding and maintenance of the institution were
donated by Don Crisanto Rodríguez, an ex-villager who has become a semi-
legendary figure. According to the story, Don Crisanto emigrated from
Becedas to Cuba in the late nineteenth century and became a wealthy
sugar planter. There he contracted yellow fever and made a *promesa*, a
vow, to Santa Teresa that if she would assure his recovery he would build
a girls' school and chapel in her honor at his native village. He was cured,
and fulfilled the promise by founding the chapel in 1889, and the Collegio
in 1898.[4]

The Colegio was, until it became virtually defunct in 1971, a source of
great pride to the villagers. It was reputed to give a better education than
the State-run village school and certainly was more prestigious. It was
attended by the large majority of village girls, even though there was a
monthly tuition of 3 to 10 dollars, depending on grade level. About 1960,
boys were admitted to the Colegio for the first time in its history, though
they never attended in as great a number as the girls. In additon to edu-
cating the village children, the Colegio operated as orphanage and boarding school for about 40 girls, placed there and supported by provincial
welfare agencies. In late 1971, just after completion of a massive, costly
building program, new governmental requirements for educational insti-
tutes and boarding schools came into effect. As the Colegio could not meet
these regulations, it was closed and today serves only as nursery school
for a handful of village youngsters.

Aside from the Colegio and associated Chapel, Becedas' institutional
buildings all lie south of the provincial highway, in the main part of the
village. The State school is, by comparison with the Colegio, extremely
modest, a one-story, four-room structure with a small adjoining yard. The
classrooms are in a bad state of disrepair and, since there are no heating
facilities, they become bitterly cold in winter. Until a decade ago, there
were six classes (two were housed in another building), divided in composition by grade level and sex. At that time, two classes were eliminated. By
mid-1970, the State had just further cut the number of classes in half,
leaving only one for boys and one for girls. This dramatic reduction in

---

[4] Apparently, this form of philanthropy was common among ex-villagers who had
become successful in the New World (Kenny 1966: 43).

school size during the 1960s initially resulted, in part, from proportionately higher enrollment in the Colegio. But considering present circumstances, it must be attributed primarily to the enormous emigration from the village, particularly by people of childbearing age.

Nearby the State school is the *Hermandad*, which contains the secretary's office and one enormous room, used as a bar and, on occasional evenings, as a meeting-place for the discussion of community business. The bar is an ongoing concern, sponsored but not owned by the *Hermandad*. Bar management rotates annually by auction. Once a year, all interested parties bid for the managerial rights. Upon paying the agreed-upon amount to the *Hermandad*, the highest bidder becomes virtual owner of the bar for a year. He provides his own labor, purchases all liquor and other refreshments for serving, and retains whatever profit he makes on the sales. As we shall see, auctions such as this are a standard village mechanism for choosing community personnel.

The other village governmental organ, the *Ayuntamiento*, is housed in the Town Hall, located just off the church square. Built in the late 1950s, this is a newer, larger building than the *Hermandad* and contains the residence of the *Ayuntamiento* secretary and his family. It is here that all legal matters—land transfers, tax payments, vital statistics registration, and the like—take place.

By far, the most imposing and impressive village edifice is the church, officially called the Church of the Immaculate Conception, but known to only a few by that formal title. Constructed during the early sixteenth century, it boasts an elaborately carved plateresque facade containing sculptured heads of the Dukes of Béjar, Don Francisco I and Doña Teresa de Zúñiga, under whose auspices it was built (Martin Angulo 1963: 532). Villagers recognize the artistic merits of the building, especially of its sturdy tower,[5] 30 meters high, which offers a magnificent view of the surrounding countryside, and of the ornate altarpiece, a copy of the one in the Cathedral of Plasencia. Located in a separate building on the church square is the Centro Parroquial ("Parish Center"), newly built residence of the village priest and repository of church documents dating from 1536 onward.

At the upper end of the village, the only site of importance to the

---

[5] Richard Herr (personal communication) suggests that the Becedas churchtower, made of large granite blocks forming a high, hollow, square-shaped belfry, is characteristic of areas in Spain where there was local ownership and control over the land. In such areas, money stayed within the community and could be spent on elaborate, expensive towers such as this one. In areas of absentee landlordism, money was drained from the community and a simpler, single-sided belfry, merely an extension of the church facade, was erected.

general community is the Plaza del Egedillo, the largest village square ringed by some of the finest village homes. In the middle of the square stands an enormous ash tree, typical of village squares throughout the Sierra de Béjar. Here, too, at the tree's base is found the most popularly used village fountain, from which the usual term for this square, Los Dos Caños ("The Two Water Spouts"), is derived. The area between the church square and the Plaza del Egedillo is generally considered the village center, and because of its *ambiente* and convenience is the most coveted residential location.

Perhaps the most startling physical feature of the village in general is the prevalence of building construction. Wherever the eye turns, work on a new edifice is in progress, and always with the use of nontraditional (and expensive) brick and mortar. When we left Becedas in 1972, the following were under construction or newly completed: a large medical center, with operating room and physician's quarters; a grocery store, with three living units, all with baths, above it; a new modern cafe; four houses to be used as permanent residences; two garages; and one enormous combination barn and storehouse. All of this work conveys the impression that Becedas has been hit by tremendous prosperity. The impression is simultaneously contradicted by the equally obvious evidence—the empty, unused houses, the dying Colegio and State school, and other manifestations of recent depopulation—that the village is a backwater, doomed to extinction.

The reason behind these seemingly paradoxical developments is, of course, that prosperity and emigration are closely interrelated. The exodus from Becedas has created the conditions necessary for the village's rising standard of living. Before explaining why this should be, however, let us turn to a consideration of migration and living patterns themselves, to show the extent and nature of depopulation as well as the ways in which daily life has been affected by the recent prosperity.

Plate 3 Victor López in front of his house (diagrammed on p. 53), and Teófilo Martín, with Becedas in the background.

III

The People: Population and Life Style

THE PUEBLO AND ITS OUTSIDERS

The people of Becedas may be divided into two basic categories: the permanent residents who were born or married into the community and make a living from its land; and the officials and professionals who, while also residing permanently in the village, were raised far away from it and live virtually as outsiders among the others. People in both groups are united by a common economic dependence on the village. The essential difference between them is their social identity.

For the first group, comprising the vast majority of the villagers, Becedas is the physical and social center of the universe. It is here that their primary source of livelihood, the land, is located. Here, too, are all their friends and neighbors and most of their relatives. Above all, their behavior is under constant scrutiny by the Becedas community as a whole, to whom they must account for their actions. Close daily contact in the nuclear setting, and the need for mutual assistance in various economic endeavors, has created in these people an acute sensitivity to their own moral status in the village. This is the group that identifies itself as the *pueblo*, the "people," of Becedas.

Unlike many Spanish communities, the Becedas *pueblo* is in many respects homogeneous. Over 85% were born or raised in the community, and the rest, who have married in, come primarily from villages within a 20-mile radius. Aside from one recently settled Gypsy family, the *pueblo* is entirely Castilian, so that the distinction they sometimes draw between themselves and other ethnic and regional groups has little day-to-day practical significance. All the villagers are Roman Catholic. In spite of varying attitudes toward the Church as an institution, everyone accepts the existence of Christ, Mary, and the saints, and undergoes the official life cycle rituals. To do otherwise would be unthinkable. Economically, although there are noticeable distinctions of wealth within the pueblo, all pueblo members work in the fields or at other types of manual labor, and no one, either inside or outside the community, has so much power over any villager that he controls his ability to earn a living. Further, only under special circumstances does wealth determine social status. Within the community, a person's reputation is based essentially on whether or not he acts in the culturally approved manner, so that theoretically all villagers have more or less the same access to prestige. This situation provides a high degree of social equality.

The second category of village residents, the officials and professionals, live physically among but psychologically and socially apart from the *pueblo* as a whole. This is a numerically small group, including only the doctor, the *practicante* (male paramedical practitioner), the veterinarian, the priest, the *Ayuntamiento* secretary, the six Civil Guards, and the several Franciscan nuns who still reside in, and guard over, the Colegio. The professionals all differ from the *pueblo* in one fundamental respect: They have advanced educational training and identify primarily with their respective occupational groups, not with the community. They reside in Becedas not because it is their place of birth or marriage, or because they are strongly bound to its people and property, but because it is where they can successfully practice their chosen professions. They consider themselves and are considered by members of the *pueblo* to be *forasteros*, "outsiders."

The outsiders are in no sense a unified group. Discounting the nuns and Civil Guards, who establish their primary social contacts from among their respective numbers, these professionals have virtually no common bonds. Relationships among them are generally characterized by social distance, and they seem to rely on their immediate families or on other professionals from nearby villages for their main social ties. The priest and the doctor, for example, are cordial toward one another but would never consider exchanging dinner invitations. Despite long residence together in

Becedas, they continue to address one another by the respectful title "*Don*" and the formal personal pronoun *Usted*. This is typical of relations among all the village professionals.

In their dealings with the *pueblo* at large, the professionals generally restrict themselves to their occupational roles. They provide the community with useful services, in return for its financial support. The priest, the nuns, and the *Ayuntamiento* secretary live largely (though not exclusively) on the villagers' donations, Colegio fees, and taxes, respectively. The medical practitioners have installed a modest socialized medical plan that assures them a regular income. In return for a small monthly fee, villagers receive all the medical care that these men can provide. Virtually all the villagers subscribe to the plan.

In additon to this purely professional relationship, the outsiders occasionally form patron–client ties with needy villagers. Their higher income and broader contacts with the outside world enable them to assume this calculatedly benevolent role. The priest has been influential in finding relatively good, well-paying city jobs or apprenticeships for young villagers. In return, the families that he has aided are known to be among the most devout and regular church attenders, many of them also participating in weekend-long, Church-sponsored *cursillos* ("little courses") in Avila to further their religious education.[1] The doctor provides select families with expensive medicines and has arranged for specialized medical care in the cities for those with uncommon ailments. For these individuals, it is taboo to visit outside medical practitioners whom the doctor has not explicitly recommended, or with whom he is known to be feuding. Other villagers do occasionally make such visits to both licensed medical men and *curanderos* (folk curers), but they do so surreptitiously, so as not to alienate a potential patron.

Despite the unequal social relationship between the *pueblo* and its outsiders, mutual residence in a closely nucleated village does create some bridges between the groups. In Becedas, as in other Spanish communities (Pitt–Rivers 1961: 7), any person who is born in the village is automatically an *hijo del pueblo*, a "child" or full-fledged member of the village. Since a number of the professionals' children were born in Becedas, they necessarily identify and have been identified with the *pueblo* and have, thus, become inextricably bound to it. The doctor's children provide a good example. His sons have, upon age, joined the village bachelor's

---

[1] These retreats usually include lengthy intimate testimonies by lay people—often doctors, lawyers, and other prestigious professionals—about their recent religious awakening. Cynics within the *pueblo* state that their fellow villagers return from the cursillos as religious fanatics, "as if they had taken a religion pill."

society, and participate fully in its activities. One of his daughters is presently in the midst of a long courtship with a young village man, and the couple is expected to marry soon. When another of his daughters died, she was given an orthodox village funeral, with the doctor and his wife participating in elaborate customs different from those in the region of their birth.

Long residence in the same community also provides limited occasions on which villagers and the professionals fall back on one another for companionship. The *Ayuntamiento* secretary and Civil Guards can often be seen in the cafes, playing cards with the village men, and the doctor's wife sometimes sits and chats with her neighbors in the street. But these instances are breaches of the usual carefully guarded social distance. The professionals live among the pueblo but can never become wholly integrated within it. They stand before the world as representatives of particular occupational groups. *Pueblo* members, on the other hand, identify fully with the Becedas peasant community.

A POPULATION DECLINE

To understand fully the economic and social life of the village today, it is necessary to examine its present and past population. In 1970, Becedas had 805 residents, divided between 397 males and 408 females.[2] These figures include only those people who live permanently within the village boundaries, or who, residing there just part of the year, depend entirely on members of the community for their subsistence. Thus, the large, but presently indeterminate, number of ex-villagers who flock to Becedas for varying periods during the summer months are excluded from the total. On the other hand, young villagers who spend most of the year away at secondary schools, but who still fully maintain their ties to the village and depend upon their parents or other village relatives for economic support, are included in the figures.

The number of village residents has declined greatly over the past generation. Table 1 shows the enormity of this change in the years following the Civil War. Looking at the fourth column of this table, it is clear that, since 1940, there has been a steady population decline. But the

---

[2] Neither my figures nor those of the Instituto Nacional de Estadística includes the Colegio boarders, who resided in Becedas until 1971. However, they do include the resident village professionals.

TABLE 1

Population and Migration in Becedas, 1940–1970

	1940	1950	1960	1970
Total births previous decade	—	328	257	122
Total deaths previous decade	—	263	150	109
Natural population increase	—	65	107	13
Total population	1303	1220	1103	805
Estimated net migration	—	−148	−224	−311
Percentage rate of migration	—	11.4	18.4	28.2

figures show, too, that only since 1950, and particularly in the decade 1960–1970, has there been a truly massive loss. In all, the Becedas population stood, in 1970, at only two-thirds of what it was just 30 years before.

There are only three possible explanations for this astounding demographic change: an excess of deaths over births in the community, emigration, or a combination of the two. We must dismiss the first and last of these explanations outright, for each of the three decades since 1940 has witnessed a natural population increase (see Table 1). Discounting any demographic alterations caused by migration, the Becedas population should have increased from 1303 to 1488 between 1940 and 1970, reflecting the natural population rise. Instead, of course, the population took a dramatic downward turn, which must be attributed solely to out-migration.

It is revealing to see which age groups are most responsible for this depopulation. Figure 1 compares the population structure of the village in 1950, prior to large-scale migration, and in 1970, by which time the effects of this population movement had been widely felt. The 1950 bar graph shows exactly what we would expect for a modern Catholic peasant community like Becedas: a population pyramid, with a large number of villagers in the lower age brackets and a comparatively small number of old people. The 1970 picture, however, is noticeably different. While the number of people 40 years old and above has remained relatively constant, there has been a sharp decline in the number of younger villagers. Among young adults, the most dramatic reduction has been in the 21 to 30 age group. In 1950, there were 202 villagers in this category, as compared with only 66 today, less than a third of that number. Within the 31 to 40 age

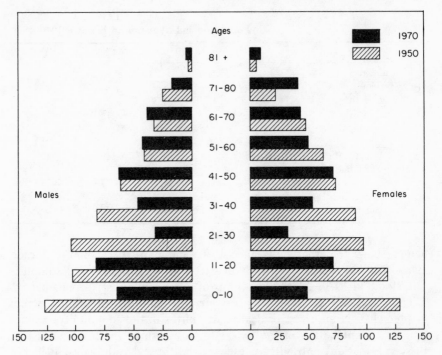

Figure 1   Age–sex distribution of the Becedas population, 1950 and 1970.

range, there are presently only 100 individuals, less than two-thirds the 166 of the early 1950s. Among children, those 10 years old and younger have suffered the greatest numerical decline. In 1950, there were 255 such children, more than double the 113 of 1972. There has also been a significant reduction in the numbers of youths between 11 and 20 years old, from 222 in 1950 to 153 in 1972.

From this analysis, it is clear that individuals between 20 and 40 years of age have left and continue to leave the village in the greatest numbers. This is not surprising, since such villagers, still young, yet nowadays economically independent of their parents, are the ones who generally recognize, and in actuality have, greater occupational opportunities in the cities. Primarily because of this large-scale migration of young adults, the numbers of village children have been correspondingly reduced. Some children have simply followed their parents and families away from the village. Others, particularly those between 15 and 20 years old, have left the village on their own to find work in the cities.

But Figure 2 shows, too, that a sharp decline in the number of village births is also responsible for the reduced child population. This decline

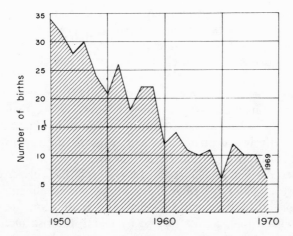

Figure 2 Number of live births in Becedas, 1950–1969.

must be attributed primarily to the migration of adults of childbearing age, though it is also true that villagers in the past decade have become increasingly concerned about limiting family size. Nowadays, it is considered irresponsible to have more than two children, and the few young village couples who have more than two are openly chided for their inability to control their sexual urge. Teodoro Márquez, a 35-year-old with five young children, is constantly greeted with the refrain, *"Atate al catre!"* —"Tie yourself to the bedpost!" Through a combination of coitus interruptus and abstention, most villagers manage to keep births down. Though they openly complain about the frustrations which these methods entail, they are willing to make the sacrifice in order to assure their ability to provide their children the best possible opportunities. Those husbands who cannot exercise control are seen as somewhat animalistic.

MIGRANT SELECTIVITY AND DESTINATION

Although it is impossible to predict whether or when a particular villager will migrate, there are several recurring patterns of migration. The earliest developed during the first decade of massive migration, from 1955 to 1965, when it was most common for the eldest children of a couple to pave the way for the entire family. Once out of school, young girls were sent to Madrid as waitresses, chambermaids, or servants in private homes; young men went to work in butcher shops, factories, or restaurants. After several years of work, siblings would have saved enough capital, when pooled, to rent and furnish an apartment for their parents and younger brothers and sisters to join them. With a residential foothold in the city, the father could find employment for himself, thereby sustaining the family in their new home.

In this early pattern, the migrants seem to have been drawn preponderantly from a single class—the landless laborers. As we shall see in the next chapter, the socioeconomic equality which today characterizes the village is a relatively recent development. Prior to the expansion of employment opportunities outside of agriculture, landless or near-landless workers in Becedas had no choice but to stay on in the village, working at seasonal, unsteady jobs for their more prosperous neighbors. With the availability of urban employment, they—the most economically disadvantaged group, with the least to lose by taking the risk of migration—were the first to go.

Although the pattern of children preceding parents has persisted, it is increasingly common for an entire family to leave the village *en masse*. This second pattern is most characteristic of independent farmers, people whose families have always owned land or who, during the mid-twentieth century, have acquired land through a combination of prosperity and expanding land supply. The exodus of entire nuclear family units has been made possible only by the prior residence of close relatives in the city, who are willing to support the migrants until they can establish themselves independently with apartments and jobs.

Similar reliance on relatives is common throughout Spain: Pérez–Díaz (1969: 163) found that, of all ex-agriculturist migrants from the Tierra de Campos (a wheat-growing region in Northern Castile), only 12.2% had no relatives to care for them when they arrived at their destination. Obviously, this second pattern could only manifest itself *after* the beginning of massive migration, when large numbers of ex-villagers had already settled in the cities. For this reason, the tendency to migrate seems to characterize some families more than others, because those villagers with migrant siblings and cousins have a ready-made avenue to resettlement. Thus, it is common to find that entire groups of from two to eight or more siblings are settled in Madrid and the surrounding area, while other equally large groups of siblings remain behind in the village.

In some instances, however, there are sibling groups whose members have all migrated, but to widely different locales. Thus, Valentín Lorca has four grown children, two settled in Madrid, one in Switzerland, and one in Buenos Aires. In this third pattern, there is little reliance on siblings or other relatives. Rather, the sibling group shares a common self-confidence which permits them to accept the risk of leaving the confines of their community and breaking close bonds with their family in order to achieve a more satisfying life style. Though the data are impressionistic, it appears that some families have provided their children with a psychological makeup fostering risk-taking and achievement orientation, and it is from these families, along with those who already have close relatives in the city, that the majority of migrants originate.

Whether children precede their parents to the city or the family moves as a unit, there has been, throughout the entire *recent* period of migration, one overriding selection criterion determining who is able to make the move: civil status. In order to earn enough money to live permanently in the city, a potential migrant must either be single, that is, responsible only for his own upkeep, or married with *grown* children, so that the family can rely on at least several breadwinners. Even if such families are well-to-do by village standards, and could receive initial assistance in the city from already established relatives, there is generally no opportunity for the husband alone to earn enough to support himself and the others in the city as well as he can in the village. This is true, despite the fact that the family might be able to earn some extra money through renting or share-cropping their village lands. A man with a young family has essentially one alternative: to continue to live in Becedas until his oldest children are able to find urban employment, at which time the entire family is able to resettle successfully in Madrid.

In order further to understand patterns of migration from Becedas, we may recall Pérez–Díaz's distinction between "universal" migration, in which individuals of a wide age range and of both sexes leave, generally as a family unit, to settle permanently in the city, and "professional" migration, in which, typically, the male household head migrates for a short temporary period to earn money and then returns to his village and family (Pérez–Díaz 1969: 89–93). The two type names are derived from the distinctive motives for migration: In the first instance, the migrant desires a completely new life style and enters into all-embracing social, economic, and legal ties to do so; in the second instance, he only forms new occupational relations, while maintaining the other spheres of life relatively unaltered.

Becedas is undoubtedly of the universal migratory type: Migration is always permanent and involves entire family units. If children precede their parents to the city, as in the first pattern, it is only with the goal of bringing them along too. A man never leaves his wife and children to work even temporarily elsewhere. Villagers recognize that, in some parts of Spain, men abandon their families for seasonal employment and claim that those of their community do not do so because they are not poor enough to warrant the sacrifice. Family solidarity, the mutual dependence —both economic and psychological—of man, wife, and children, is so great that only extreme poverty could, in their minds, justify even temporary severance of the conjugal unit. Though such abject poverty did exist in 1950, it was at a time when opportunities for outside employment were minimal. Since Spain has undergone its economic transformation, villagers have prospered and greatly improved their standards of living. At least in the 1960s, it was this prosperity which provided them the extra margin of security, permitting them to make a permanent move to the city.

Along with standard patterns of migration, villagers have a fairly standard destination: Madrid. In his excellent analysis of the factors influencing the destination of migrants in the Tierra de Campos, Pérez–Díaz found a correlation with village size. Migrants from large villages (with over 1000 population) are more likely to go to foreign countries and cities farther from home than are those from small villages. In explaining this phenomenon, Pérez–Díaz recognizes that an essential part of the migration process is risk-taking. Those from larger villages and towns are likely to experience more cultural variability and have more communication with the outside world than those from small *pueblos*. The former group, therefore, will be more willing to maximize their risks by straying farther from home into culturally remote areas than will the latter.

This analysis helps to explain the Becedas pattern. Since Becedas has traditionally a small, tightly knit, relatively insulated society, its migrants have chosen to settle in the closest large city with expanding job opportunities. Madrid, only 3½ hours by car, permits migrants to maintain close contact with the village, thus minimizing the shock of acute environmental change. The risks of leaving the *pueblo* are great enough without thrusting oneself into a totally alien milieu, far from family, friends, and all that is familiar. Madrid's proximity to Becedas, as we shall see in greater detail later, permits potential migrants to make exploratory sojourns to the city, to investigate occupational and residential possibilities, and to acquaint themselves with the atmosphere of Spain's largest metropolis. Once they actually make the move, migrants further minimize risks by retaining their landholdings—sharecropping or renting them, but not selling them—long after they have made the transition to city life. The knowledge that they can fall back on village farming as a last resort is comforting, as are their constant visits back to Becedas to oversee landholdings. In no sense, then, does the move to the city represent an abrupt change for migrants, though once they have permanently settled in Madrid, they never return to Becedas for extended residence. Never again can village life provide an adequate substitute for the comforts and glamour of the city.

OCCUPATIONAL STRUCTURE AND VILLAGE COMMERCE

Despite the fact that Becedas is a peasant community—its culture is a local manifestation of a general national culture, and its villagers rely on and produce for large urban centers, whose influence is felt at every turn— most *pueblo* members seldom leave the community for daily affairs. The people of Becedas usually take trips outside the village only on special occasions, such as visits to fiestas, cattle fairs, or relatives in Madrid. Daily life is, for the most part, acted out wholly within the boundaries of the village terminus.

This general lack of mobility is sustained by two aspects of village organization: the occupational structure and the commercial system. Occupationally, the large majority of villagers are full-time farmers (*labradores*), who themselves till the land. Some villagers, however, combine agriculture with a specialized trade, thus providing the community with necessary goods and services. Villagers buy all their bread from the two village bakers and grind their grain at the two village mills. There are several part-time tailors, who specialize in sewing the ubiquitous men's corduroy suits, and part-time shoemakers with small but relatively well-equipped repair shops. There are, further, a part-time blacksmith and a solderer, who fixes iron implements. The two village barbers, both part-time, pull teeth and repair wrist watches, as well as performing their usual function. There are two carpenters, one part-time who operates a sawmill and the other who manufactures and repairs most of the village carts and farm implements. A couple of masons specialize in building the carefully constructed stone walls that enclose the small fields of the village terminus. Four other men are construction workers who, due to the village's recent building expansion, have kept at this occupation almost full-time in the past few years. There is also a State-paid mailman, who makes twice-a-day deliveries. When we add to this list all the medical personnel who live in the village, it is clear that the variety of services offered to the people of Becedas within their own community is fairly extensive by peasant standards.

Similarly, the village commercial system provides the community with all its important food staples and manufactured products. During the 1960s, milk came to be regarded as a daily necessity, at the very least for young children and sick people, and ideally for healthy adults as well. Until 1971, milk was provided by several villagers who raised *vacas suizas* ("Swiss cows"), a variety bred for its large milk-producing capacity. Further, several vendors from nearby communities made the daily trek on donkeyback to Becedas, thus supplementing the village's own milk supply.

In mid-1971, a large milk-processing and bottling firm from Plasencia began coming daily to the Sierra de Béjar to collect milk. They pay the State-regulated price (in 1972, 10 pesetas per liter) and will purchase in any quantity available. Thus provided with a reliable outlet for marketing milk, a number of Becedas villagers have been stimulated to buy and keep Swiss cows, and by the summer of 1972 over 50 villagers were selling milk to the company on a regular basis. The vast majority of these farmers owns only two or three cows; only two villagers have large enough herds to warrant using the large tin milk cans provided by the firm. Still, as a result of this development, milk has become superabundant in Becedas, and milk vending by outsiders has altogether ceased.

Meat, too, came to be regarded as a daily necessity during the 1960s, and, to meet this demand, there are four butchers, one specializing in pork, another in beef, and the third and fourth handling a melange of lamb, chicken, goats, and pork. Each of the former two slaughters at least once a week and in wintertime considerably more often; the latter do so less regularly. The butchers sell the best cuts of meat to shops in Béjar and El Barco, usually reserving the inferior portions for village sale.

In addition, food and manufactured products of all kinds are sold in the village's permanent commercial establishments, which include two grocery stores, two clothing and dry goods stores, three cafes, and a hardware store. There is even a branch of a nationwide savings bank in the village, which is operated by the practicante, and a relatively well-stocked pharmacy, owned by a nonvillager but run by a young unmarried village woman.

The grocery stores, in particular, sell previously unavailable products, like bananas and frozen fish, which in recent years have become extremely popular. One grocer offers trading stamps similar to our own Green Stamps, and villagers diligently save for prizes which are chosen from an elaborately illustrated catalogue. The other food store is a licensed tobacco shop as well and was recently remodeled on the style of a self-service market. Among the unlikely products available at these stores are shampoo, shoe polish, detergent, and house paint. Colgate toothpaste, Ponds cold cream, lipstick refills, razor blades, and low-grade toilet paper are also sold. Packaged foods include Knorr instant soups, Royal brand pudding, and Dubble-Bubble chewing gum. Three brands of canned pineapple, from the USA, Malaysia, and South Africa, are in stock. Despite the fact that these items are all infrequently purchased luxury goods, their mere presence in Becedas indicates the wide range of available merchandise. It also shows the great extent to which the Becedas economy has been penetrated by and become involved in a worldwide market.

At the village's clothing and dry goods stores, one can literally buy all necessary apparel for the entire family. There is a good supply of underwear, work clothes, yard goods, and kitchen wear. Even such items as pajamas, neckties, sports jackets, costume jewelry, bedspreads, and inexpensive children's toys are found in limited quantity. The single village hardware store carries all kinds of kitchen implements and agricultural tools and has recently introduced the sale of chairs and bed frames.

In addition to the permanent commercial enterprises, itinerant vendors come weekly to the village in small vans, selling a number of ordinary food items, like eggs, cheese, olives, and fresh fish. Periodically, larger trucks from all over Spain also arrive stocked with clothing, yard goods, linens, bedding, furniture, kitchenware, and shoes, which are put out for display in the Plaza del Egedillo. By and large, these *ventas ambulantes* ("movable salesstands"), as they are known, merely duplicate, at reduced prices, what is already available in the village stores. Every so often, however, the village stock is expanded by such visits, as when pottery vendors from Alba de Tormes and Cespedosa in the province of Salamanca arrive to sell. On these occasions, the Plaza is particularly crowded with buyers.

Even this brief survey of occupational specialization and commerce in Becedas will suffice to indicate the surprising variety of goods and services regularly available to villagers. No wonder that repeatedly one hears the proud refrain, *"Aquí hay de todo"*—"There's everything here." For this reason, in ordinary day-to-day living, villagers are rarely forced to leave the community and thus practically never do so. It is interesting that this overall lack of mobility has produced various psychological and physiological effects among the populace, with widepsread apprehension about travel and a general tendency toward motion sickness. Numerous Becedas villagers even become ill at the *thought* of a car ride and are forced to relieve themselves at least every 15 minutes when actually inside a moving vehicle.

We may speculate that the village's diversified occupational and commercial system originally developed in response to the harshness of the Sierra terrain, which seriously limited access to large economic centers. Hemmed in by forbidding mountains and restricted by lack of adequate transportation facilities, Becedas villagers have, with few exceptions, learned to supply their own needs from within the community. This generalization even extends to marketing, a process which has for centuries required peasants in most parts of the world to travel to commercial centers. The people of Becedas, however, have always had the option of remaining inside their community for marketing transactions.

Until the late 1940s or so, villagers sold their cash crops to middlemen of the Sierra region, who came directly to Becedas to buy the produce. These middlemen, many of whom were from the nearby village of Medinilla (see Map 1), would pack the produce in large wooden carts and transport it to Béjar, where it would be loaded on trains to be distributed to large cities throughout Spain. Until the early 1950s, too, villagers benefited from an extensive barter system with the traveling vendors who even then came regularly to Becedas. With inferior quality produce, which could not be sold in bulk, a villager could purchase all kinds of clay kitchenware, as well as figs, grapes, and other fresh fruit. On occasion, one could even barter one's own or one's daughter's hair for other items; vendors would sell the cut tresses to wigmakers.

This is not to say that villagers never left the community for commercial transactions. Men would have to go at least several times a year on horse or donkey to Béjar to sell surplus or inferior garden and cash crops in the weekly market. It was a rare farmer, too, who did not attend one of two of the annual cattle fairs in El Barco and Béjar. If business did not warrant the visit, the need for diversion did. Even the women of Becedas had their annual jaunt to town. In the years before the Civil War, there was a four-passenger horse-drawn coach which traveled several times a week between Béjar and El Barco. Each woman would take this coach once a year to Béjar, always making the trip on a Thursday, the large market day. She carried with her a huge sack, into which she would pack all the supplies she had purchased for the coming year—needles, thread, cloth, blankets, and other necessities not then available for sale in the village. The yearly trip was a fixed institution, necessary to the maintenance of the household.

Now, village shopkeepers either go in their own cars to towns and markets to bring foodstuffs and manufactured items to the village, or else have these items delivered directly to them. There is no pressing need for women to make the trip for supplies to Béjar, though a number of them still go there occasionally, seeking out lower prices and greater variety than is available at home. On the other hand, only a handful of men now bring produce themselves to the Béjar market for sale, for the trip takes up a full day and yields, on the whole, very small profits. Three or four villagers still make the trek on horse or donkey, requiring them to awaken at 4:00 in the morning in order to arrive at 8:00 or 8:30. This still leaves them the 4-hour return trip in the afternoon. One Thursday, Marcos Tejeda made the trip in the pouring rain and arrived home drenched after selling only 8 kilos of apples for a total of less than a dollar.

Other marketers point to such experiences and thus justify the extra expense of going by bus. But this means of transportation also has disadvantages. Besides eating up a good portion of the day's profits, it requires the villager to wait aimlessly from 1:00, when the market locks its doors, until 7:00, when the bus makes the return to Becedas. For this reason, even those villagers who personally make the trip to market do so only occasionally, just to sell the inferior produce which would otherwise wastefully lie rotting in their barns. Such marketers are today drawn from among the poorest villagers, who have more time than their fields require and fewer animals than can consume the goods.

By far, the most prevalent marketing method today is a modernized version of the traditional system. For sale of the main cash crops—pears, apples, and potatoes—a handful of villagers operate as middlemen, buying from their fellow villagers and selling to large-scale purchasers from the outside who come directly to Becedas in trucks. The village middlemen are known as *comisionistas*, because they make *comisiones*, or contracts, with the outsiders, most of whom are Southerners—from Badajoz, Seville, or Córdoba, areas where crops such as those produced in Becedas are rarely grown. This distribution system places villagers in a precarious, vulnerable position. Should truckers not come, or should the truckers who arrive earliest in the season offer unreasonably low prices, farmers have little recourse but to wait and hope that others making better offers will arrive later in the year. Becedas farmers thus play a passive role imposed on them by their marketing system.

For the single farmer, the only locus of profitable marketing is Becedas itself. On the one hand, a farmer could never make a profit selling all his cash crops in local markets, for Béjar and Barco are already flooded with similar produce from villages all over the region. On the other hand, no farmer grows enough to be able to find a decent nonlocal marketing outlet on his own. The only reasonable alternative is to sell to the truckers. Thus, paradoxically, though villagers are involved in a world market system as never before, regularly purchasing manufactured items from Madrid and abroad and selling to distributors from distant parts of Spain, commercial activity still takes place mainly within the confines of the village. The widened economic network has not pushed the people of Becedas outside their community. If villagers today have a widened social network, it is, as we shall see, primarily the result of one development—migration.

STANDARD OF LIVING

As may be surmised from portions of the preceding discussion, the standard of living in Becedas is presently high relative to many other peasant communities the world over, and in fact, has been constantly rising since the mid-1950s. This trend can be well-documented by an examination of residential quarters and diet.

No two houses in Becedas are laid out or equipped in precisely the same way. Nonetheless, they do have more or less a standard form, which the oldest villagers remember as being common even when they were young. The houses are generally three stories high, including a low attic. The first story is made of stone, the second of adobe (sun-dried mud brick), constructed within a wooden Tudor-like frame. There is usually a long, second-story balcony running along the front of the building. In older houses, this is made of wood, in newer ones of concrete and iron. The second and third story floors are almost invariably wooden. Inside, walls are plastered and whitewashed, and most homes also have a plastered facade, though this is a development did not begin until around the mid-1950s. Residences generally have a small barn (*cuadra*) leading off from one side or in the back of the house.

In most homes, the first floor of the residential part of the building is comprised only of a large combination kitchen–dining room with a stone fireplace, a small pantry, and a separate room for the storage of firewood, potatoes, and dried meat. The second floor generally contains two bedrooms, one or both of which have alcoves, just large enough to accommodate a bed and perhaps an end table. A few of the oldest, poorest homes have kitchens on the second story rather than the first. The hearth in these houses consists of a stone slab embedded in the wooden floor; smoke escapes through apertures in the tile roof. Occasionally a modernized older home may contain a second-story hearth, but also a bathroom and a well (see Figure 3).

House furnishings have traditionally been minimal: in the kitchen, a stone washbasin, a round table with five or six straight-backed chairs, and a tall wooden cabinet with glass windows for the display of family dishes and knickknacks; in the bedrooms, beds, an end table or two, a wardrobe closet, and a wooden chest, with or without drawers. Crucifixes, calendars, and faded portraits of the saints adorn the walls. This is the essential format of the houses as they have existed throughout the present century.

The years since 1955 or so have witnessed considerable improvement in the overall quality and furnishing of the homes. Traditionally, there was always a dirt floor on the ground level of the living quarters. In 1970, of

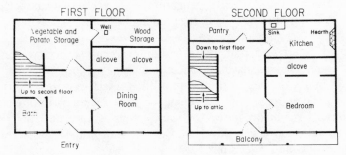

Figure 3 Home of Sr. Víctor López and Sra. Catalina Hernández.

the 230 permanent residences in the village, only 54 (23% of the total) had a ground-level dirt floor. The other homes had the floor covered wholly or partially with cement (45%), tile (17%), stone (12%), or wood (3%). Traditionally, cooking has always been done over the open hearth. By 1970, however, only 50 households (22%) relied entirely on this primitive method. The majority of residences (70%) used butane gas stoves for cooking, and the remainder (8%) iron wood-burning stoves, in this region called *cocinas bilbainas* ("Bilbao stoves"). Most villagers with gas stoves retain the fireplace for heating, as well as for cooking whenever there is a live fire available. A small number of homes are equipped with both gas and wood-burning stoves. The gas stove, which has become common only in the past three years, is an enormous work-saver both for women, who can heat food quickly without having to build a fire and who can assume a comfortable, upright cooking posture, and for men, who are now responsible for collecting only half as much firewood as in previous years.

During the 1960s, too, a number of items that are luxuries by any peasant standards came to grace Becedas homes. Of the residences, 38 (17%), have acquired simple valveless toilets, which drain through pipes into the village streams. Another 7% now have wells and water pumps, which provide them with running water; in these homes there are bona fide flush toilets. The large majority of villagers, however, still draw water from the village streams and fountains and relieve themselves in chamber pots, barns, and fields. Due to the increased awareness of urban mores, villagers seem particularly sensitive about the lack of toilets and say that they are waiting only for the imminent State installation of running water to add this convenience to their homes.

A majority of houses (78%) now have radios, and a substantial 20% have televisions as well. This contrasts with only 8% of the households having radios in 1957, when a geographical survey was made (Esteban Sánchez 1957), and none having televisions until the first was installed in 1960.

It should be stressed that all these improvements and conveniences—finished floors, cooking devices, toilets, radios, televisions—did not begin to appear in the village until the mid-1950s. Relatively few houses are fortunate enough to possess every one of these material improvements. Most houses have incorporated the least expensive and most practical of them—concrete floors, gas stoves, and radios—but still lack the real luxuries like toilets and televisions.

It is worth noting that there is a core of about 22% of households that have incorporated none of the recent advances. Since some of the poorest villagers have at least a gas stove and radio, we may surmise that there is a psychological rather than an economic motivation behind this extreme conservatism. Many of these households are made up of very old couples or widowed individuals living alone, who simply cannot break away from established living patterns. Others of this group are middle-aged or young but are afraid to depart from their former style of life. These people are criticized by other villagers as being miserly and *miseres*, downtrodden, living a self-imposed, impoverished existence.[3] But, despite the

---

[3] Significantly, Foster found a similar group of extreme conservatives in Tzintzuntzan, Mexico, which he refers to as the "submerged quarter" because they include about 25% of that village's population (1967a: 301–302). In another Mexican village, located in the state of Morelos, Fromm and Maccoby (1970: 59) state that 28% of all households still live at bare subsistence level, exhibiting none of the recent material improvements shown by the large majority of domestic units.

presence of this conservative element in Becedas, the household data point to a remarkably improved living standard and to relative prosperity in the years since the late 1950s or early 1960s.

The villagers' diet showed similar improvement over the same period. Until 1950 or so, most people had to content themselves with a diet consisting mainly of bread, potatoes, and fatback. Sometimes for the noon meal, a bit of codfish or rice was added for flavoring. On special occasions only, such as Holy Week or the patron saint festival, villagers would indulge in some bacon and eggs. People speak bitterly of those days, and it is today's changed diet which most represents to them the recent improvements in the living standard.

Nowadays, all villagers are able to eat meat or fish at least once daily. For *almuerzo*, the morning meal, it is popular to consume coffee and milk with bread and sugar, or *leche mingá*, bread soaked in milk. Milk with bland crackers is the most common breakfast for children and old people. Only a few villagers still eat *sopas* for breakfast. Made with bread soaked in a mixture of water, garlic, and bacon drippings, this dish is a symbol of former impoverishment, and those who take it do so out of habit, not necessity.

The largest meal, the midday *comida*, is frequently a *cocido* stew, made with garbanzo beans, potatoes, and small chunks of meat. Other common *comidas* are hake, breaded with egg and flour, meatballs, similarly prepared, and pork with beans or rice. Noodle soup is a usual supplement to the meal. For *merienda*, the late afternoon snack, villagers eat bread with cheese, *chorizo*, sausage, or, for the children, chocolate or jam. Children and old people sometimes have a snack of egg omelette or thin slices of fried beef. The evening meal, *cena*, is generally small. Villagers finish off leftovers from the noon meal and combine these with *leche mingá*, omelettes, salt cod, or bland cooked cereal.

Chicken, almost never consumed during the years prior to the 1950s, is now served regularly on festive occasions—Holy Week, Christmas, and the patron saint's day. Frozen fish, which has been stocked in village stores only since 1965, has become particularly popular because of its low price. To be sure, by American standards, this diet may seem monotonous. But by village standards, it represents real luxury. Villagers today honestly believe that no one in the world eats as well as they.

Correlated with dietary improvements has been a significant and sharp decline in infant mortality (Table 2). In the decade 1930–1939, 43% of all live births resulted in death prior to 1 years of age. In the following decade, this percentage was reduced only slightly, to 42.3. Then, from 1950 to 1959, the figure was cut significantly to 28.9%, and in the last

TABLE 2
Infant Mortality: Number of Infant Deaths
Per Live Births, 1930–1969[a]

Decade	Number of live births	Number of infant deaths	Infant deaths per hundred live births
1930–1939	188	81	43.0
1940–1949	170	72	42.3
1950–1959	135	39	28.9
1960–1969	68	4	5.9

[a] Source: Register of Births and Deaths, Becedas Ayuntamiento.

decade, from 1960 to 1969, only 5.9% of live births in Becedas resulted in infant mortality. This striking record must be attributed to improved diet and, concurrently, better medical knowledge and attention.

Fundamentally, of course, it is greater prosperity that is responsible for all the changes in the living standard. People say that money "flows" (corre) more than ever in the village. It is for this reason that villagers now live in better homes, eat a more varied and nourishing diet, and can afford the medical and professional care necessary to keep their children alive. To be sure, more than a few villagers still hesitate before consulting a doctor out of fear of the resultant cost in professional fees and medication. But more and more, villagers travel to Béjar, Salamanca, Avila, and even Madrid to seek the advice of medical specialists. Most people never scrimp when the health of a child is at stake.

Again, we are confronted with the seemingly incongruous evidence that a village that is rapidly losing its population, and in this respect is dying, should simultaneously be experiencing a burst of prosperity. But, as we shall see, emigration is a fundamental source of improved living in Becedas.

CENTRIPETALITY AND CENTRIFUGALITY IN VILLAGE LIFE

The analysis thus far indicates that Becedas is developing dual tendencies in its relationship to the outside world. On the one hand, we are confronted with evidence of a centrifugal force, thrusting villagers into ever-increasing integration with larger surroundings. Villagers, to a greater degree than ever before, rely on manufactured products and other items that they themselves cannot produce, and are now deeply enmeshed in a world market system. They also migrate in large numbers, indicating an underlying dissatisfaction with village life, and the inability of the Becedas economy to satisfy fully the changing aspirations of all its inhabitants. At the same time, however, the centripetal phrasing of village activities, which is characteristic of the traditional Castilian *pueblo* (see p. 17), has been retained. Though the content of commerce and exchange has changed to keep pace with the developing Spanish economy, the occupational and commercial structures have responded by enabling village residents to carry out daily life within the familiar community framework. Depopulation and economic change have not destroyed the village's sociocentrism.

To understand why let us first examine the motives for migration. Most important is the attraction of a better income and a more comfortable material existence. The vast majority of ex-villagers find employment in factories, fruit and meat markets, hotels and restaurants, private residences, and similar situations where they carry out largely manual work. But even this type of employment provides an income which far exceeds that which can be earned in the village. When Faustino Pradera moved to Madrid, he found work as a part-time garage attendant at 12,000 pesetas (about 170 dollars) per month. By comparison, his village income would not have exceeded 60,000 pesetas for the entire year. Equally important, urban income appears sure, steady, and independent of the vagaries of weather and market, conditions which constantly burden those who remain behind in the village.

Moving to the city also means the acquisition of modern conveniences: stoves, refrigerators, gas heaters, bathtubs, and toilets, not to mention luxuries such as radios, telephones, televisions, and automobiles. Further, there is easy access to a wide array of bars, movies, theaters, parks, and other centers of diversion. The city has more *ambiente*, "action," than the *pueblo* and, almost for this reason alone, is to be preferred over the restricted and comparatively uneventful life of the village.

The people of Becedas migrate not only to improve their lives, but also to assure that their children will have better lives, for the urban milieu provides opportunity for education and advancement. Ex-villagers who are now engaged in urban unskilled labor expect their children to become skilled workers, or even professionals. For all that is needed, in their view, is that educational institutions and employment opportunities be available, and, presently at least, this is the case in the major Spanish cities.

Due to the widespread introduction of radio and television in Becedas since the mid-1950s, villagers have become increasingly aware of the attractions of the city and of the limitations inherent in village life. Close contact with city relatives, who have prospered far more than any Becedas farmers, has made this message more immediate and compelling. At the same time, however, economic and family circumstances still limit the number of people who can successfully leave the community and settle elsewhere. The result is that those who have been left behind have tried to provide themselves with the trappings of city life—the material symbols of urbanism—while remaining within the community.

The motives for change are, of course, complex. It is not simply because villagers enjoy modern conveniences and a higher standard of living that they have improved their houses and furnished themselves with a variety of new manufactured items and processed foods. The prestige of eating certain new foods, like fish or canned fruits, and of acquiring modern appliances also plays a role. Realizing the cultural and economic limitations of Becedas, villagers are anxious to display to themselves and migrants alike that they too can modernize, and that they are not willing to postpone gratification until the day when resettlement becomes feasible. In other words, by modernizing, the people of Becedas demonstrate a basic commitment to life within the community, whatever their long-range plans may entail.

There is yet another motive for emulation. Villagers, for the most part, still maintain an essentially sociocentric mentality. Becedas is the center of their world, the locus of daily life, and they are anxious that it should remain as much so as possible for migrants as well. To attract migrants back to the community, for however short a visit, means that villagers must meet certain basic requirements. They must install bathtubs and toilets, which migrants openly state as a necessity. They must provide migrants with the toothpaste and toilet paper to which the new urbanites have also grown accustomed. In short, they must replicate the city milieu, however imperfectly, so that migrants will neither ridicule nor ignore them. And increasingly, migrant standards become internalized; villagers themselves now perceive many of these manufactured items and conveniences as requirements, too.

Becedas has thus remained the *patria chica*, the "little country," for villagers. Their standard of living and material life approximate those of the city more than ever before. Yet their exchange activities and daily living habits remain centripetally phrased. They have also succeeded in making the community a magnet for ex-villagers, who, as we shall see in subsequent chapters, visit Becedas regularly several times each year. Despite the undeniable dispersal of the populace, the village remains the primary source of identity for its inhabitants. Recent material changes have, for the time being at least, preserved the viability of that identity.

Plate 4   Planting potatoes.

IV

The Village Economy: Property and Production

LAND AND CROPS

Farmland in Becedas is of generally low quality. A recent government survey reports that the agricultural land in Becedas is of poorer quality, measured by productivity, than half to two-thirds of the land in the rest of the province (Ministerio 1965). Considering the relatively limited productivity of Avila as a whole, this is indeed a poor record. The soil in Becedas is thin and rocky, the terrain broken and uneven. Not surprisingly, land parcels are small and, throughout much of the village terminus, are arranged into complex natural and man-made terraces. In one sense, this physical setting has been advantageous to the people, for it has mitigated against the formation of large-scale absentee land ownership, which is characteristic of many more fertile regions of the country. But in the current context, small land parcels are distinctly disadvantageous and limit the possibilities for technological modernization. The land's only blessing is that it is well-watered, both by rainfall, concentrated in the winter and spring months, and by the melting snows of Peña Negra.

In Becedas, land is classified according to its use. *Huertas*, or orchards, and *linares*, treeless land parcels, both fall within the category of *regadío*, or irrigated terrain. Two kinds of cultivated land are *de secano*, dry farmed: *tierras*, which are generally planted with wheat or barley; and *cerraos* (from standard Spanish, *cerrados*), which are devoted to rye and are progressively being laid waste due to the abandonment of rye cultivation.

In addition to cultivated land, much of Becedas's terrain is more or less naturally productive. The largest portion of the village terminus consists of dry scrubland, loosely called the *"Sierra,"* where the *ramos* (Spanish broom) that are used to kindle fires grow wild. Further, there are extensive, privately owned *matas*, woodlands of scrub oak trees, that provide the villagers' main source of firewood. Pastureland is furnished by *praos* (i.e., *prados*), which are small, privately owned meadows, and by communal *pastos*, the property of corporations of villagers and of the municipality as a whole. None of these lands requires sowing, but all of the pasturelands demand controlled irrigation for full productivity. Table 3 lists the approximate area and percentage of the village terminus occupied by each of these land types.

Although *huertas* and *linares* comprise little more than 8% of the total land area, it is this terrain that provides the villagers their main source of livelihood. Becedas's primary cash crops are apples and pears, grown in the *huertas*, and potatoes and navy beans (*pipos blancos*), sown in the *linares* and in the *huertas*, under the shade of the fruit trees. Potatoes are usually sown in one field for three or four consecutive years, after which the land is exhausted, and navy beans are substituted for a year or two. Most people also sow some barley in the *linares*, alternating this crop with potatoes. But unlike the other products, this grain is used almost exclusively as animal feed, not for market sale.

TABLE 3
Land Use in the Municipality of Becedas, 1965[a]

Land type	Hectares	Percentage of total area
Huertas	157.20	5.01
Linares	104.75	3.38
Tierras	75.04	2.42
Praos	349.44	11.26
Pastos	192.83	7.40
Matas	239.00	6.52
Sierra	1983.58	63.63
TOTALS	3101.84	100.00

[a] Adapted from a 1965 survey of the Ministerio de Hacienda de Avila. The folk land typology has been substituted for the scientific terminology used in the State document.

In addition to these primary crops, villagers always put aside a small corner of several *huertas* and *linares* for the production of vegetables, such as cabbage, lettuce, onions, tomatoes, carrots, and green beans, that are generally reserved for home consumption. Also destined for family use is the valued fruit of the huge walnut trees that dot the village terminus. Walnuts, formerly an important secondary product of Becedas, have lost virtually all their importance as a cash item. Most of the trees were sold at high prices for their wood a generation ago.

Without doubt, the emphasis on the production of four main crops— apples, pears, potatoes, and navy beans—represents the culmination of a process of agricultural specialization that took place throughout the years from about 1910 or 1920 to the 1970s. As already noted, flax (or *lino*, from which the term *"linar"* is derived) was one of the village's most important crops during the eighteenth and nineteenth centuries. As factory-made cotton and woolen fabrics became popular in twentieth-century Spain, home-produced linen could no longer compete, and flax production was entirely discontinued in Becedas, as in all of the Sierra de Béjar. Similarly, grain production, once carried out on a relatively large scale in Becedas, diminished rapidly during the years from the 1940s and 1950s to the 1970s. This period has witnessed a steady increase in land consolidation and agricultural mechanization throughout large areas of Spain, where flat, dry, treeless terrain has permitted these advancements. Unable to compete with grain production in these regions, the people of Becedas transformed some of their secondary crops—fruit, potatoes, and beans, which all require the water that Becedas' environment can provide—into primary cash products.

Interestingly, these agricultural changes are all reflected in Becedas' place names. As throughout much of Spain (Foster 1960: 56), land parcels in Becedas are grouped into well-defined territories of varying size, each with a distinctive name that may or may not reveal the actual status of the land today. For example, El Prado de las Monjas ("The Nun's Meadow") and El Prado del Obispo ("The Bishop's Meadow") presently belong to villagers, but undoubtedly were once the property of individual clerics or of the Church, probably prior to the large-scale sale of Church lands in the 1830s. Similarly, there are numerous territories, all of which today contain irrigated orchards, whose names reveal that they were formerly areas of dry grain agriculture. Such territories generally carry the term *"cerrao"* (for example, Cerrao Magán, Cerrao Mancebo) or *"tierra"* (Tierra la Juma). Another large area of irrigated orchards is referred to as Las Eras ("The Threshing Floors"), reflecting its past use in the cycle of grain production. Even today, we can witness the continuation of this process of agricultural specialization, as formerly dry-farmed land parcels are brought under irrigation and planted with apple and pear trees.

Until the 1960s, Becedas' rich water supply, an anomaly in arid Castile, gave the villagers a competitive advantage in the production of specialized crops. Since the Spanish government embarked upon ambitious irrigation projects throughout dry Spain (Flores 1969: 181–193), harnessing potentially powerful, but heretofore dormant, water supplies, the village economy is in a considerably weaker position. Areas that were, in the late 1960s, brought under irrigation, and in which land parcels were consolidated and agriculture mechanized, can now produce the same crops as Becedas, but much more cheaply. Becedas farmers suffer when potato prices drop to 2 pesetas per kilo; farmers in other areas prosper at the same price.

For this reason, the people of Becedas have already begun slowly to abandon potato and navy bean cultivation. Since 1971, when the Plasencia dairy outfit started coming to the village and farmers began purchasing Swiss cows for milk production, they have been turning more and more to the cultivation of fodder crops, especially clover and cabbage, but also, in smaller quantities, alfalfa. Although these crops require an abundant water supply, the availability of water can no longer be the sole criterion for specialization in Becedas. Rather, it is a combination of water availability and mountainous terrain, suitable for herding, that now determines the course of agricultural developments. With the introduction of more cattle, Becedas can no longer resist turning increasingly to pasturage-oriented crops. The steady abandonment of grain cultivation over the past generation was, therefore, only the first of a long series of agricultural adaptations to the modernization of the Spanish economy.

THE AGRICULTURAL CYCLE

In Becedas, the rhythm of life is determined by a relatively fixed yearly cycle of productive activities that is still measured largely by reference to the religious calendar. Villagers know that potato planting should be completed by the day of San Marcos (April 25), and that community-controlled irrigation commences on the day of San Juan Bautista (June 24). Weather prediction, upon which many agricultural decisions are based, is discussed in a similar framework. It is said for example, that:

> *El agua por San Juan*   Rain on San Juan
> *Ni da vida ni da pan.*   Yields neither life nor bread.

and:

Por San Blas la cigüeña veras   Look for the stork on San Blas
                                 [February 3]
Y si la vieres, año de nieves.   And if you see it, there will be
                                 a year of snow

Older villagers still believe in the *cabañuelas*, a method of prognostication once widespread throughout Iberia (Riegelhaupt 1967). In the Becedas variant of this belief, weather conditions during the first 12 days of January are supposed to predict the entire year's climate, with January 1 corresponding to the month of January, January 2 to February, January 3 to March, and so on. This method of prediction, however, has recently fallen into disrepute as being "backward," so that it no longer openly determines most villagers' agricultural decisions.

Because of the harsh and unstable climate, the agricultural year is unevenly divided into periods of relative dormancy and intensity of productive activities. Winter in Becedas is a time of relative agricultural inactivity. The days are cold and short and often snow-filled, so this is the season for retiring to bed early, rising late, and generally spending a lot of time indoors. In the fields, men occupy themselves with necessary, though subsidiary, tasks like collecting and chopping firewood, gathering leaves to make cattle "beds" in the barns, making charcoal to feed the ubiquitous *braseros*, and constructing and repairing irrigation ditches. Those who have sown navy beans the previous year spend much time at home with their families at the painstaking work of shelling and sorting.

By mid-February, longer days and improved weather permit the beginning of a new agricultural year. Villagers begin visiting their fields regularly to prune the trees and to cover the ground with manure, which is transported from the barns for use as fertilizer. Currently, too, many villagers devote this period to the planting of new fruit trees, which are shipped directly to Becedas middlemen from as far away as Zaragoza.

Full-scale agricultural production really begins only in mid-March, when farmers prepare their fields for sowing. Land parcels must be plowed between three and five times before the hard rocky soil is ready for planting. Because the plow lacks mold boards, fields are worked crossways to break up the soil most effectively. Consequently, Becedas, like most Mediterranean communities, has square-shaped land parcels, so different from the predominant northern European strip pattern, which has resulted from plowing in only one direction with the use of a mold board plow (Bloch 1966: 21–63; Foster 1960: 58).

By mid-April, the fields are generally ready for sowing. Beans, potatoes, and grain are all planted in a 2- or 3-week period, after which villagers begin several operations which occupy them through midsummer. First, they must spray their trees with chemical insecticides. A few of the wealthiest villagers own gasoline-propelled sprayers, but most people use simple hand-pump devices. Each field must be "cured," as this operation is called, seven or eight times. In addition, the sown parcels must be weeded. This is accomplished both with a plow (in the operations known as *aricar* and *a dar tierra*—"to strike earth") and by hand with a hoe (in the operation called *a dar entre parra y parra*—"to strike [earth] between one grapevine and another").

By far the busiest agricultural season lasts from mid-June through mid-July. In this period, villagers are especially occupied with irrigation and hay collection, as well as with the ordinary tasks of spraying and weeding. During late June and July, when water is most abundant, each field is irrigated once a week, the optimal amount. Due to the complex village irrigation system, which will be fully described in the next chapter, farmers never know more than a few hours in advance when they can irrigate which field. This, plus the delicacy with which irrigation must be carried out, makes the operation particularly burdensome. Haying, also, is accomplished under a great deal of both physical and psychological pressure After the long grass is reaped, it must be dried out in the sun "for two *siestas*," that is, for two days, before it can be collected and stored for use as animal feed during the long winter. The threat of rain is ever present. If the cut hay should get wet, a large part of it will rot, and the rest will lose much of its nutritional value, therefore rapid collection is necessary. When haying is completed, villagers who have sown grain begin to reap and thresh it, tasks that generally last through the first week of August. The land makes so many demands on human labor during early and mid-summer that villagers cannot even rest from work on Sundays during this period. Aside from a short afternoon nap, men are at work in the fields from sunrise to sunset, and sometimes beyond.

The work pressures become considerably less acute during the final weeks of August. Spraying and irrigation continue, but at a slower pace. Farmers prop up the sagging branches of the fruit trees with long forked poles, known as *horcas*, and collect apples and pears which have fallen to the ground to be used as animal feed. But this is mainly a period of re-cuperation and of preparations for the four-day patronal fiesta which begins on August 27.

In mid-September, the pace once again quickens as villagers begin the *recolección*, or fruit harvest. This is a period of intensive labor, but, unlike the weighty aura surrounding hay collection, irrigation, and threshing, the fruit harvest is marked by a spirit of lightheartedness and gaiety. Villagers say that they never tire or run out of energy at this task, even though they spend all their daylight hours in the fields.

The *cosecha*, or bean and potato harvest, immediately follows the *recolección* and lasts into early November. This is backbreaking labor, more burdensome than the fruit collection, but villagers are spurred on by the knowledge that they will soon receive monetary payment for the year's work. After the beans and potatoes are in, the weather once again turns bitter and the work cycle shifts to a period of dormancy. There is little to be done now but await the arrival of buyers from the outside.

AGRICULTURAL TECHNOLOGY

The people of Becedas are extremely self-conscious about their methods of working the land and are well aware that the traditional technology greatly inhibits their productive capabilities. Most agricultural tools and techniques in Becedas have a pan-Mediterranean base and can be traced historically through several millenia. On the other hand, the village has recently witnessed some technological changes that have been at least temporarily beneficial to the populace.

In Becedas, animal and human labor provide the main source of energy. Most farmers own at least one or two beasts of burden, which are used both as pack animals and for work in the fields. Plows are drawn primarily with *vacas de trabajo*, "work cows," by horn yokes (Figure 4), as is typical in Castile. These animals are preferred to oxen for their greater docility, and also because they periodically provide their owners with milk and calves, the latter of which are sold at animal fairs in Béjar and El Barco. Their main disadvantage is that they are expensive to maintain, so that less prosperous villagers must content themselves with horses or donkeys. Frequently, people who own work cows will also own a horse or donkey to be used in threshing, in carrying small cargos of firewood, and for traveling to neighboring villages or distantly located fields.

Fields are plowed with the *arado dental*, the most common Spanish

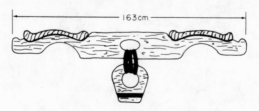

Figure 4   Cow yoke, Becedas.

plow, particularly characteristic of the Castiles (see Figure 5).[1] Despite
the plow's relative simplicity, the depth and width of the furrows can be
regulated somewhat by the use of dowels (*orejeras*) which are inserted at
varying angles into holes in the wooden foundation (*dental*) of the iron
plowshare (*reja*).

Threshing methods in Becedas date back over 2000 years. All threshing
is carried out with the *trillo*, the *tribulum* of ancient Rome. This is a
simple wooden sledge whose underside is covered with short flint blades
of varying lengths that are serrated for increased sharpness. A vertical
pole at the front of the sledge permits its attachment to a team of animals.
For their faster pace, horses are preferred to cows in threshing. The operation generally requires the work of two individuals: one who drives the
team over the grain while riding the *trillo* (either standing, or seated on a
wooden crate or soft sack); and the other who continuously turns the
grain, thus progressively exposing more of it to the *trillo* blades and to the
sun. The drier and the more brittle the grain, the more easily it is threshed.

When this is accomplished, the grain must be winnowed in the operation known as *limpiar* ("to clean"). With wooden shovels and rakes, the
ground grain is tossed into the air. The kernels drop straight to the floor,
while the chaff is carried off by the wind and deposited a few feet away.
The kernels are further extracted through the use of a simple, wooden-
framed sieve. The entire operation is best carried out in the early morning
or late evening, when the winds blow strongest, but often the work is
prolonged by unusually calm air. When this occurs, people sleep outdoors
on the threshing floors, waiting for winds and protecting their grain from
theft by man or animals.

Unlike this threshing operation, which has been used over a wide area
since antiquity, Becedas' irrigation methods are, to my knowledge, unique

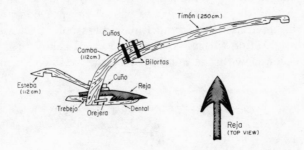

Figure 5 The Becedas plow.

---

[1] Caro Baroja (1949) has made the most extensive and valuable study of Spanish
plow types and their distribution.

to the immediately surrounding region. Villagers today, as traditionally, use three methods of irrigation, which are classified according to the different patterns of furrows and valves in the fields (see Figure 6). Two of the methods, *a palaera* and *a cantero*, are suitable for more or less level terrain. The third, *de tablero*, is used for fields situated on an incline. In all three systems, the water flow is regulated by small gates made of sod and stone. In irrigating any field, a farmer must continually knock down and rebuild these simple gates, which he accomplishes only with the use of a hoe.

Changing economic conditions have influenced the use of the two methods suitable for level fields. Of these two methods, irrigation *a cantero* is by all accounts the most productive. Because, in this method, the furrows are broken into smaller units, the method allows most control over the water flow and hence yields the best and most abundant crops. It also requires the most time and effort on the part of the irrigator. Prior to the

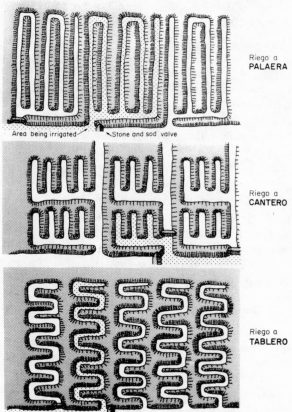

Figure 6   Irrigation furrow patterns.

1960s, this was by far the more popular of the two methods. Since most villagers controlled small amounts of land, if any at all, it was important to make each parcel yield as much as possible. However, with the acquisition or control of larger quantities of land, a phenomenon which will be discussed in more detail later, villagers must sharply restrict the amount of time they can devote to each small parcel. For this reason, they have been switching increasingly to the inferior *a palaera method*. Even though fields produce significantly less under this system, it requires less work than the other and thus provides extra time for work on a greater number of fields. In the end, for a busy farmer today, it pays to irrigate *a palaera* rather than *a cantero*.

Other more far-reaching agricultural changes came to the village during the 1960s. The scientific spraying of fruit trees, for example, is an introduction that has vastly improved the quality and size of the harvests. This horticultural advancement was encouraged by local-level workers from the Ministry of Agriculture, which established a branch office at El Barco as late as the early 1960s. Since spraying is inexpensive and provides such obviously improved crops, the people of Becedas willingly adopted the method. No villager today goes without it.

Grass reaping is the only agricultural activity in Becedas that has become truly mechanized. Traditionally, and up until 1960 or so, villagers relied entirely on the scythe (*guadaña*) for this operation. All the reaping in the village was done by 15 or 20 *coritos* (literally, "timid ones") who were among the many landless villagers who made their living by working for others. Using a scythe is a highly developed skill and is considered particularly onerous, so most villagers pay *coritos* to reap rather than learn to do the job themselves. At present, there is a serious labor shortage in Becedas, and most people are unable to find workers to do the reaping for them. The shortage has been considerably eased by the appearance of mechanical reapers, nine animal-drawn and five gasoline-operated, all purchased by the wealthiest villagers. While the owners of these machines rent them out at 250 pesetas per *peonada* (the area of grass that one man can reap in a day, using a scythe), the few individuals who do still hire themselves out to reap by scythe charge 350 pesetas to do the same work. Although it is generally conceded that the hand-reaping job is superior to machine reaping, the price is simply too high. So most villagers now either rent a machine or struggle along on their own, trying to learn the new, difficult skill of scything. It seems that only a slight majority of the villagers presently use machine reapers. But in the context of such an overwhelmingly traditional agriculture, this change is significant, particularly since it has arisen in response to conditions brought about by migration.

LAND TENURE

In Becedas, there are three types of land tenure: outright ownership, rental, and sharecropping (*a medias*). In general, when cultivated land is used by someone other than the owner, it is sharecropped rather than rented. Meadows and woodlands, on the other hand, are rented, since they do not produce easily divisible goods. Leases on the land last one year and are made by verbal agreement. The traditional time for rental payments is Christmas Day.

Although there is no written evidence to substantiate the claim,[2] informants are unanimous in stating that, until the mid-1950s or early 1960s, relatively few villagers owned a large proportion of the land. The majority made their living by working for others as *jornaleros*, "day laborers," though they might have also owned one or two small plots of their own. Economic equality existed in that no individual was so wealthy that he could live exclusively from the work of others. But within the village context, there were significant differences in wealth, and the people were divided into *ricos* ("rich ones"), those who owned more land than they themselves could cultivate, and *pobres* ("poor ones"), those who owned little or no land and had to work for the others.

Now, the situation is considerably altered. Table 4 lists the numbers and proportions of villagers who work land under the various systems of tenure. From this statistical breakdown, it is clear that ownership and control over land is different from what it was traditionally. All but 13% (categories b, c, and g) of the individuals presently active in farming own some or all of the land they work. Further, the vast majority (74%) control a great deal of land through renting and sharecropping. Although these forms of nonproprietary control always existed to a limited extent in Becedas, their use became much more widespread during the 1960s. Consequently, the number of full-time day laborers has decreased dramatically, with only two individuals, both bachelors, presently making their living in this fashion.

The change to more evenly distributed land ownership and control has resulted from the recent exodus from the village. Some migrants have sold

---

[2] The village census, which is carried out every decade, contains an entry for every villager's occupation. A distinction is usually made in Spanish between two kinds of farmers, the *jornalero* ("day laborer") and the *labrador* ("small proprietor"). While the Becedas census uses both these terms, I have determined that the criteria by which they have applied to one individual or another have been totally subjective, unfortunately rendering the "hard" statistical data virually useless.

TABLE 4
Distribution of Land Tenure Systems
among the Becedas Population, 1970

System of tenure	Number of active farmers	Percentage of active farmers
a. Own all land worked	45	26
b. Sharecrop all land worked	10	6
c. Rent all land worked	3	1
d. Own and sharecrop all land worked	30	17
e. Own and rent all land worked	32	18
f. Own, rent, and sharecrop all land worked	47	27
g. Rent and sharecrop all land worked	8	5
TOTALS	175	100

their landholdings outright to landless villagers after securing permanent positions in the cities, while others have retained their landholdings as a source of rental or sharecropping income. As of 1970, 96 of the 175 active farmers in Becedas, or 55% of the total number, worked land belonging to recent migrants on a sharecrop or rental basis. At that time, the large majority of absentee landowners lived in Madrid, the destination of most Becedas migrants, but many also resided in provincial capitals like Salamanca, Avila, Caceres, Badajoz, Santander, and Barcelona, and a few as far away as Caracas and Buenos Aires. Obviously migration has given land ownership or control to villagers who previously had no such opportunity.

Correspondingly, migration has created a serious labor shortage. Former day laborers now work the land they themselves control, as already noted. As mentioned in Chapter 3, many others, without a permanent economic stake in the village, were among the first to respond to the expanding urban job market and began leaving Becedas as early as the late 1950s and early 1960s. Now there is effectively more land than can be productively worked by the inhabitants and it is this unusually high land–labor ratio which is essentially responsible for the much altered distribution of land ownership and control.

A few concrete cases will clarify these recent developments. Let us first look at what becomes of land that was previously farmed by migrants:

1. Francisco Pozo. In late 1969, Francisco took his family to Madrid, where he obtained a job as garage attendant. Previous to his move, Francisco owned four agricultural plots and sharecropped five others. Now, he retains ownership of his four plots, which are worked on a sharecrop basis by a village cousin. The five plots that Francisco formerly sharecropped himself have been taken over by a different cousin under the same tenure

system. Since neither of these cousins has relinquished any of the lands he previously worked, they both have considerably expanded their resources as a result of Francisco's move.

2. Emilio Tormes. When Emilio and his family left the village for Barcelona at the beginning of the 1970s, he owned only two *praos*, but sharecropped five other plots belonging to large landholders of the village. All of this land is of extremely low quality, so that Emilio's two *praos* are presently abandoned, no one wishing to rent them. Three of the previously sharecropped plots have similarly gone to waste since their owners can find no one to work them under any system of tenure. Although the final two plots have limited productive value, the owner, for lack of other laborers, half-heartedly took upon himself the burden of cultivating them.

Thus, as a result of the rural exodus, so much land has become available that villagers can now afford to be selective and choose to farm only the most productive plots. Landowners who have more property than they themselves can handle are forced to let their worst lands go to fallow. Excess land and the labor shortage thus tended to bring about increasing economic equality among villagers during the 1950s and 1960s. Just as landless villagers are now controlling more and more property, large landholders are limited in their productivity by the shortage of workers. Consequently everyone tends to farm just what he and his immediate family can manage on their own.

The case of Julio Ramírez illustrates well how previously landless workers have been able to benefit from the current economic situation. At the beginning of the 1950s, Julio owned no property and was among the poorest villagers. All his earnings came from work as a *jornalero*. Even today, villagers remark how his young sons were driven by hunger to steal milk by drinking it directly from the teats of other people's cows. Eventually Julio's wife inherited one plot. As his sons grew older, they were able to join Julio in work as day laborers, and the family thus saved enough to purchase two more plots, which were sold by migrants. In 1966, they began to sharecrop five more plots belonging to a migrant. Now, the land has passed to the hands of this migrant's daughter, who lives in Madrid, and she plans to sell it to Julio. Julio's family is considered in excellent financial condition, and they live in one of the newest, most well-equipped houses in the village.

It is significant that villagers who control property through renting or sharecropping really think of that property as their own. A renter or sharecropper more often than not refers to a certain plot as "mine." For this reason, many months often passed before I realized that particular *huertas* and *linares* belonged to migrants, rather than to the individuals who farmed them. Not only do villagers conceive of such land as their own, but also they are acquiring more actual—not only perceptual—control of the property. In 1950, the most common sharecropping arrangement was an exact division of the costs of production and of the harvest between the owner and the sharecropper. Now, because of the high value of his labor, the sharecropper often gains a slight economic advantage from the arrangement. On sharecropped orchards, it is becoming more common for the sharecropper to receive half the fruit crop, as he would have before, as well as *all* of whatever is grown on the ground. Increasingly, too, owners of sharecropped plots are paying for more than half the cost of production, for example, covering the entire price of manure for fertilizer rather than just half. Whereas, as late as the 1960s, owners always decided what crops would be planted on their property, now the decision almost always rests with the sharecropper. Thus, even when the farmer does not own the land he works, that land is virtually "his own."

The foregoing analysis in part explains the correlation between migration and a rising standard of living in Becedas.[3] Through the sale of agricultural parcels, as well as the extension of sharecropping and renting, the distribution of village property has become much more equal than before, giving the majority of villagers a source of income that was unavailable in 1950. Further, by specializing in particular crops and using some new horticultural methods, villagers have profited considerably. For all these reasons, villagers now have more money at their disposal than ever before. Until the 1950s, most villagers needed to borrow money at high interest rates in order to subsist for the several months preceding harvest. Now, virtually no one borrows, except for major projects like rebuilding a house. An old, retired village carpenter complains that he usually had to extend long-term credit if he expected to have any customers at all. Now this man's son, who carries on the trade, reports that villagers invariably pay him promptly. It is the economic change resulting from migration which is immediately responsible for this newfound village prosperity; as we shall show later, the economic development of Spain as a whole is ultimately responsible for Becedas' rising living standards. In following chapters, we shall discuss some social and psychological ramifications of the changing village economy, as well as other factors related to migration that have tended toward the villagers' financial well-being.

---

[3] The same development may be noted in the southern Italian town of Franza, where emigration has produced two strikingly similar results to those in Becedas: (1) the creation of a fluid land supply, and (2) the infusion of wealth from the outside. Both have led to markedly higher standards of living in the community (Lopreato 1967).

ECONOMIC EGALITARIANISM AND
COMMUNITY IDENTITY

As we saw in Chapter 1, social scientists have labored under the notion that small communities in a developing society undergo a process of economic atomization and internal differentiation. There is, according to this view, a unilineal progression from equality to hierarchy and from individual self-sufficiency to complex division of labor. Our thinking on this matter has, of course, been strongly influenced by Durkheim's *Division of Labor in Society* (1964) in which he described the evolution from a state of "mechanical solidarity"—in which social cohesion is accomplished through the likeness of parts and functions, and all individuals strongly resemble one another in their status, activities, and ideas—to a state of "organic solidarity"—in which parts and functions differ, and individuals are bound to one another through the mutual dependency that arises out of specialization of status and role. This idea was adopted a half-century later by Redfield (1941, 1947) who applied it specifically to the analysis of peasant communities undergoing change. Frankenberg (1966), Halpern (1967), Anderson and Anderson (1964, 1966), Pérez–Díaz (1969), and others later saw the same process at work in small European villages everywhere from Denmark to France to Yugoslavia.

Has Becedas followed the same route? By all expectations, our village should conform to the overall scheme. Urban contacts have become more intimate, village agriculture has undergone increasing specialization in response to changing market conditions, and there has even been limited mechanization as well. According to prevalent theories, these and other similar developments should have been accompanied by a rise in the degree of individualization and heterogeneity within the community. Yet, just the opposite has occurred.

Of course, the progression from mechanical to organic solidarity within any society may be gauged along any number of dimensions, including the ideological, social, and legal. Here, we are interested primarily in economic changes, and it is clear that at least on two counts mechanical solidarity has increased in Becedas. First and most important is the obvious egalitarianism of the community in comparison with the past. Migration has created a situation in which both land ownership and land control have become more evenly distributed within the community than ever before. The traditional division between *ricos* and *pobres* has become obsolete; while *ricos* have been deprived of the labor supply upon which they depended to sustain their superior position, *pobres* have disappeared altogether. "Now," the people say, "we are all the same." Everyone shares a middling status as independent proprietor, and the effective interdependence between landless and landed villagers has been totally eliminated.

Second, the division of labor within the community has been correspondingly reduced, and for much the same reason. In previous years, the poorest villagers not only hired themselves out as reapers but also carried out almost all the tree planting and pruning of all Becedas. During the 1960s, those who specialized in these tasks either left the community or came into substantial landholdings of their own. Only at exorbitant prices will they now agree to leave work on their own fields to perform these tasks. As a result, the majority of villagers have had to learn to carry them out by themselves. Even the price of hiring a mechanical reaper is too expensive for many.

Because more villagers now have more land to care for, occupational specialization has also declined in the non-agricultural sector as well. The several village barbers still cut hair but no longer pull teeth, as was their traditional role. Villagers today entrust this task only to Béjar dentists. Nor do the Becedas shoemakers and tailors operate in any but the most minimal way, for even though they charge less for their services than do their city counterparts, they no longer can afford to take time from the care of their newly acquired fields. Once again, the mutual interdependence of people within the community that is implied in the concept of organic solidarity has been effectively reduced.

A great paradox lies behind these recent developments. For if we take a national, rather than local, perspective, it is clear that the organic solidarity of Spain as a whole has increased. Becedas and hundreds of small communities like it were once highly self-sufficient, providing themselves with considerably more of the necessary foods and services than they now do. Agricultural specialization and increasing involvement in the national economy has actually enhanced Becedas' economic dependence on cities and outside agencies. At the same time, the dependence that the village as a whole experiences in relation to urban centers has had the effect of reducing the dependence of community members on one another. Recent economic circumstances have fostered a situation in which everyone is occupationally more like everyone else than ever before. Never has the economic similarity of family units in Becedas been greater than at present.

The outcome of these dual tendencies—economic egalitarianism and the decreasing division of labor—has been to enhance the feeling of community identity and solidarity. Because all villagers share more or less the same life circumstances, they can easily identify and empathize with one another. As Durkheim would put it, there now exists a mutual attraction of the social molecules through similarity and likeness; a state of mechanical solidarity is in evidence. It is not only that people do the same things and share the same status, but also that they are all equally affected by the increased dependence on the outside world and by the pressures which that dependence has produced. No longer do some villagers have more advantages than others. All are struggling with and responding to new market conditions, attempting as best they know how to adapt their inhospitable terrain to the demands of an expanding national economy. They all now are in the same sinking boat—and they know it.

Plate 5 Haying.

V

Some Social Aspects
of Economic Organization

THE FAMILIAL BASIS OF PRODUCTION

Throughout much of western Mediterranean Europe, the most common production unit is the nuclear family. Whether in agriculture, pottery-making, or other subsistence activities, a man working in conjunction with his wife and children is generally able to provide all the labor necessary for his subsistence. To be sure, individuals invariably become bound to those outside the nuclear family through blood, marriage, friendship, or ritual kinship. But in the economic realm, each nuclear household usually forms an isolated unit in the productive process, wary of cooperating with other such units on any but the most fleeting basis.

While the situation in Becedas conforms in part to this overall picture, it would be an oversimplification to say that here families operate purely as economic isolates. Rather, we may distinguish three separate kinds of economic units, each with a distinct social underpinning. First, there is the nuclear family, living in its own household and having an internal organization for the performance of subsistence activities. In terms of the variety of activities carried out in Becedas and the time devoted to these, this type is, without doubt, the most important economic unit in the village. Second, there are explicit and implicit contracts for economic cooperation made voluntarily by friends and relatives from separate nuclear families. Such mutual assistance is limited to the performance of several specific agricultural tasks. Finally, there is the Becedas community as a whole, organized for the control, care, and periodic redistribution of communal resources. The economic activities which fall under community jurisdiction are, like those of the second category, few in number, but cooperation here is mandatory, imposed on individuals by the entire village for the benefit of all.

In Becedas, the nuclear family household, as a discrete unit, clearly bears the main burden of production. Within the family there is a relatively well-defined division of labor by age and sex. The heaviest, most time-consuming production tasks are relegated to the men. Generally, only men prune, spray, plow, irrigate, and ride the *trillo*. Women though proudly claiming liberation from farm labor, in actuality share certain major tasks with their husbands. Man and wife work alongside one another in the fields to sow beans, winnow grain, and harvest all the major crops. In these activities, there is virtually no distinction between the labor roles of the sexes.

In other instances, men and their wives work together but perform different operations. In sowing potatoes, for example, a man walks along the furrows chopping small holes with his hoe, while his wife follows, depositing the sliced potato tubers into the earth. The roles here are never reversed. Generally, too, it is the woman's responsibility to sort the apples and pears as they are picked from the trees. While women do harvest fruit from the lowest branches, only the men climb the enormously high, specially designed ladders (known as *burros*, "donkeys") necessary to reach the highest branches of the tall pear trees.

At times, the sexual division of labor seems to be guided more by the final goal of an operation than by its intrinsic nature. For example, both men and women know how to slice potatoes and are culturally permitted to do so. But almost invariably, it is the woman of the household who slices potatoes in preparation for sowing, just as it is the man who slices to provide potatoes as feed for the draft animals, since it is primarily his responsibility to care for cattle. Obviously, there is nothing inherently masculine or feminine about potato slicing; the activity simply falls within distinct sexual domains, depending on the final goal of the operation. Similarly, both men and women know how to handle a hoe. However, women use this tool only to plant beans, never to sow potatoes, when the hoe is invariably wielded by the man.

The sexual division of labor is never so rigid that boundaries cannot on occasion be crossed. The situation is precisely that described by Pitt–Rivers (1961: 86) for an Andalusian town: Certain activities are more appropriate for one sex or another, but men would not be considered effeminate nor women masculine if it should become necessary for them to carry out tasks ordinarily assigned to people of the opposite gender. It is common, in fact, for old or recently ill men to take up some women's activities, and for women to substitute for their husbands when the men are tied down with other chores. If, as often happens, a woman should have to assume responsibility for the irrigation of a *huerta*, she is never ridiculed. It is simply assumed that, not being particularly skilled in the task, she will perform it less well than her husband, who has greater experience and strength than she. But it is far preferable for her to do the job than to let the parcel go dry.

Due to varying degrees of economic necessity, families differ as to the amount of productive labor required of children. Nowadays, with jobs opening up in the cities, people are becoming increasingly aware of the positive value of education and are reluctant to withdraw their children from school, even temporarily, to make them work in the fields. It is considered foolish, even cruel, to prepare a child for a future of farming. Everyone aspires for his children to leave the village; "All this is going to die" or "I don't want my son to learn the work of the fields" are the phrases most commonly heard from parents with regard to their children's futures. In Becedas, to prepare a child for farming is to condemn him to a life of continual hardship with few material rewards.

Nonetheless, from the sheer necessity for their labor, all children are expected to help their families whenever time permits or agricultural requirements dictate. This is uniformly true during the fruit harvest, when even the relatively meager physical strength of children can be of considerable economic benefit. As the saying goes:

El oficio del niño es poco,	A child's work is worth little,
Y *el que lo pierde es un tonto.*	But he who doesn't take advantage of it is a fool.

Whenever children of either sex are called upon to work, they are generally assigned the lighter women's tasks. Not until a boy is at least 15 or 16 years old is he permitted to manage the plow or ride the *trillo*, both of which require a good deal of skill and strength. The only job regularly assigned to young boys (in this, girls are exempt) is to take the family's cows and horses to pasture in the early evening (in summertime), or to return the animals to the village barns. And they are usually free from this chore during winter, when their fathers have plenty of time to do the job themselves.

In any case, it should be stressed that the fields are primarily the adult man's domain. Women and children are merely helpers, called upon in relatively specific circumstances to supplement the man's labor. To women and children, agricultural activity is subsidiary, and the amount of time they spend in the fields is considerably less than that demanded of their husbands and fathers. If family production could be carried on without their services, they would doubtless refrain altogether from participation in agriculture. But then, the household would not be an economic enterprise, and the farmers of Becedas could no longer be termed "peasants," in the strict sense.

INTERFAMILY COOPERATION

In Becedas, there are two prominent occasions on which individuals of different households combine to assist one another: the hay collection and the potato harvest. In both instances, the cooperation is completely voluntary, at least in theory, and is devised to fulfill labor needs that the nuclear family alone cannot provide. In both, too, friendship and kinship bonds are the source of recruitment for cooperative endeavors. The main difference between them is the nature of rights and obligations among the cooperating individuals.

As already noted, haying is one of the most psychologically and physically intense agricultural activities in the village. The constant threat of rain falling on the cut, dried hay means that it must be collected rapidly and placed as quickly as possible in the village barns for storage and consumption throughout the long winter. Haying lasts for about 3 weeks every year, during which time a man may have to cut and clear hay from any number of fields, varying from only one or two for the less prosperous villagers, to eight or more for the wealthiest. The job is arduous, tiring, and unpleasant. It is the work of men alone; women never participate.

In order to collect hay from a field as rapidly as possible, a man calls upon friends, neighbors, and relatives to form a work team. No money exchanges hands for this service. The only expense an individual incurs is the provision of food for his helpers during the period of their labor. When the operation lasts all day, the usual amount of time for a single field, his wife carries both the noon and the late afternoon meals out to the field for the entire group. If the project lasts only a morning, the workers are provided the noon meal alone; if accomplished in a single afternoon, they are given only dinner.

By asking people to work for him, an individual automatically obligates himself to reciprocate the labor for the others. The value of the meals in no way compensates a man for a day's work, especially during this peak agricultural season. Rather, people help in haying with the expectation that they will be similarly aided. For this reason, during haying season, if a man is fortunate enough to have a couple of slack days, free from the ordinary agricultural tasks, he will usually offer his labor to those who are about to collect hay. In this way, he obligates the others to work for him later on, thus, in effect, creating for himself a reserve labor force.

Haying teams generally consist of five to seven individuals. The important social bonds in any team are always between the person whose hay is being collected, on the one hand, and each of his workers, on the other. In other words, even though more than two individuals comprise each team, the basis for team recruitment is essentially dyadic. A man chooses his helpers from among a labor pool consisting of all his friends, neighbors, and relatives. Those who eventually come to work for him on any one day may or may not have close social ties with one another. The important thing is that they each, individually, have a social bond with the person for whom they are collectively working and from whom they can expect similar services in the future.

Over a period of days, what results from this recruitment pattern is a string of work teams, each with a different but overlapping membership. Figure 7 illustrates the typical structure of such teams over a 3-day period.

On the first day, Ego recruits four people, let us say Friends A, B, C, and D, to help him hay. On the second day, Ego reciprocates by helping to harvest hay for Friend A, who has also asked three other men, D, E, and F to join the team. On the third day, Ego and Friend A find themselves together again, working for D, to whom each is independently obligated for such service. In this fashion, an elaborate network of haying

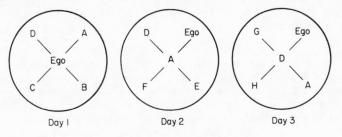

Figure 7 Team membership in haying.

teams is established throughout the village. Each individual is actually obligated to assist only a limited number of people with haying, but in the process he finds himself working and clearing alongside of numerous other villagers, who have similar obligations to these people. In this way, the network of economic reciprocity not only reinforces existing social ties but also establishes a basis for social integration among the villagers in general.[1]

Essentially, the pattern of reciprocity in haying is one important expression in Becedas of the dyadic contract which Foster (1961a, 1963) has shown to be a structural feature of peasant societies throughout the Mediterranean and Latin America. As in Tzintzuntzan, Mexico, such contracts in Becedas are "informal or implicit, since they lack ritual or legal basis. They are not based on any idea of law, and they are unenforceable through authority; they exist only at the pleasure of the contractants" (1961a: 1174). In Becedas, two men who are friends, neighbors, or relatives are under moral pressure to assist one another in haying. But the cooperation between them is completely voluntary, and it is necessary to the continuance of their social relationship that it be conceived as such.

When informants are asked, "If you help Fulano to collect hay, will he help you later on?" they invariably reveal a reluctance to answer the question directly. People become uncomfortable at the implication of forced assistance and, after hedging a few moments, state, "Perhaps," or "Not necessarily, but maybe." Although pairs of individuals definitely are obligated to cooperate, it is a functional requirement of their social relationship that the obligation never be explicitly stated, lest the mutual aid appear too openly a commercial bargain. For in Becedas, as in Alcalá de la Sierra, social relationships, especially among friends, must *appear* free from economic interest or exploitation, even though they actually require the performance of reciprocal favors (Pitt–Rivers 1961: 138–139).

For this reason, villagers are ambivalent in their attitude toward cooperation in haying. They know that the continuance of a positive social relationship requires them to assist others in the task. But at the same time, they frequently resent the demands on their labor during a period of intense argicultural activity. Since it is morally forbidden to calculate

---

[1] A strikingly similar pattern of voluntary cooperative work teams exists in rural Ireland, where it is known as "lending a boy" (Arensberg 1959: 64–70), and in villages of the Loire Valley, France, where the grape harvest (*vendange*) provides the occasion for reciprocal labor (J. Brandes n.d.: 35–37). As in Becedas, workers in Ireland and France are fed their meals by the recruiting farmer during the day of service. In Serbia, a cooperative work group (*moba*) forms for mutual aid in wheat reaping. Here, too, the laborers are provided food and drink by the host family (Halpern 1967b: 66).

a man's labor in haying as if it were an economic commodity, people usually help one another to different degrees. It often happens that a man assists a friend to clear four entire fields, while only receiving half a day's labor in return. Several villagers, particularly those with nonfarming occupations like carpenter or storekeeper, have no hay to collect, yet are constantly called upon by others to help in this task. Such individuals cooperate because they know it is part of their role as friend, neighbor, or relative to do so. But they cooperate reluctantly, and with a feeling that they are being exploited. Indeed, it is generally true that people with few animals, hence little hay, assist more than they are assisted. And since those with relatively little land have more time to devote to hay collection than do their economic superiors, they consequently find themselves recruited more often than they consider just. Almost never is an even balance in reciprocal labor struck between any two individuals.

A very different type of relationship among cooperators characterizes the second form of voluntary mutual assistance in Becedas, that of the fruit and potato harvests. Here, extra labor is needed not so much because of weather requirements as because of marketing demands. Since outside buyers appear in the village spontaneously and unannounced, people find it advisable to have all of a single crop sorted and ready for sale. Whether one harvests early or late in the season, it is better to collect all one's potatoes in a 2-week period than to prolong the process over a month's time. Further, farmers' crops mature at different times. Trees in different sections of the village yield fruit at varying rates, and some villagers prefer to wait longer than others before harvesting their potatoes. For these reasons, farmers generally have some free time to assist one another in collecting the crops.

Until the mid-1950s or so, when there were a good number of landless laborers, mutual assistance in harvesting was virtually unknown. The villagers who controlled extensive amounts of land hired others for a fixed daily sum to help them collect the crops. Today, some large landowners still hire workers, but the labor pool is furnished almost exclusively from the neighboring village of Neila, whose farmers sow grain, operate under a different agricultural cycle from Becedas, and are, therefore, available for employment during Becedas' peak harvest season. Because of massive migration, however, the tiny village of Neila can furnish only a handful of workers.

To solve the labor problem, Becedas farmers have in recent years resorted to mutual assistance. As in haying, reciprocal labor is provided by friends, relatives, and neighbors. Unlike haying, however, both men and women participate in the work, so that the labor contract is generally made between couples rather than between individuals. Further, as in systems of exchange labor throughout the world (Erasmus 1956: 445–449), the amount of labor given and received is carefully calculated. If one couple works two full days for another, they can reasonably expect an equivalent amount of service in return. Although there is no written legal code that can be brought to bear on violators of this norm, people understand, verbalize, and generally adhere to this principle of equivalence. This contrasts strikingly with the informal, implicit exchange of haying.

Unlike hay collection, too, recruited harvest workers must provide their own meals during their days of labor for others. Even though the field owners and their workers labor together all day on a particular plot and take breaks to eat together, each couple furnishes its own food. Clearly, then, mutual assistance in the fruit and potato harvest is a much more individualistic enterprise than it is in hay collection. Time and labor in harvest cooperation are viewed as precise economic commodities, to be exchanged in equal quantities between pairs of workers. And because of this principle of equivalence, villagers do not claim that they are called to labor unjustifiably or that they are being exploited. Here, social ties are openly harnessed for purely economic ends, and everyone is aware of his exact rights and obligations vis-à-vis a work partner.

This essential difference between mutual assistance in the harvest and in hay collection may best be explained by the distinct origins of both types of cooperation. Cooperative hay collection is a completely traditional practice, passed on through the generations to meet a common labor shortage. For hay collection, the nuclear family would never be sufficient. Some form of outside assistance is mandatory because of the difficulty of the task and the urgency of its completion. Cooperation, in this case, is simply the most advantageous method of completing the job. People stress the cooperative nature of the enterprise, the need to assist one's friends, neighbors, or relatives, lest their hay become worthless. Working for others becomes one's duty, an expression of care and affection. To reveal economic self-interest, however much this actually exists, is viewed as selfish.

The harvesting of fruit and potatoes, on the other hand, can be and frequently is carried out by the single nuclear family. To work for others or to take extra hands oneself is merely a wise management of time in a peak agricultural season. As already noted, under the traditional system, when there was an adequate labor force, those who could afford to hire workers did so; the others merely carried out the task themselves or worked for others. Today, virtually everyone owns or controls enough land to make some outside assistance in harvesting economically advantageous. At the same time, few villagers are so free from the burden of their own fields that they can work steadily for others. To meet the common labor shortage, brought on by migration, farmers resort to cooperation, which in this case is really only a substitute for the old hiring system. In effect, the economically rational guidelines of the traditional practice—so much work equals so much money—have carried over into the new system, so that villagers actually charge one another, in terms of man hours, for assistance in the fields. This careful accounting is consonant with the nature of fruit and potatoes as cash crops, as opposed to hay, which is never marketed. In no sense do villagers feel that it is or should be their disinterested duty to help someone else with his fruit and potato harvest. The money economy here has merely been transplanted by a barter of labor.

COMMUNITY CONTROL OVER AGRICULTURAL RESOURCES

As already noted, there are in Becedas a number of publicly owned resources that all members of the community may draw upon and use for personal economic gain. These include the water of the village streams, necessary for irrigation, and a good deal of land, in the form of threshing floors, pastures, roads, and paths. All of this property, though exploited on an individual basis, falls under the jurisdiction of the community as a whole. It is the community which is responsible for the preservation and maintenance of these resources, as well as for apportionment of the rights over their use.

The most elaborate system of community controls and organization in Becedas is that associated with water rights and irrigation. For 9 months of the year, from October through June, any villager is permitted to divert water, at will, from the streams of his fields. Throughout the three summer months, however, the village streams come under tight community control. This is the period when water is scarcest and, at the same time, in greatest demand. The community organizes to solve two essential problems: to clean and repair the irrigation ditches in order to assure the maximum flow of water, and to partition rights to the use of the water among all village farmers.

Initially, the most important task is to fortify and repair the four main water arteries, tributaries of the Arroyo Becedillas, that are the source for all the subsidiary irrigation ditches traversing the fields. These arteries, upon which all villagers rely for water, must be cleared of accumulated silt, rocks, and garbage, and be banked on both sides with sod and rock in order to prevent water from being wasted through escape and overflow. This is accomplished by an annual communal operation known as *hacer las presas* ("building the dams"). Traditionally, the *Ayuntamiento* organized the event, but since the Civil War, the responsibility has fallen primarily to the officers of the *Hermandad*. On the day of San Juan, or as soon thereafter as the weather permits, it is announced by *pregón*[2] that the men should prepare themselves to *hacer las presas*. At dawn the following morning, the church bells call all workers to the Plaza del Egedillo, where the men are informally divided into several work groups, each assigned to a particular irrigation site. The groups lack formal leaders, but the officers of the *Hermandad*, exempt from actual physical labor on this occasion, individually march from site to site, making sure that everyone who is supposed to work is present and that the task is progressing reasonably. The entire operation lasts little more than 2 hours, and by 8:30 A.M. everyone is working in his own field.

There are clearly defined rules as to who participates in this communal project. All farmers who own and work irrigated land are required to contribute to the work force one male at least 14 years of age. If such land is sharecropped, the labor contribution is the owner's responsibility; if it is rented, the renter is responsible. Everyone, regardless of how much land he owns or works, is required to provide the labor teams with only one worker. If he himself cannot attend, he must find a substitute, either an eligible household member or a hired worker, to replace him. Here are a few typical problems and solutions that villagers face:

1. Marcelino Talavera is fortunate to have an able-bodied son of 15. Like everyone else, Marcelino finds himself in peak agricultural season at the end of June, having to reap, hay, spray fruit, and engage in reciprocal labor operations. When it is time to *hacer las presas*, he continues his normal agricultural routine and sends his son as a legitimate replacement. This is standard procedure for someone in Marcelino's position.

2. Pedro Torres has a wife and four children, all under 5 years old, and the family lives with his aged, recently widowed mother. Both he and his mother own irrigated land and must each, therefore, send a qualified representative to *hacer las presas*. Pedro goes on his own behalf; he recruits his brother-in-law, Germán, a miller who is free from the labor

---

[2] The *pregón*, or "announcement," is a community information mechanism widespread in Castile. In Becedas, any individual or group can make a public announcement by paying 10 pesetas to the *aguacil*, who marches through the village, toots a small tin horn at strategic points to call attention to himself, and then reads the message aloud.

obligation, to go on behalf of his mother. Germán performs this service free, as an expression of aid to his family.

3. Carlos Trapero, a baker and farmer, has only one son, a boy of 10. Since Carlos must spend the early morning hours baking, he must find an eligible substitute to fulfill his work obligation. Lacking a suitable and available relative or friend to call upon, he is forced to hire a young teenager, at the price of 75 pesetas,[3] to act as his surrogate. Though he pays the wage reluctantly, it is preferable to his forfeiting the earnings from morning bread sales.

It is essential to note that villagers comply with the work regulations not because of an altruistic desire to help the community at large but, rather, in order to avoid punishment. He who shirks his obligation to send an eligible worker to *hacer las presas* is required later in the summer to carry out a *full* day's labor on the main water arteries, at repairing, clearing, or doing whatever other jobs seem necessary. This punishment can mean a serious economic loss, considerably more than just the 2 hours required during communal labor. For this reason, virtually no one ignores his duty to attend personally or to send an appointed representative on the communal workday.

This communal work project marks the beginning of rigidly partitioned water rights. The water that passes through the village must be divided not only among the Becedas farmers, but also between Becedas and other nearby villages. According to traditional agreement, between the days of San Juan (June 24) and San Miguel (September 29), Becedas is obligated to share its rich water supply with Gilbuena and Junciana, which are located on dry mountain slopes several kilometers north of Becedas and lack an independent source of irrigation water. Each week from dawn on Friday until 4:00 P.M. on Saturday, three of the four main water arteries are left untapped by Becedas farmers to pass through to the other villages. (Becedas retains control over the fourth artery during these days.) To obtain these water rights, it is said, Gilbuena and Junciana centuries ago presented Becedas with the reputedly fine clock which sits in its churchtower. But this gesture apparently was insufficient to assure unwavering commitment to the agreement, for two representatives from Gilbuena and Junciana spend every Friday and Saturday in Becedas, trying to protect and guard their villages' water. Even among the people of Becedas, it is assumed that, without the watchful presence

---

[3] For some years prior to 1969, the official rate of exchange was 60 pesetas to the dollar. In 1970, the exchange rate became 70 pesetas to the dollar and then dropped again by 1972 to 63 or so.

of these outsiders, water would be diverted illegally to Becedas fields.

All of Becedas' water supply, aside from the small portion siphoned off to the other villages, must be divided equitably among Becedas farmers. To regulate this division, the villagers employ a system of annually chosen public irrigators called *aguadores* (literally, "water men"), There is generally a total of six *aguadores*, five regulars and one head, the *vigilante*. For the purposes of irrigation, cultivated land is divided into five distinct territories of varying size. The five regular *aguadores* draw lots for assignments to these territories. It is the responsibility of each *aguador* to devise an irrigation schedule for his territory and to advise farmers with landholdings there when it is their turn to irrigate. The *vigilante's* job differs from that of the other *aguadores*. He oversees the entire irrigation operation by controlling the relative flow of water to the five territories, obstructing the flow to one in order to speed the flow to another, so that all cultivated terrain receives a more or less equal amount of water. He is also in charge of unlocking the main water valves (from the small reservoirs in which water collects during nighttime) early in the morning and shutting them again at the end of each day.

The position of *aguador* is difficult and time-consuming, and *aguadores*, like most villagers with authority, generally suffer a good deal of criticism. In Becedas, unlike other parts of Spain,[4] when it is a person's turn to irrigate, he can use as much water and time as necessary. For this reason, irrigation schedules can never be worked out more than a few hours in advance, and it is difficult to find people in order to notify them of when they can be at a certain field for irrigation. Most of the *aguador's* work consists of trudging through the countryside in the heat of summer, searching for farmers. When an individual is finally located, he will likely as not complain about being called away from one job to do another, or about being given either insufficient or premature notice as to when he can irrigate. The *vigilante* suffers even greater disfavor than the regular *aguadores*, for every time he obstructs the flow of one artery to increase that of another, those affected negatively by the decision protest vigorously, even though they know that a subsequent adjustment of the water flow will probably work toward their own benefit.

To compensate for this criticism, the position of *aguador* is relatively lucrative. Every Saturday, all six *aguadores* make a round of the village, collecting money from each farmer who irrigated during the previous week. The amount of money varies directly with the amount of land

---

[4] In parts of the *vega* of Valencia, an irrigation schedule specifying the precise amount of water allotted to each farmer was the traditional method (Costa 1915: 536).

irrigated. The total is then divided equally among all the *aguadores*, *vigilante* included, regardless of the relative amount of work accomplished by each. Most of the money is earned early in the summer, when water is abundant and all fields can be irrigated at optimal frequency, about once a week. Later on, when water is scarce and fields have to last 2 or 3 weeks without irrigation, the *aguadores* earn less. But in general, the work pays well.

For this reason, there has traditionally been a much greater number of candidates for the position of *aguador* than there were places available. To choose their *aguadores*, the community, until 1969, always resorted to a standard device: the lottery. Sometime in June, the *Hermandad* would call a special evening meeting of all farmers who wished to be *aguadores* during the coming summer. Their names were written on small pieces of paper, which were crumpled, placed in a beret, and drawn in public by a *Hermandad* officer. The first six individuals to be drawn were the year's *aguadores*. From among themselves, these six would then, by consensus, choose the oldest or most experienced to be *vigilante*.

Due to changed economic conditions, the social organization of irrigation now differs markedly from what it was as late as the mid-1960s. In the past, it was the landless laborers or those with just a minimal amount of land who became *aguadores*. They were the only ones who could afford the time. Though the position of *aguador* is lucrative, much more so than day labor, it could never compensate a man for the loss of crop earnings. Therefore, those with enough land of their own to keep busy throughout the summer would never consider entering as candidate for *aguador*. The post would simply be too time-consuming.

Currently, because landless laborers are virtually nonexistent in Becedas and the vast majority of villagers either own or control a good deal of land, there has been a serious scarcity of *aguador* applicants. In the 1960s, adjustments were made to suit the new conditions. First, the position of aguador was transformed into a half-time post. There are now ten *aguadores*, five pairs of men operating in effect as five full-time *aguadores*. Each pair divides its time as it sees fit, one pair of men alternating weeks of work, another alternating every 2 days, and so on. This arrangement permits the *aguadores* to have at least some time to devote to their own fields, which makes the position considerably more attractive to landholders. Second, the position of *vigilante* has altered. Now, one of the five pairs of *aguadores* is chosen by lot to operate as *vigilante*. *Vigilante* duties are heavier than formerly. In addition to regulating the water flow, the *vigilante* is assigned control over the irrigation schedule of one of the five irrigation territories and must operate just like any other *aguador* with respect to this territory. To be sure, the territory is the smallest and easiest of the five. But because of the extra labor added to the post, it is no longer as desirable as it once was. This probably accounts for the present choice of *vigilante* by lot. The old consensus method failed when new duties were added, and no one would accept the post voluntarily.

The labor situation in Becedas is now so changed that villagers seriously doubt that the *aguador* system of organizing irrigation can remain in effect for more than a few years. In June 1970, the community suffered extreme difficulty in getting enough applicants for *aguador* to permit irrigation to begin. When the *Hermandad* first announced that *aguadores* would be paid 8 pesetas per *fanega*,[5] only two or three individuals volunteered, and on a half-time basis at that. After the price was raised to 9 pesetas, the highest on record, just enough volunteers stepped forth to fill the available positions. For the first time in the villagers' memory, the lottery was not used to choose *aguadores*. There was simply insufficient competition to warrant its being called into service.

In the 1960s, because of similar labor problems, several other villages in the Sierra de Béjar had to discontinue the *aguador* system entirely. In these villages, advising of irrigation schedules is now done *por vecinos* ("by neighbors"), as it is known. Adjacent fields are irrigated in turn, just as in Becedas, but here the irrigators themselves advise one another when they can irrigate. There is no single individual to coordinate the operation. Becedas farmers consider this method much inferior to their own. Because *aguadores* are paid according to the number of *fanegas* irrigated, they are motivated to cover as much terrain each day as possible. Thus, little time elapses between the irrigation of two adjacent *huertas*, providing the most efficient use of the community water supply. In the substitute system, farmers have no direct material interest in the number of plots irrigated each day, so that several hours sometimes elapse between the irrigation of two *huertas*, leading of course to the loss of valuable water. In spite of the advantages of the *aguador* system, it seems likely that Becedas, like its neighbors, will soon be forced to abandon its traditional mode of organizing irrigation for want of the laborers necessary to sustain it.

In addition to regulating the village water supply, the Becedas com-

---

[5] The *fanega* is the traditional unit of land measurement in Becedas, as in most of Spain, though the size of the unit varies tremendously from region to region. Properly considered, the *fanega* is measured by the land's productive capacity rather than by its actual size. On irrigated land in Becedas, the *fanega* is equivalent to the amount of land on which 100 kilos of potato tubers may be sown. Thus, the actual areal extent of the *fanega* varies even from one site to another within Becedas, depending on the quality and nature of the terrain.

munity also exerts control over agricultural land resources, specifically threshing floors and public paths and roads. Here, the control is less pervasive and more fleeting than in the case of irrigation, for only a portion of the villagers use the communal threshing floors, and community work on public byways lasts but a few days. Nonetheless, these are further instances in which public property, though exploited individually, is subject to community regulation in order to promote the general welfare.

In Becedas, there are two large, uncobbled communal threshing floors, one located adjacent to the cemetery at the lower end of town, the other at the opposite, uppermost end of the village. The former is considered to have a better threshing surface, but the latter receives stronger breezes and, therefore, is preferable for winnowing. Unlike the case of water, the village does not have a monopoly on threshing facilities, and a number of farmers consistently elect to do their threshing in some privately owned conveniently situated meadow. Most villagers who sow grain do, however, choose to thresh at one of these two main sites, usually the one closest to their barn and residence.

The use of these threshing floors is governed by lot, the drawing generally taking place just before threshing season in mid- to late July. Each of the two communal sites is sectioned into 20 to 30 separate parcels (*eras*) with the aid of simple stone markers. On the appointed day, at dawn, everyone who wants a parcel to use that season gathers at the threshing floor of his choice. Pairs of farmers, generally close relatives, team up to share the parcels, but it is necessary for only one person of each team to attend the drawing. Each plot is assigned a number, and the numbers are written on small pieces of paper which are, once again, crumpled up and placed in a beret. Everyone chooses a lot, thus earning the right to use the parcel to which his number corresponds. The officers of the *Ayuntamiento* organize and supervise the drawings.

Given the relatively small amount of grain grown in Becedas, everyone is assured of obtaining a portion of the threshing floor; lots are used merely to assign individual plots rather than to limit the number of people who can use the threshing floors. The partnership arrangement in the use of plots, made feasible because each person produces a small amount of grain, more or less guarantees that everyone who wishes to thresh on the communal floors will be able to do so. In any case, all villagers, regardless of whether or not they participate in the lottery drawing, ultimately have the right to use of the floors. Whenever a plot is unoccupied by the person to whom it is officially assigned, any other villager has the right to its use.

Only one of the two threshing floors is actually the property of the

Becedas municipality. The other is owned by a corporation of eight villagers, all of whom have either inherited their shares in the corporation or purchased them from a retiring member. Interestingly, even though the corporation nominally owns the threshing floor, village tradition places stringent limitations on its disposition. From San Miguel (September 29) to San Juan (June 24), the owners may put the ground to any purpose they wish, and, in fact, they do employ it for several months as pastureland. But from San Juan to San Miguel, the three summer months, the land is regularly expropriated by the community for threshing purposes. On one other occasion, too, the community asserts its control over this land: Every Easter Sunday the threshing floor is converted into a picnic ground, where families and groups of young, unmarried men and women flock for a traditional get-together, known as the *Hornazo*. And, because the land must be preserved for both threshing and the *Hornazo*, the share holders in the corporation, both individually and collectively, are denied the right to partition the ground permanently into smaller parcels. Here, the community clearly asserts its traditional claim to the land; private property is controlled and used by the villagers for their common benefit, and for the benefit which might accrue to their progeny.

The Becedas community takes charge of the maintenance, as well as the use, of public land. Just as villagers must donate their labor to fixing the main water arteries, so too they are required to devote a day's service to work on the main roads and paths that traverse the village and fields. Public roadworks, organized by the *Ayuntamiento*, are always carried out in late August or early September, just prior to the fruit harvest. There is an economic justification for this scheduling: At harvest time, the apples and pears must be transported on large wooden-wheeled carts (*carros*) from the fields to the village houses and barns for storage until sale. In order to make this short journey as smooth as possible, thus minimizing the amount of bruising of the fruit, the main surfaces along which the carts roll must be repaired and evened.

Traditionally, and until 1969, the *Ayuntamiento* would announce in advance the day for public roadworks, and a male representative from every household would be required to attend. As in the case of irrigation service, the villagers would break up into small groups, each of which was assigned to a particular work area. Attendance was mandatory on penalty of a fine or similar work later on, during harvest time itself.

During the 1960s, there had been growing dissatisfaction with this system. All the household representatives would meet at the appointed time and go off for the day's labor on the roads, but, for lack of a serious feeling of responsibility, the men would pass the day chatting and taking cigarette breaks, so that very little productive work was accomplished. Then, in 1970, the *Ayuntamiento* decided to institute a new system of communal roadwork. Each day, a small group of 10 or 12 men was called up for service on a limited road area. The method of recruitment, called *por calles* ("by streets"), involved advising people on the basis of house order. That is, on one day, men from the first 10 houses on a block were called up; the following day the next 10 houses were required to send their representatives, and so on.[6] The entire project took several weeks for completion, but it was believed that, when men work together in fewer numbers, they can be more easily controlled and that, therefore, this goal would be achieved more efficiently. In fact, careful control was now exercised through the constant pressence of an *Ayuntamiento* officer —either the vice-mayor or one of the councilmen (the mayor is in charge of recruitment)—while the work was being carried out.

It should be stressed that community works projects, on both irrigation ditches and roadways, affect only that portion of the community resources which all Becedas farmers are to one degree or another reliant. The vast mazeway of short, narrow paths and irrigation ditches that weave through the fields must be cleaned and repaired privately, with each individual responsible for those sections most directly affecting his fields. Alternatively, several individuals, all reliant on the same ditch or lane, may get together for a half day of repair work. But community action, mandatory and sanctioned, is necessary only for those major arteries that benefit all village farmers more or less equally and for which no individual responsibility may therefore be assigned.

PASTURAGE ORGANIZATION

In Becedas, there is a generally favorable ratio of cattle to meadow, so it is unnecessary for most villagers to practice fully transhumant herding. About 5 or 6 of the most prosperous villagers, all owning between 20 and 50 head of cattle, regularly ship part of their herds south during

---

[6] The rotation of communal responsibilities by house order is a widespread Castilian practice. It has been described by Freeman (1970) for a hamlet in the Sierra Ministra, where house rotation, called the *adra*, is used in gravedigging, irrigation, public works, and other activities.

winter to the fertile pastures of Extremadura,[7] but, on the whole, Becedas' land is sufficient to support its livestock.

The municipality has three kinds of meadow: privately owned, corporation-owned, and communal. Most villagers with horses, donkeys, or cows own or rent small private meadows whose disposition and use they control completely. Regardless of how much private meadowland a person may have, however, he is likely to rely on communal or corporation-owned meadows for at least part of the year's grazing, and both these property types are subject to strict regulations.

There are two large corporation-owned pastures, El Regajo and Las Quemadillas, both located on the slopes of Peña Negra. Each corporation is comprised of about 50 members. Changes in membership take place smoothly through inheritance or sale, but the total number of shareholders may never be increased, lest the land be insufficient to accommodate all the members' cattle. Grazing on the corporation pastures follows a fixed annual schedule. On May 13, cows and horses are brought up to the pastures where they are kept to graze for exactly a month; then the pastures remain clear from June 13 until July 13, when the animals are once again brought up to feed on the regenerated grass. Finally, on August 13, all cattle are cleared from El Regajo and Las Quemadillas until the following May when the cycle is renewed (snow and frost make these pastures useless during the long winter).

There are, in addition to these corporation pastures, two large communal pasturelands owned and managed by the municipality as a whole. Any permanent resident has the right to graze his cattle on these lands. In the pasture known as La Sierra, there are two consecutive grazing periods, from April 1 to San Juan and from San Juan to San Miguel. For an annually fluctuating fee (in 1970, it was 180 pesetas per animal), a person may graze his animals in La Sierra during either or both of these periods. This sum also entitles a person to graze his cattle on the village-owned wastelands, the small strips of unused, mostly barren ground that skirt the roads and paths of the terminus.

The second communal pasture, La Dehesa ("The Meadow"),[8] receives cattle from June 13 through July 13, precisely the summer period when

---

[7] The few transhumant herds in Becedas are generally transported by means of truck and rail. One villager, however, regularly walks his cattle to and from Malpertida de Plasencia, just east of the city of Plasencia in Caceres. A second villager sends his herd walking to pastures as far as Badajoz, but he himself does not accompany them on the trek.

[8] The word *dehesa* is usually the generic Spanish term for "meadow" or "pasture," but, in Becedas, it is used as a proper noun as well as to denote a particular portion of land.

both corporation pastures are unused. Because most plowing is accomplished by mid-June, and people can afford to let their cattle out to pasture at this time, grazing on La Dehesa reaches massive proportions. On June 13, the day of San Antonio, there is a large movement of cattle out of the village and up to the communal meadow. The event is celebrated by a special early morning mass, attended primarily by the village men, in the hope that San Antonio, patron of cattle, will protect their animals throughout the coming month. After the mass, the men carry an image of the saint in procession through the village streets. Interestingly, no such mass and procession mark the transfer of cattle to corporation or private pastures. The San Antonio celebration clearly bolsters the collectivist landholding tradition. Here, the village as a landholding group finds support in common religious ritual.[9]

In addition to the common ownership and use of pastureland, the Becedas community provides itself with pasturage personnel. For the period of cattle grazing at La Sierra and La Dehesa, cowherds (*vaqueros*), one for each pasture, are needed for full-time care of the animals. Every spring, at no fixed date, an auction is held among all villagers who are interested in the position, and those who bid the lowest salary are awarded the job. Precisely the same method is used by the two village pastorage corporations to hire cowherds for El Regajo and Las Quemadillas.

The community as a whole is also responsible for the annual choice of a goatherd (*cabrero*) to take the village goats out to pasture daily. In Becedas, every household usually owns one to three goats, kept primarily as a source of milk and extra income (from the sale of newborn kids). At the end of December, the usual auctioneering procedure is used to choose the village *cabrero* and, as in the case of cattle, the person who makes the lowest bid gets the job.

Until about 1960, large numbers of villagers with little or no land of their own coveted the job of *vaquero* or *cabrero*. Now, however, there is considerable difficulty in finding people to fill the posts. Just as the position of *aguador* became half-time, permitting each individual to work at agriculture as well, so too *vaqueros* and *cabreros* began taking half-time posts, with pairs of men equally dividing both the work and income from each full-time position. In addition, because so few people have bid for the jobs, there has been little competition, and salaries have soared. In 1969, the *cabreros* earned 22 pesetas per goat each month, but in 1970, there was a real danger that no one would accept the position. After con-

---

[9] Similarly, Freeman (1968) has shown how virtually all instances of corporate action are (or were traditionally) supported by religious ritual in the Castilian hamlet of Valdemora.

siderable persuasion on the part of the community at large, a pair of villagers finally took the job at 40 pesetas, virtually doubling the preceding year's salary.

In 1970, most villagers predicted that, within the next few years, the post of *cabrero* would disappear entirely from Becedas, leaving each family to pasture its own goats or to give up raising the animals altogether in order to avoid the nuisance and extra work. It took little time for the prediction to come true. In 1971, no villager would accept the post, so all goat-owners had to take turns at pasturing the entire village flock. In order to avoid this unpleasant chore, large numbers of households immediately sold or slaughtered their goats. The nearly 300 goats that belonged to villagers in 1970 dwindled to only 54 by the summer of 1972.

A similar fate had earlier befallen pig raising in Becedas. Until 1962, there was a village *porquero*, chosen annually by auction, and charged with the daily pasturage of one or two pigs owned by each household. Eventually, the price of keeping a *porquero* became so exhorbitant, due to lack of competition for the post, that the position was dropped entirely. Today, many fewer villagers keep pigs than formerly, and those who still have them raise them on their own, indoors, feeding them grain and commercially prepared feed. The expense, the dirt, and the nuisance of rearing the animals in this manner have caused many villagers to abandon the enterprise completely. People prefer to purchase pork, just as they may, in the future, prefer to purchase milk regularly rather than to rely on their own animals for the product. These developments are just other manifestations of the overall labor shortage and rising standard of living that have resulted in Becedas from massive migration.

ATTITUDES TOWARD COOPERATION AND COMMUNITY ORGANIZATION

In order to understand fully how villagers view their economic system, it is necessary to place this system in spacial–temporal perspective. The work of Joaquín Costa (1915) amply demonstrates that the corporate–collectivist tradition in agriculture and pasturage has a long history in Spain. Among the regions in which common property ownership and control are most widespread and pervasive, Costa includes the Asturias, the Pyrenean zone, and the West, extending from León and Zamora south through the villages around Alburquerque in Badajoz (1915: 40–41). Becedas, of course, is located in this western area, of which Costa writes, "The land, wholly or in part, is held in common by the members of the respective villages, but . . . the exploitation of the land is not carried out in common, but rather through individual lots, at the account and risk of each villager" (1915: 40–41; my translation). In addition, in this area, area, there is generally found "regular and periodic distribution of the land among the participants." (1915: 335–336).

With respect to irrigation, Costa describes elaborate community organization and controls, principally in the eastern *vega* of Valencia, but also in the Pyrenees, where special officers called *regadores públicos* ("public irrigators"), analogues of Becedas's *aguadores*, regulate the flow of water by turn from one parcel to the next (1915: 535–536). Many of the collectivist arrangements that Costa mentions have doubtless disappeared since the turn of the century, when he wrote; many, in fact, were eliminated prior to his study as a result of mid-nineteenth-century liberal legislation (1915: 331). Nonetheless, even today we can find prominent vestiges of the communal tradition, which has been described at least for eastern Castile (Kenny 1966; Freeman 1970), and for Zamora (Arguedas 1968). Collectivism in Becedas, then, is merely a local manifestation of a widespread and deeply entrenched Spanish and, to judge from the works of Jorge Dias (1948, 1953), pan-Iberian mode of economic organization.

Further, in Becedas, cooperation and collectivism are basically a pragmatic response to extant conditions. Unlike many peasant societies, in which the nuclear family can function economically without the assistance or cooperation of outsiders (Foster 1961: 178), farmers here cannot operate adequately without extrafamilial assistance. Hay collection, potato and fruit harvesting, labor on the primary irrigation ditches and roads— all these, as already noted, are instances in which one man with his wife and children are simply insufficient to accomplish the job in the best and most efficient manner. Moreover, where there is community-wide organization and control, it pertains with few exceptions to communally owned resources—threshing floors, pastures, streams, and roads. In the domain of private ownership, the community with few exceptions leaves jurisdiction over the property entirely in individual hands.

Cooperation and community organization in Becedas, then, have their bases in these pragmatic considerations and in the adherence to traditional modes of operation. Under no circumstances may they be attributed to a "natural" expression of altruism or communalism on the part of the villagers. For in Becedas, as in Java, where similar group and exchange labor forms are found, cooperation is based on "a very lively sense of the mutual value to the participants of such cooperation, not on a general ethic of the unity of all men or on an organic view of society which takes the group as primary and the individual as secondary" (Geertz 1962: 244).

Paradoxically, it is the villagers' deeply imbedded individualism, and their recognition of it, that makes community organization essential. As one informant put it, "If it weren't for the *aguadores*, we would be at one another's throats during irrigation time, each fighting for as much water as he might get, without regard for the next villager. In other words, the collectivity organizes itself to protect the rights of all the individuals of which it is composed. Without such organization and control, economic individualism would lead, in the eyes of the villagers, to chaos and violence.

Villagers are also well aware that their acceptance of the system is based on stringent sanctions, both diffuse and organized, to use Radcliffe-Brown's terminology (1965: 205–211). If a person who is recruited to collect hay refuses to do so with little or no reason, he knows that he will lose the potential and necessary aid of the recruiter in some future enterprise of his own. Such refusal, if carried to an extreme, may even lead to social ostracism, for as we have seen, the network of economic cooperation bolsters and is one important expression of social relations between friends, neighbors, and kinsmen. In the case of communal works projects, of course, there is a formal mechanism for the punishment of those who refuse to lend assistance. It is unlikely that attendance on these projects would be very high if there were no organized sanctions to assure it.

Moreover, cooperative work ventures, though an integral and traditional part of village life, are invariably accompanied by complaints and petty resentments. Those villagers with little or no hay secretly object to helping others to collect theirs. Small landholders feel that they should share less of the communal labor burden than more landed villagers who, because of their greater use of streams for irrigation water and roads for fruit transport, derive greater benefit from the work. People cooperate, but with an overbearing sense of duty and obligation, albeit often concealed on the surface. Generally, villagers communicate the feeling that they are being somehow shortchanged by communal work projects. Only rarely do they openly discuss the personal benefit they derive from such participation.

Yet, it should also be noted that when new economic opportunities present themselves, villagers sometimes do fall back on their collectivist traditions. In 1968, the Agricultural Extension of the Ministry of Agriculture, with an office in El Barco, offered the villagers a government-subsidized plan of insecticide spraying. According to the plan, the Extension would provide the villagers for free with several gasoline-operated sprayers (much more thorough and efficient devices than the hand-pump variety) and with a large proportion of the chemical insecticides. In that year, the community decided to accept the government-sponsored plan and, by a majority vote, made participation in the plan obligatory among all farmers with orchards. Work groups were formed among all villagers, who operated the sprayers on a rotating basis, systematically spraying all the trees in the terminus.

When the summer was over, everyone agreed that community-organized spraying was considerably cheaper than the old method, and that the trees also had received a more thorough dousing of chemicals than formerly. But there were serious complaints about the care given to the fields. According to reports, the spray teams walked cautiously on their own fields, while those belonging to others were trampled needlessly or were otherwise abused or neglected. Not surprisingly, when the government renewed its offer in 1969, the community rejected the plan outright, and individuals reverted to the hand-pump method.

In 1970, the Extension Service offered the villagers a variant of the original spraying plan. The Extension would provide five gasoline sprayers, the entire first insecticide treatment given to the trees, and 75% of the cost of subsequent treatments. Participating farmers in rotating groups of three would share the labor of operating the machines, and everyone would be paid 250 pesetas on the days he worked. The costs of labor and insecticides would be borne by all participating members, in proportion to the number of trees belonging to each. Four organizers of the project were chosen by lot from among all participating members. The main difference from the 1968 arrangement was that entrance into the spraying project would be voluntary.

Surprisingly, 152 of the 250 farmers who needed to spray in 1970, or 75% of the total, entered into the collective plan. Another 8 farmers had bought their own gasoline sprayer the previous year on a cooperative basis, so only about 22% of the farmers with orchards sprayed insecticides individually in that year. Most of the people who entered into the plan did so, they said, in order to save money. The 1969 reversion to individual spraying had shown that the Extension plan was a financial boon to the villagers. The case is interesting because it provides an instance in which cooperation and organization were *not* necessary to accomplish the job. Rather, the collectivist action was seen as preferable to individual spraying and was chosen voluntarily by the large majority of villagers.

Given the villagers' basic individualism, how may we explain this relatively large-scale acceptance of community action? First, of course, there was the demonstration effect. Villagers had tried the collectivist and individualist modes of spraying in consecutive years and had chosen the former course on the basis of rational economics. More important, perhaps, villagers were beginning to sense that they represented a dying way of life and were particularly fearful that their traditional technology would cause them soon to be priced out of the national market. Accepting the government spraying scheme at least offered them the opportunity for mechanization, albeit partial and minor, which they saw as the only hope for maintenance of a viable agriculture in Becedas. Finally, we should remember that, to the villagers, collectivism forms a traditional model for economic organization. If it is not always the ideal mode of operation, it is at least reliable, and works. The formation of labor teams, the choice by lot of a four-man coordinating committee to run the project, the rotation of work responsibilities—all of these elements were incorporated into the community spraying plan and have exact analogues in traditional village collectivism. Here, then, is a case in which basically individualistic peasants seized upon the familiar organizational techniques of communal agriculture and applied them to a new economic problem. By spraying collectively, the villagers saved money, modernized, yet relied on well-known cultural forms. It was the fear of disappearing and being left behind, combined with a sense of familiar social organization, that motivated and permitted the villagers to make this technological advance.

COMMUNITY INTEGRATION AND COMMUNITY LABOR

In his now classic article, "The Occurrence and Disappearance of Reciprocal Farm Labor," Charles Erasmus (1956) surveys the vast literature on cooperative work in peasant societies throughout the world and determines that the conditons which give rise to this type of labor organization are becoming progressively obsolete. Increasing monetization, agricultural specialization, and intimate involvement in a commercial market system, he argues, have all created the need for labor efficiency and have induced in farmers a desire to accumulate the highest possible profits. Under such economic circumstances, people are no longer interested in maximizing social goals, and using cooperative work to solidify relationships within their community. Rather, their main consideration in the organization of production activities is to accomplish the necessary work at the least expense. Reciprocal farm labor, which often requires large outlays of time away from one's own fields, which also involves considerable cash outlays for feasting one's workers, and which provides no guarantee of obtaining the best available labor force, then goes by the wayside. Exchange labor is replaced by cash hiring, and economic relationships become increasingly independent of and divorced from social bonds.

Erasmus' analysis, of course, is a reincarnation of one aspect of Redfield's folk–urban continuum, especially as the continuum was originally presented in *The Folk Culture of Yucatan* (1941). In this seminal work, which ranks four communities along a scale measuring their degree of isolation from the outside world, Redfield found a positive correlation between the importance of monetization and specialized commercial agriculture, on the one hand, and individualistic, noncooperative production organization, on the other. This correlation is part of Redfield's evidence that economically isolated, subsistence-oriented communities are more cohesive—or "organized," as he put it—than are those involved in a commercial market system. In more isolated settlements, cooperative labor teams, formed on the basis of social ties between the participants, provide a crucial source of community integration and solidarity absent in highly commercialized villages and towns.

Does Redfield's and Erasmus' developmental view (which, as we have seen in Chapter 1, has become adopted generally in contemporary community studies) also apply to recent changes in Becedas? Our Castilian *pueblo* provides a rich source of data against which we may test prevalent generalizations. For here, as in other peasant communities around the world, there is substantial evidence over the past century of increasing agricultural specialization and commercialization. Farmers have progressively abandoned certain crops, either wholly or partially, in favor of others that suit the particular environmental advantages and limitations in the Sierra de Béjar, and that prove to have the greatest cash value. In conjunction with these changes, there has been an increasingly greater involvement of Becedas agriculture within the national, and even world, market systems. Has the organization of production activities in the village kept apace and become correspondingly more individualistic, as we might anticipate?

To answer this question, we need only review the way Becedas farmers have changed their labor commitments during the years since 1950, specifically with regard to the relative degrees of hiring, on the one hand, and interfamily cooperation and communalism, on the other. As we have seen, the traditional, premigration system of production organization included a good deal of wage labor. Landless or near-landless villagers were required, particularly during the peak agricultural seasons, to hire themselves out on a daily basis to proprietors who owned more land than they themselves could manage. Further, landless laborers could be counted on to become *aquadores*, goatherds, and pigherds, thus assuming communal responsibilities, but always for a fee.

The massive rural exodus has altered this situation markedly. Now that land has become available and everyone can farm as much terrain as he and his family can manage—but no more—the pool of available day labor-ers has dwindled to virtually nothing. Only two adult men, bachelor brothers, now may be considered to earn their living by wage work. Simi-larly, villagers no longer can afford the time away from their own fields to hire themselves out for community posts, and it is this new development which has precipitated the decline of widespread family pig and goat raising in the village. Even the traditional irrigation system, upon which the fate of all Becedas agriculture depends, has been threatened as a result of the labor shortage. There is no doubt that hiring today plays a less important role in the organization of production than ever before.

At the same time, there has been a significant increase in the amount of interfamily cooperation and communalism within the village. In addi-tion to haying, which has always been, and continues to be, a main focus of cooperative activity, Becedas farmers now rely on this mode of labor organization for the fruit and potato harvests as well. In fact, there could be no better example of what Erasmus calls "exchange labor" than the reciprocal arrangements that have become a part of these harvests; pairs of friends, neighbors, and relatives trade equivalent amounts of labor on one another's fields. This system, far from disappearing with increasing commercialization, has actually expanded at the expense of more im-personal hiring practices found traditionally.

Communalism has experienced a similar expansion. In addition to the wide array of communal regulatory and work activities found both traditionally and contemporaneously, villagers now band together for insecticide spraying. Even though work teams are paid for their services, they are not comprised of a special class of landless laborers working full-time at the job for hire. Rather, all farmers who participate in the spraying plan rotate labor responsibilities, which, at least in theory, benefit all of their privately owned fields equally. A similar kind of labor rota-tion is now practiced among families that still maintain goats, and, as described, this system has replaced the traditional hiring of landless labor-ers as full-time goatherds.

By any reasonable estimate, then, the Becedas data contradict the usual developmental sequence described for numerous other peasant communi-ties around the world. Becedas has become increasingly less isolated and more involved in a commercial market economy. Yet, instead of a cor-responding rise in individualistic modes of production and breakdown in cooperative and communal forms, we find that precisely the opposite has occurred. Insofar as labor arrangements are concerned, farmers pool their energies more than ever before.

By far the most crucial reason for this development is the recent labor shortage created by migration. As we have already seen, a considerable variety of production activities in Becedas require more hands than any one family can provide. While this situation has not altered during the years since 1950, hired labor is no longer available. Not out of devotion to some pristine communalistic or altruistic ideal but, rather, because of concrete labor needs, villagers have had to band together for mutual economic well-being. To be sure, Erasmus long ago recognized that "labor shortages may be . . . [a] reason for the persistence of exchange labor within a money economy, for in some areas it may not be possible to obtain sufficient labor even for wage payments" (1956: 466). Yet the Becedas experience reveals not only a retention of interfamily cooperation but, more importantly, an extension of it under conditions of labor scarcity.

The village's basic technological stagnation has also figured importantly in changing labor organization. Mechanized agriculture, which enables a single farmer to carry out the activities of several farmers within a shorter period of time, is often cited as a factor in the individualization of labor and in the breakup of cooperative and communal work enterprises. Becedas, with its mountainous terrain, has not been able to consolidate plots to the point at which tractors and other heavy farm machinery would be viable. Farmers have seized upon mechanization, in terms of reaping and insecticide spraying, to the extent that it has been possible. But whereas in the one case—reaping—mechanization has done nothing to change the balance of individualistic versus cooperative work patterns, in the second instance—insecticide spraying—communalism has actually increased.

How have all these changes affected community solidarity and identity in Becedas? Perhaps the most significant development has been the intensification of economic networks through an increase in work obligations among kinsmen, friends, and neighbors. Not only do farmers rely on one another more than ever before, but also their social relationships have been infused with an increasingly economic dimension. At least as much as in the past, and probably even more so, Becedas' economy is embedded in its society. In turn, the increased interpersonal dependency in agricultural production, the solidification of social bonds through economic exchange, as well as the recognition by all farmers that they are battling against the same market forces, have all fostered a sense of common identity. As long as a Becedas farmer remains in the village, the welfare of his family depends, as it never has, on his recognition of the common fate and dependency that he shares with his fellows.

Plate 6 María Ovejero and children sorting pears.

VI

Family and Household

HOUSEHOLD STRUCTURE
AND COMPOSITION

In Becedas, as in villages throughout most of western Mediterranean Europe, the ideal household is composed of the nuclear family, a man with his wife and unmarried children living alone in a separate dwelling. The nuclear household is the main source of an individual's social and psychological security. *"En casa hasta el culo descansa"*—"in your own house, even your backside rests," is how people put it. It is recognized that, under the protective wings of the single family unit, a person can be himself and can relax from the pressures and insecurities that inevitably characterize relations among all villagers outside this unit. In every way, the nuclear family is thought to be the best and most natural domestic group.

Actual living arrangements in Becedas reflect domestic ideals. Table 5 lists the distribution of household types by kinship composition. In 1970, of the total 235 households, 149 (63%) were made up of the simple nuclear family. Another 24% included variations of what I have called the "fragmented family," a man or woman living either alone or with their unmarried children or unmarried siblings. In contrast, only 10% of the households could be termed "extended" or "joint," because they contained parents or unmarried siblings living with a married couple.

Clearly, the figures show a numerical preponderance of nuclear family households. Of these, the large majority consist of a man and woman with their children, even though there are 39 instances of couples living entirely alone. For some unexplained biological reason, 21 of these couples, most of them in late middle years of life, have been entirely childless, the woman never having given birth. The remainder are old villagers, whose children either have married and moved out or have left the village for permanent residence in the city.

Everyone professes to want children, and most women give birth within a year or two after marriage. If a newly married couple remains childless for several years, it is assumed that the union will be barren. Often, such a couple will form an unusually strong emotional bond with a niece or nephew who, generally before 5 years of age, comes to live with the aunt and uncle *como hijo (a)*—"as a son (or daughter)." In 1970, there were five such cases in Becedas. The child's actual parents, who invariably have at least two or three other children, relinquish him willingly, usually because of financial necessity. This form of adoption is never made official,[1] and the child is completely aware of his biological relationship to all the adults involved. Though the cost of the child's upbringing falls entirely upon the adopting aunt and uncle, he receives no greater share of their inheritance than he would ordinarily be entitled to as nephew (or niece).

In Becedas, too, a surprisingly large number of men and women never marry. In 1970, there were 24 men and 26 women over the age of 30, approximately 10% of all villagers in this age bracket, who had never married. A similar situation is found in the Zamoran village of Bermillo, where it is reported that an "extraordinary and alarming quantity of unmarried men and women exist" (Arguedas 1968: 101). Yet in Becedas, as in Bermillo, this phenomenon is not considered a problem, and everyone "is accustomed to view the existence of numerous bachelors and spinsters as a natural fact, a normal characteristic of the pueblo" (Arguedas 1968: 294). The primary drawback of bachelorhood or spinsterhood, according to villagers, is that there is no one to care for the lone individual after the death of his or her parents. In Becedas, unmarried women, fully capable of running a household by themselves, generally live alone or with unmarried sisters after parental death. When faced with the same situation, however, a bachelor is likely either to move in with a married sister and

---

[1] This is in contrast to adoption practices among barren couples in rural Japan (Embree 1939: 81–85), where adoption is designed to provide an heir for the family patrimony.

TABLE 5
Household Composition, 1970

Household types	Number of households
I. Simple nuclear family with variations	
A. Husband wife alone	39
B. Husband, wife, and unmarried children	110
II. Extended family with variations	
A. Type I.A. with married child and child's spouse and unmarried children	5
B. Type I.A. with one parent of either spouse	4
C. Type I.B. with wife's mother	9
D. Type I.B. and unmarried sibling of one spouse	5
III. The fragmented family unit	
A. Man alone	8
B. Woman alone	24
C. Type III.A. and unmarried children	6
D. Type III.A. and brother	1
E. Type III.B. and unmarried children	13
F. Type III.A. and sister(s)	4
IV. Other[a]	7
TOTAL	235

[a]"Other" includes woman with boarders (2 households), married couple plus servant (1), married couple plus niece (1), nuclear family plus servant (1), widow plus nephew (1), and widower plus children and mother-in-law (1).

her family, or to solicit the aid of some close married female relative, who is then responsible for cleaning his house and providing him the day's major meal.

In Becedas, it is said that *"El casa'o, casa quiere"*—"The married person wants his own house." Because of domestic ideals, extended family living is relatively rare, and where it exists it is designed to resolve serious financial or social problems. Sometimes newly married couples move in with the parents of either spouse for a short time after marriage, to enable them to accumulate enough money for the rental or purchase of a house. In this case, everyone in the domestic group eats together and shares food expenses, though lodging is provided free to the young couple. The period of such joint residence is 1 or 2 years at most, after which time the new couple establishes an independent household. As we shall see in Chapter 8, however, weddings usually provide newlyweds with enough capital to start out immediately on their own, so even this temporary postmarital joint residence is an exception to the usual practice.[2]

---

[2] In contrast, I found that in Tzintzuntzan, Mexico, where newlyweds are not endowed with a large capital outlay at the start of married life, they are generally required to reside patrilocally for 1 or 2 years before setting up their own household.

The extended household is most frequently formed in order to care for the aged. As long as an elderly couple is able to care for themselves, it is considered preferable for them to do so rather than to rely on married children. If they should become incapacitated, however, their married children and respective families are required to come live with them on a rotating basis, for anywhere between 1 and 3 months at a turn. Thus, a married son and his wife and children will pack most of their readily moveable belongings and bring them to the house of his parents for the several months' period, during which time their own house remains un-inhabited. When their turn is finished, they move back to their permanent residence, and a sibling with his or her family will come to live at the parents' house. After all the brothers and sisters of a family have taken their turn, the cycle is renewed, until the death of one of the parents. Thus, at any point in time, the parents' household is extended, though the household membership is in continual flux.

As long as both elderly parents are alive, it is considered heartless to break the continuity of their lives by asking them to leave their home. After one parent dies, however, the disintegrated nuclear unit no longer justifies the maintenance of a separate household, and the widowed in-dividual must accommodate himself to the homes of his or her children. Again, the responsibility for parental care is divided equally among all married siblings. But, in this case, the widow or widower is the mobile unit, moving in turn from the house of one child to another every several months, while his or hers remains closed and uninhabited. This practice establishes a curious situation in which there is an extended household at any one point in time, but the actual site of the household, as well as its membership, constantly changes.

Villagers view this latter system as dehumanizing, for when an indi-vidual has no permanent home base, a private domain in which he has at least minimal control over his life, he is considered less than a complete person. For this reason, widows, who are accustomed to the daily tasks of running a household, generally try to reside alone rather than to rely on their children. Not surprisingly, it is much more common for helpless widowers, untutored in carrying out domestic chores, to enter into a mobile existence.

A completely stable extended household forms under just one special circumstance: when there is an only child. In this case, the lone married son or daughter and his or her family reside permanently with the widowed parent, usually in the parent's house, and often before personal disability of the old person makes the arrangement necessary. Whenever married children live with their parents, they always eat together and divide the cost of the food. But in this instance alone, there is a total merger of economic functions, and the household becomes extended for purposes of production and marketing, as well as of residence. Nor is there any exact division or accounting for the cost of food. The arrangement is facilitated by the fact that inheritance, usually divided equally among all siblings, goes entirely to the only child. Thus, the parents' estate, including all land, furniture, and the house, is in reality as much the child's as the parents', though official title to the property remains in the hands of the latter. The stable extended family, then, is a convenient arrangement based on a sensible assessment of the future. Since only children are rare, however, this domestic situation is uncommon; in 1970, there were two such cases.

The preponderance of nuclear family households, the large number of single-member households, and the fleeting, impermanent nature of most extended households, are the major factors contributing to the small size of most domestic units. Table 6 lists varying household sizes and the numbers of households and village inhabitants they represent.

The numerical breakdown shows that 635 persons (78% of the total village population) live in households of 5 members or fewer. Still more striking, the average household contains only 3.4 members.

Since Becedas is made up of poor Catholic peasants, one wonders about the unusually small household size. A partial explanation is migration which, as already noted, has drained the village of a high proportion of its population, particularly of those in the childbearing years. Among adults with older children, it is rare to find a couple without most of their children residing either permanently or temporarily away from the village, and there are 12 village couples whose children are *all* either married or otherwise settled in cities throughout Spain. Another 17 families have children who are either studying or completing military service in distant locales.

TABLE 6
Household Size, 1970

Number of household members	×	Number of households	=	Number of villagers
1		32		32
2		56		112
3		35		105
4		49		196
5		38		190
6		12		72
7		7		49
8		5		40
9		1		9
TOTALS		235		805

Numerous other couples with from three to nine children have just one child—the youngest, the intellectually dullest, or the most physically handicapped—still resident in the village. The rural exodus obviously has had a tremendous impact on household size.

But, in addition, with increasing urban opportunities and the hope for material advancement, most young couples wish to have as few children as possible in order to give their children the greatest possible advantages. Adults who reside in the village like to think of their situation as temporary; if the children can be educated for city jobs, if they can "escape," as it is said, then they will certainly fulfill the filial duty and bring the parents along with them as soon as finances permit. Hence, now it is considered something akin to economic and social suicide to have more than two children. Primarily through a combination of abstention and coitus interruptus, young married adults attempt to limit births, which in turn affects household size. According to all evidence, these are relatively recent practices, begun as late as 1956 or so. Thus, it is clear that the opportunities for migration and greater material well-being have provided the main motivation for birth control in Becedas, just as similar factors have influenced family size among rising middle-class populations in more developed countries.

FAMILY ROLE RELATIONS AND SOCIALIZATION

Ideally, Becedas family life is guided by a strict dominance–submission hierarchy, in which the father is the ultimate source of all authority, the mother maintains the household and caters to the wishes of her husband, and the children respect and obey the cues and commands of their parents. As the saying goes,

En los tiempos de querer	During the time of loving [i.e., during courtship]
La mujer es la que manda,	The woman is the one who orders
Y en las puertas de la iglesia	And at the church doors [i.e., upon marriage]
Los papelitos se cambian.	The roles are changed.

In Parsons' (1955) terms, the husband's role is that of instrumental leader of the nuclear unit, making decisions that involve the relationship of the family to the outside society, while the wife's role is that of expressive leader, maintaining orderly relations between members of the family and caring for the general emotional well-being of the household.

In Becedas, as in communities throughout Spain (e.g., Lisón Tolosana 1966: 144), the husband derives authority from his position as *vecino*, "household head." It is in the role of *vecino* that he acts as legal representative for his family. He alone votes in municipal elections for *Ayuntamiento* and *Hermandad* council members, and he alone is responsible for paying taxes and for protecting the family's rights over property and person. In any legal disputes over land, whether the land actually belongs to the man or to his wife, it is he who is called upon to argue the case before community officials. As principal economic provider, the husband, in theory at least, has control over all matters concerning the disposition and use of family property. And it is true that no woman would ever presume to make a major decision affecting the family property or assets without first consulting her husband, though as indicated shortly, in minor day-to-day financial transactions, the woman actually plays the dominant role.

Just as the husband is legal head of the family, binding its members together as a single unit in relations with outsiders, so is the wife the central emotional figure, the person around whom all family affect and activities coalesce. *"El que tenga madre, que no le llore nadie"*—"He who has a mother, may no one cry for him" is how the saying puts it. Whenever a husband or child dies, it is tragic for all the surviving family members, but so long as the wife is alive, there is hope that the integrity of the household as an independent, ongoing social unit may be maintained. For house and home, respectively the physical headquarters and psychological expression of family life, are her domain. Thus, when referring to a particular house, villagers will always call it by the name of the wife, not the husband, saying, for example, "I'm going to the house of Margarita," even though Margarita's husband is actual owner and just as much a resident of the structure as she.

A woman's primary duty is to maintain her house in good order and to provide her family with food and decent clothing. Nowhere is this role better encapsulated than in the village census, where invariably a married woman's occupation is listed either as *"domicilio"*—"house"—or, even more telling, *"su sexo"*—"her sex." In the popular mind, as in actuality, the female status means automatic association with the home.

This is not to imply that housewives are seen as economically unproductive, for neither are they unproductive nor are they thought to be. As a minor example, we may remember that a good portion of a woman's working day is devoted to the tasks of knitting, darning, and sewing. Far from being idle, leisure-time activity, a woman's handiwork is of crucial psychological and economic importance to the family. In Becedas, as throughout Spain, family pride is dependent on and reflected in well-mended, cared-for clothing, for torn, filthy garments bring shame upon the individual and his family. And in a society in which new clothing is purchased only on very special occasions, the meagre family wardrobe is comprised largely of mended and remade garments. When a sweater becomes too small, the yarn is unwound and reknit to a larger size, being mixed in the process with low-grade cotton strands. If the sweater becomes worn at the elbow or cuff, the sleeve is cut off and a new one attached. Every bit of old cloth is treasured for future patching and piecing. Thus, a father's torn undershirt may provide the material for his daughter's underpants, while a mother's old dress may become pajamas for her son. This is all essential, significantly productive activity, work by definition, so it is never engaged in on Sunday, the day of rest.

Since the house is the woman's domain, it is she, too, who has primary responsibility for the care and early socialization of the children. Until a child is 4 or 5 years old, by which time she is said to have attained *sentido* ("sense" or "judgment"), socialization is concerned largely with controlling aggression and inculcating proper sexual identification. In Becedas, young children are permitted, indeed encouraged, to express anger openly. Tens of times each day, parents and other adults provoke children to hit animals, hit one another, and, more surprising still, hit adults, including the parents themselves. When a mother scolds her baby for being mischievous or engaging in unsafe activities, the child reacts by crying or throwing a tantrum. Almost immediately, a third individual, usually a neighbor, appears on the scene, scoops the child up in her arms, holds him close, and firmy grabs his right arm, saying *"Tonta Mamá, boba Mama, pégale a Mama"* ("Crazy Mommy, silly Mommy, hit Mommy"), all the while guiding the child's hand in an aggressive forward thrust, though never permitting the hand actually to touch the mother's body. The mother either ignores the child and goes about her business or, equally often, laughingly asks the child, *"Me pegas? Me pegas?"*—"You're hitting me? You're hitting me?" Never does she discourage such third-party sympathy, nor the open expression of anger.

If the child is old enough to walk, a similar method is used. On one occasion, 3-year-old María José was severely scolded by her mother. She ran out of her house crying and was immediately picked up by a neighbor, who, as is usual in such cases, told her that her mother was foolish, unkind, and unreasonable. Then, she guided the child's hand in a hitting motion, even though the mother was not present. Children at this age, and even more so when they are younger, are not expected to have moral judgment, so it is irrelevant whether or not they are in reality being punished justifiably. The important thing is to enable them to feel and express aggression toward their parents. And the method does at least achieve the short-run goal of quieting children for the crying generally stops within a few moments after the child gains the adult's sympathy. Shortly after each incident, parent and child hug and become completely reconciled, until the next divisive encounter.

Young children receive no such sympathy when it appears that they are beginning to identify with the opposite sex. To the contrary, they are usually ridiculed into playing the appropriate sexual role. One day, 5-year-old José Luis was walking in the street with his shirt tails hanging out over his pants. When his mother noticed this, she ran to him and began shooing him into the house, all the while spanking him lightly on the backside and saying loudly, so all present could hear, "Everyone is going to laugh at Luisito because his shirt is hanging out. Everyone is going to say that his shirt is a little dress, and they're not going to know if he's a little girl or a little boy." In other words, the mother was warning her son that if he refused to dress like a proper male child he would be ridiculed; she was citing the necessity of neatness for establishing clear sexual identity.

On another occasion, four siblings, three girls and their 5-year-old brother, were being prepared for a wedding. Following recent Spanish peasant custom, the little girls were all doused in cheap cologne water, after which everyone present began telling them how cute they were and how darling they smelled. The little boy, receiving no attention at all, took the bottle of cologne and applied it to himself in generous quantities. When he proudly stepped up to exhibit his newly acquired scent, his parents became visibly upset and told him loudly that cologne was only for little girls, that everyone was going to call him *marica* ("sissy"): "They're all going to say Angelín is a little *marica*, a little *marquita*." By causing the poor child embarrassment, they hoped to impress upon him the fact that sexual boundaries should not be transgressed, and that he should, in the future, distinguish carefully between male and female behavior.

The techniques of controlling aggression and instilling proper sexual identity not only show how the people of Becedas deal with these universal childbearing problems, but also dramatically illustrate the way in which shame, rather than guilt, is used to guide behavior. Because children learn early that it is acceptable to get angry at a parent and to express their hostility openly, they are relatively free of the pent-up guilt feelings that often accompany similar emotions in other societies. Unlike the Japanese, for example, for whom guilt feelings play a role in parental manipulation of a child's behavior (De Vos 1960), the people of Becedas rely primarily on ridicule to control the actions and attitudes of their children. It is understandable, then, that Becedas, like most communities of Mediterranean Europe and Latin America, is a shame-oriented rather than a guilt-oriented society. For, as we shall see in the next chapter, the people of Becedas conform to ideal or expected behavior patterns because violation of the rules evokes severe criticism or other negative reactions from the community at large. There is little inner motivation, through a deep-seated moral sense of right or wrong, to behave normally or correctly. In the socialization patterns just described, we see the psychological basis for the formation of this personality type.

In their early years, children begin to learn that different roles are appropriate to each of the sexes. Later, however, after they have acquired *sentido*, they get a greater opportunity actually to play out these distinct roles. Here, the parental treatment of sons and daughters varies greatly. Sons, to be sure, are periodically expected to help their fathers with agricultural work. But, as already noted, these occasions are minimal and occur only when there is an absolute shortage of hands. Until a boy is at least 14 years old, the age at which his formal education generally terminates, his parents give him little responsibility. During the course of the day, he may run an errand or two, or he may voluntarily amuse himself by watching and assisting his father in the performance of some minor household repair. But in general, aside from school hours, he is given free reign to do as he pleases, which usually means playing outside with other boys. Parents are forever running and screaming after their sons to come to dinner or to be off to school. Young boys are expected to exhibit such irresponsible and carefree behavior, and often a mother or father seems to delight in the childish transgressions of their sons.

In contrast, daughters are burdened with a large number of household responsibilities. Outside of school hours—during summertime, on weekends, or whenever they are free on weekdays—girls assist in the upkeep of the house. Girls as young as 7 years old may be seen washing dishes and clothing, mopping floors, and cleaning walls, while those a few years older help with the family cooking. Daughters also assist in the care of their younger siblings, feeding, changing, and entertaining them. In short, they become, as Díaz describes it for Mexico, "little mothers" (1966: 84). They do have free time, but, like adults of their sex, this falls mainly on Sundays. It is no wonder, then, that women often express a preference for having female children. Girls not only lighten the household workload but may also be counted upon to take over household maintenance whenever their mothers become ill.

The overall effect of this differential treatment of children is to make girls much more independent and self-reliant than their brothers. Left alone in the world, a teenage boy of Becedas would no doubt fare much worse than a girl of the same age. For, unlike his sister, he remains totally ignorant of and unpracticed in the mundane chores that are necessary for physical maintenance. This is why, later in life, sisters and other close female relatives are inevitably called upon to assist with the upkeep of a bachelor's or widower's home.

When the domestically untutored son marries and establishes his own household, he invariably retains his basic dependence on an adult female. The wife replaces the mother as the provider of nourishment, but both women have essentially the same guiding role in the man's life. The husband hands over all his earnings to his wife, virtually as soon as he receives them, for she is the person responsible for the family's primary capital outlay—the purchase of food. On Sundays and feast days, the woman gives her husband a small token sum to spend on drinks in the bar. And, of course, if agricultural products must be bought, she also provides him a suitable amount. But, in almost all cases, it is the wife who does the actual budgeting and who has real control over the purse. The husband, remaining aloof from the petty commercial transactions of daily life, never really knows the exact state of the family kitty. Because of this self-imposed ignorance, he unconsciously abdicates power over household finances.

Becedas men are so dependent on their wives that they even rely on them for so simple and routine a matter as getting dressed. Every Sunday morning, the wife lays out a fresh set of clothing for all the household members. A husband never chooses what he is to wear, nor would he know how to go about making such a momentous decision. One Sunday afternoon, I walked into Alberto's house; he was to have changed his clothes to accompany me to a village bar. Instead of finding him ready, as was usual, I found him dejected and moping, his head on the table, his outfit still unchanged. "What's the matter?" I asked. The problem was that his wife had left the house to visit her parents and had forgotten to lay out his fresh set of clothing. Alberto was completely immobilized. His wife's negligence was equivalent to a personal rejection. Even though he might have looked for and chosen the clothing himself, he preferred instead to sit around the house in a depressed state, waiting for his wife to come home and assume her proper role. His reaction to this situation was no different from that of any helpless, dependent young child.

This profound and prevalent male dependency helps to explain an important phenomenon in Becedas: late marriage. In this village, as in rural Ireland (Arensberg and Kimball 1968: 99–102), and Europe generally (Hajnal 1964), both men and women marry late as compared with peasant averages in other parts of the world. Table 7 shows the marriage age of all persons married in Becedas from 1940 to 1969.

It is clear from the table that the overwhelming majority of persons of both sexes marry at age 25 or over. Men, in particular, exhibit this pattern, with about a fourth to a third of the marriages being contracted after the age of 30. The second marriage of widowers accounts for only three of these cases, while a mere seventh or so of married males were under 25 at the time of their union. Further, during these three decades, not a single Becedas man got married before the age of 20.

The pattern of female marriages is somewhat more complex in that the record indicates a trend toward increasingly older marriage ages. The percentage of females contracting marriage after 25 years of age increases markedly from 54% in the decade 1940–1949 to 63% in the decade 1960–1969. (In other words, during this period the percentage of women marrying before age 25 drops from 46 to 37%.) The reason for this change is discussed fully in Chapter 9. Here, it is sufficient to note that, for both sexes and for all decades, there is undeniable conformity with the overall European pattern of postponed marriage.

Unlike some European societies, for example, the rural peoples of Greece (Campbell 1964: 82; Friedl 1964: 66), late marriage in Becedas cannot be explained in terms of economic motives. For, as we shall see shortly, virtually all villagers are assured a large capital reserve at the time of marriage. Rather, this phenomenon must be explained, at least in part, by male dependency on the mother and by the reluctance of mothers to relinquish their tight hold over their sons. Every mother knows the saying:

Hija que casas, hijo que ganas,   If your daughter marries, you gain
                                                                     a son,
Y si es hijo, hijo que pierdes.   But if it's the son, you lose him.

TABLE 7
Marriage Age, 1940–1969

Decade		No. marriages of persons under 25	No. marriages of persons 25–29	No. marriages of persons over 30	Totals
1969–1960	M	7 (10%)	36 (51%)	27 (39%)	70 (100%)
	F	26 (37%)	30 (43%)	14 (20%)	70 (100%)
1959–1950	M	14 (16%)	53 (58%)	23 (7%)	90 (100%)
	F	32 (35%)	46 (51%)	12 (4%)	90 (100%)
1949–1940	M	14 (13%)	57 (55%)	13 (32%)	104 (100%)
	F	48 (46%)	44 (42%)	12 (12%)	104 (100%)

As already noted, when a son marries, his wife assumes the role that his mother previously played in his life. With the son no longer physically and psychologically dependent on his mother, the primary bond between them is severed and their relationship dwindles to mere formalities of exchange and visits on relatively rare occasions. It is this severance of the bond that the mother fears and tries to forestall. Not only are mothers reluctant to relinquish their hold over their sons but, more importantly, the sons become aware of and anxious about their mothers' possessiveness. It is largely because sons develop ambivalent attitudes toward their mothers, resenting their dependence on them, yet fearful of hurting them by leaving, that marriages are postponed until late in life.

There is a good practical reason why a mother fears separation from her son. As already noted, later in life the mother will in all probability live temporarily in the home of her son and daughter-in-law. In this situation, there is always tension and disagreement between mother-in-law and daughter-in-law, who are trapped in one another's company for hours on end and who generally have different ideas about how a household should be run. Mothers constantly complain about ill treatment, real or imagined, by daughters-in-law. It is primarily because of this psychologically uncomfortable situation between the two women that it is considered wise to have frequent rotation of filial responsibility for old people. Better for brothers and sisters to have 1- or 2-month turns taking care of their parents than to stretch the period of extended household living over 6 months or a year.

As we have seen, women also marry relatively late. Given that a fourth to a half of female marriages have been contracted prior to the age of 25 over the past generation, the data are not as striking as in the case of men. To be sure, parents, especially mothers, greatly value the economic contribution of their daughters to household maintenance and, for this reason, are often reluctant to see them married. But late female marriage is most likely a function of late male marriage. In Becedas, children of both sexes begin serious courtship early in life, between 14 and 17 years of age. More often than not, sweethearts are close in age, with the girl perhaps a few years younger; their relationship remains stable over a long period of time—as much as 10 to 15 years in many cases—until the actual legal union of the couple in marriage. Since the boy is usually the reluctant party, constantly prolonging the relationship yet postponing the final step, both he and his girlfriend consequently marry late. In some cases, men and women enter into courtship only in their late twenties or early thirties; here, the courtship lasts but a few months and the couple is said to marry *por recojerse* ("to take refuge" [i.e. from bachelorhood]).

Whatever the precise courtship pattern, parents, especially mothers, are not as fearful of losing their daughters as they are their sons. Paradoxically, because of the daughter's greater independence, she is not as likely psychologically to abandon her mother. A son, when he marries, finds a mother substitute in his wife and, therefore, severs ties with his real mother. But the emotional relationship between mother and daughter changes very little after her marriage. After marriage, to be sure, a daughter is no longer the household helper. But at least she may be counted on to remain loyal to her parents and concerned about their welfare. Thus, it is said:

La hija al pie de la camisa	Your daughter right by your side,
Y la nuera mas afuera,	Your daughter-in law further away,
Te cierra la puerta;	She shuts the door on you;
Y la hija te la abre.	And your daughter opens it for you.

The mother's attitudes toward her children, then, are intimately bound up with her anticipation of the future. At the moment of truth, when in old age she must call on her children for help, the daughter will welcome her with open arms, a role for which her childhood training has prepared her. The son, on the other hand, accepts responsibility for his aged parents only as a matter of duty; neither he nor his wife is expected to have true concern for their welfare. For, unwittingly, in the course of socialization, during which the mother maintains and guards her dominant position over the dependent males in the family, she has assured that her son's future loyalties will lie elsewhere.

INHERITANCE

In Becedas, there is a simple inheritance rule: All children, regardless of sex, relative age, or place of residence, divide the property of both parents equally. In the case of a childless couple, nephews and nieces inherit their property in equal parts. The property of a bachelor or spinster is divided in the same manner among his or her siblings, or, in the case of deceased siblings, among the siblings' children.

The precise time of property division varies under different circumstances. Everyone prefers to hold legal title to his property until death. In this manner, he hopes to assure the loyalty and obedience of all potential heirs. Children, however, often come into real control of their inheritance shares before parental death. For example, when it becomes obvious that a man can no longer effectively farm his land, he permits his property to be divided among his children, while still retaining the deeds in his own name. The children then work the land, which is in reality theirs as long as they live, on a sharecrop basis, thus providing the parents with an income. Widows, automatic heirs to their husbands' property, usually permit their children to work their inheritance shares outright. In this case, each child provides the mother equally with a small monthly cash payment, which effectively provides her a steady, though meagre, "salary" (*sueldo*). The widow is, therefore, freed from the responsibility of making crop sales, a procedure with which she is entirely unfamiliar. In all these arrangements, monetary transactions or crop transfers between parents and children are executed with minute exactness. After the death of both parents, the de facto inheritance shares of children are legalized by changing the official property titles.

The actual method of property division is designed to insure absolute equality among all heirs. Children gather at the parental home and make a careful list of all the family belongings, including land parcels, house, barns, furniture, clothing, and household items—radios, clock, gas stove, and the like. The prospective heirs then group all the items into what they, by consensus, consider to be equal shares (*lotes*). The number of shares, of course, corresponds to the number of heirs. Sometimes, no exactly equal division of property is possible. In this case, shares carry monetary stipulations, stating, for example, that the person who gets Share 1 must pay the receiver of Share 2 cash to the amount of 5000 pesetas; or, that the receiver of Share 3 is entitled to collect 2000 pesetas from all the other heirs. In addition, considerations such as the distance of a field from the village or the potential resale value of a land parcel are taken into account when calculating the value of shares. As might be imagined, the formation of shares is a sensitive matter, involving a great deal of bickering among siblings. But since it is in all their interests to make the shares as equitable as possible, the process usually takes no more than a single afternoon. The task accomplished, each share is carefully written out on a separate piece of paper and numbered. The papers are crumpled up, placed in a beret, and drawn, in no particular order, by all the heirs. At least two nonkinsmen, usually neighbors, are called upon to witness the drawing, thus assuring that no one can claim unfairness or improper procedure.

Frequently, more than property is at stake in an inheritance drawing, for children may inherit a specialized occupation and with it a distinctive life style. For example, Carlos Trapero's father was for most of his adult life both a baker and a farmer, with considerable landholdings. Just before his death, his property was split by lot among his three sons. Carlos drew the bakery and a small orchard, while his two borthers came into a number of land parcels. Consequently, Carlos devotes most of his time and energy to the bakery and only a little to his orchard. His brothers, on the other hand, are full-time farmers. Thus, the lottery determined the whole course of Carlos's life: a small but steady income earned through daily bread sales accompanied by freedom from concern over unpredictable weather. In contrast, his brothers usually enjoy greater income, but they face the uncertainties of all farmers.

The results of the inheritance lottery are not necessarily final. Sometimes, the siblings' individual life circumstances cause them to prefer one kind of property over another. A brother with a large number of cattle might favor a meadow over an orchard; a sister, married to a man without his own residence, might strongly desire the family house over any land at all. In these cases, pairs of siblings sometimes exchange lots after the drawing, each inheriting the share drawn by the other. But this smooth rearrangement of fortune is accomplished only rarely, when there is more or less equal desire on the part of two heirs to obtain the other's property.

More often, a drawing bestows unequal benefit, when seen from the standpoint of the siblings' individual life circumstances, and yields an undercurrent of hostility and resentment among heirs. An example illustrates the almost inevitable problems of such "equal" division. Exactly 7 days after their father's death, Miguel, Antonio, and Lorenza drew lots for the family inheritance. The main family property was divided into three equal shares: Share 1 was the parental house, in extremely good condition and very centrally located; Share 2 consisted of three large *huertas*; Share 3 was a small meadow and an older, rather decrepit house that, at the time, was being rented from the parents by Lorenza and her family. To equalize the lots as much as possible, the person who drew Share 3 would receive 5000 pesetas from the person who drew Share 1, and 3000 pesetas from the person who drew Share 2.

Though the three shares were all approximately equal in value, clearly Share 1 was the most desirable. Miguel, with a good house of his own, wanted the parental house to convert into a bar, for the future welfare of one of his sons, a mentally ill child with no prospects of migrating. Lorenza, with no home of her own, wanted either Share 1 or Share 3; her husband is village bailiff and they have no need for agricultural or pasture land. Antonio, who has neither children nor a house of his own, also wanted Shares 1 or 3; to be burdened with more land and more work, when there was no prospect of leaving the fruits of his labor to progeny, was a dismal prospect at best.

In the end, Miguel drew the parents' house, Antonio drew the meadow and lesser house, and Lorenza drew the three large *huertas*. The outcome was advantageous to everyone but Lorenza, who now had an excess of land, useless in her specific circumstances, but no house. Upon completion of the drawing, Lorenza immediately broke into tears, screaming that she would have no place to live, that she and her family would be homeless, and so on. Out of pity, Antonio, one of the most soft-hearted of villagers, on the spot offered to switch shares with her. Now Antonio was to be given the *huertas* and Lorenza the second house and meadow.

The whole affair ended on a distinctly sour note. Within hours, Antonio was regretting his decision to switch, attributing it to a momentary emotional lapse. Both Antonio and Lorenza were hopelessly envious of Miguel's good fortune and, at the same time, resentful that Miguel, the day after the drawing, shut down the parental house completely. It was painful for them to see the house they had been reared in closed so finally, with no immediate prospect of occupancy. In this case, as in numerous others, the lottery system produced a cold equality, without regard to practicality or actual life circumstances.

VILLAGE–URBAN FAMILY TIES

As already mentioned, virtually every Becedas family has close relatives now living outside the village, many of them in provincial capitals, but most in Madrid. Some ex-villagers have what may be considered lower middle-class occupations, such as schoolteacher, secretary, or semiskilled office worker. The vast majority work as butchers, vendors, cab drivers, factory workers, or at other unskilled or semiskilled labor. All these migrants, regardless of their present socioeconomic position, maintain close bonds with their families in the village. As in Greece (Friedl 1959), the villagers' most meaningful and intensive urban contacts are with or through their kinsmen in the city.

Direct, regular contact with urban kinsmen generally takes place within the village itself. Because many of the Madrid migrants own cars or have ready access to the direct taxi service linking city and village, they make the 3½-hour journey back to the village whenever a sufficiently long vacation permits. All migrants prefer to visit during the summer months, when the cool mountain climate offers them relief from what they consider a scalding city. August, particularly late August, witnesses the greatest migrant influx, as ex-villagers flock to the village to participate in the 4-day patronal fiesta honoring Santa Teresa. Often a nephew or niece will come early in the summer, spend a month or two in the village, and then return to Madrid in August with his parents, who visit for only 1 or 2 weeks. Because of the constant coming and going, it is impossible to make an exact numerical calculation of this summer influx. However, the general impression is that the vast majority of Becedas households receive at least one set, if not a continuous string, of visitors from Madrid during these months.

An only slightly less popular occasion for village visiting is provided by the *matanza* ("slaughter"), which for any given family takes place over a 2- or 3-day period, any time between late November and late January, when the weather is coldest and, hence, the freshly killed meat least likely to spoil.[3] Many families still follow the traditional practice of buying a piglet in late spring and raising it for the winter slaughter. Most, however, have abandoned this practice and simply buy a full-grown pig, or desirable portions thereof, from a village butcher just prior to the *matanza*. In any case, the word *matanza* refers less to the actual slaughter of the animal than to the social event itself, the few intensive days of preparing and curing the meat into hams, bacon, and several varieties of sausages, which are eaten throughout most of the coming year.

The *matanza* is easily the happiest occasion for any family, a time of plenty, when relatives gather for large banquets and assist one another with the preparation and curing of the animals. Frequently, city relatives have an actual monetary investment in the *matanza*: A migrant may purchase a piglet, have it raised by a sibling at his (the migrant's) own expense, and come to the village for the curing; or, alternatively, he may share the expense of one animal with a village relative by purchasing the piglet, while having the villager pay for the cost of feeding. Migrants generally trust and prefer the quality of village-prepared meat to that which they can purchase in the butcher shops of Madrid. For this reason, they go out of their way to "make the *matanza*" in Becedas.

When migrants visit Becedas, they usually stay in the home of some close relative—parents, siblings, or aunts and uncles. Sometimes, because of marriage or migration away from a home, a house will have extra beds to accommodate guests. More frequently, a house contains just enough beds to sleep its own regular occupants, so when relatives visit, children, and even adults, double or triple up. Rarely are there any complaints about lack of comfort in such situations. To the contrary, villagers seem more than willing to sacrifice a modicum of comfort in order to enable their guests to stay with them. In Becedas, no matter how small a house,

---

[3] Such family pig slaughters are a common feature of rural life throughout Mediterranean Europe. The practice is reported by Pitt–Rivers (1961: 85–86) in Andalusia, and by Deane (1965: 28–47) in Corsica. To my knowledge, the best and most complete study of a Spanish *matanza* is provided by Taboada (1969), who writes in great detail about all aspects of the slaughter and feast in Galicia.

it seems sufficient to accommodate an unlimited number of family guests, at least for a short period of time.

As the rural exodus hastens, more and more migrants are retaining their village residences, remodeling or rebuilding them to be used as summer quarters for themselves or their children. Of the 361 houses in Becedas, an astounding 98 (27%) belong to outsiders, all ex-villagers. Of these 98, 35 are vacant, 27 are rented to permanent village residents, and 36 are already used as summer homes. Since the beginning of migration, the value of village houses has risen rapidly, principally because of their newly perceived potential as summer residences. Rare is the migrant who is willing to sell his house at a price most villagers could pay. Rarer still is the permanent villager who wishes to sell a second, unused house. He would rather retain the property in case he or a child should move to Madrid and want it for summertime use. Homeowners have even become reluctant to rent houses, lest there be difficulty in asking a tenant to vacate. Because of migration, then, property values within the village nucleus have soared at least as much as the value of agricultural and pasture land, for the same reason, has dropped.

In addition to having extensive contact with city relatives who come to the village, the people of Becedas occasionally visit kinsmen in Madrid. Such visits are likely to take place only under several specific circumstances. First, widows and widowers who migrate from the house of one child to another generally spend part of the year with children in Madrid. If a widow has four children, for example, two of whom live in Becedas and two of whom live in Madrid, she probably will spend 3 months of each year in the house of each, hence, 6 months in the village and 6 months in the city. All elderly people who "float" in this manner spend the winter months in Madrid so as to avoid the harsh Becedas climate. Even when a widow is able to care for herself, if she lives alone in the village, she is likely to visit children in Madrid between December and February. In this way, old people are able to maintain contact with city relatives while, at the same time, taking refuge from the most physically trying aspects of village life.

Occasionally, too, villagers make short visits to Madrid. Young people, free from agricultural tasks in the winter, stay with aunts and uncles in the city during Christmas time. Whenever a villager is referred to a medical specialist in Madrid, he is put up at the home of a relative. If the person should require a long period of convalescence, he stays with his city kinsmen for a longer period of time, up to several months. In all these ways, kinship ties enable the people of Becedas to have direct contact with the urban environment.

The constant movement between Becedas and Madrid is facilitated primarily by excellent door-to-door taxi service. A young man, an ex-villager in his late twenties who now lives in Madrid, owns and operates a limousine that he drives exclusively between the village (and some of the neighboring communities) and the capital. Such service is common in *pueblos* of the Sierra de Béjar. In summertime, when there is greatest demand for travel, the driver makes the round trip daily, bringing and taking *Madrileños* to and from the village. In winter, when there is less traffic, he makes the trip only two or three times per week, except during the Christmas holidays, when he again has full bookings and does the round trip every day. The cost is 200 pesetas (about 3 dollars) each way, plus a 25-peseta tip, in all a significant, though hardly prohibitive, amount. For the price of a small tip, too, the driver delivers packages (agricultural, meat, and baked goods from the village, canned goods, clothing, and packaged sweets from Madrid) between village and city relatives, especially during the Christmas and Easter holiday seasons.

Structurally, then, kinship relations provide the main avenue of contact between the village and the city. On occasion, one hears of migrants who no longer return to Becedas, who have, for all practical purposes, severed ties with their native *pueblo*. In these instances, it is invariably found that the migrants no longer have close kin residing in the village; in other words, their entire families have already moved away. On the other hand, virtually all villagers today have at least some close relatives living in Madrid and other large Spanish cities. Because of the continuing and increasingly intense contact with these kin, it may be said that the villagers' primary outside contacts now lie with Madrid. The connection with Béjar and El Barco, important as it may have been historically and culturally, is no longer foremost among the people of Becedas. Nowadays, the main urban influences stem directly from the capital.

URBAN LINKS, FAMILY SOLIDARITY, AND COMMUNITY IDENTITY

The evidence presented in this chapter and elsewhere reveals the undeniable fact that the Becedas populace is more dispersed today than ever before. True, the physical dimensions of the village have not changed significantly over the past several generations, and the community's discretely bounded, highly nucleated aspect has been preserved. Yet, socially, its edges have become permeable and indistinct, even to the point of making it difficult to determine precisely who is a village resident and who is not. Migration, as well as the constant interaction between those who live most of the year in the city and those who live most of the year in the village, have combined to break down the traditional neatly confined social network. Does this mean that Becedas has already become totally integrated within and engulfed by the wider society, thus losing its sense of separate identity? There are several indications that this has not happened and that the continuing importance of family ties to villagers and migrants alike is the main reason why.

At the outset, we should stress that in Becedas, contrary to developments elsewhere in Europe and throughout the peasant world, family ties have actually been strengthened with increasing migration and modernization. A generation ago, when peasant studies first took firm hold among anthropologists, Redfield (1947) characterized the folk world in part by its strong sense of familism and by the strength of its kinship ties. Contact with the city, Redfield (1941: 187–228) said, brings about individualization and family disorganization, manifested in part by the fact that each person no longer calculates his behavior in accordance with its economic and social ramifications for a wide number of relatives. This idea has been seized upon by observers of contemporary European peasantry from Denmark (Anderson and Anderson 1964: 106–108) to Yugoslavia (Simic 1973: 134–142), where developments do seem to parallel what Redfield originally identified in southeastern Mexico.

In Becedas, however, migration and urban contacts have had the opposite effect on family sentiment and unity, and for a number of reasons. First, the often extreme economic competition that characterized relations between siblings in the traditional setting has become considerably reduced. Extensive migration has eased land pressure not only within the village generally, but also within family groups, whose property divisions often resulted in a precarious existence for each heir. We have already seen one instance in which animosities among siblings were engendered by property division, even though this division was equal. Significant in this case is that none of the heirs was a migrant. Where sibling groups contain migrants, as is true in the vast majority of village families today, all siblings still inherit equally, but the migrants free their land at reasonable rental rates or sharecropping terms to their village brothers and sisters. As a result of the more plentiful land supply, an important source of competition among village siblings, on the one hand, and between villagers and their migrant relatives, on the other, has been eliminated. Migrants and villagers alike have benefited from the situation in their own way and, in the process have become more dependent on one another than in the past.

Second, villagers are now more sensitive to the potential economic utility of kinsmen than ever before and, as a result, are more careful to avoid disputes and maintain amicable relations with them. Until the 1960s, patron–clientage was never an outstanding feature of Becedas social structure. To the extent that such ties existed, they were confined primarily to relationships between the *pueblo* and its influential professionals (see pp. 39–40). In contemporary times, however, migrants have become more and more like patrons to their village relatives, providing them with clothing, interest-free loans, medical advice, and a place to stay in Madrid. They also provide, as we have seen, the main avenue through which villagers can find jobs and housing when they or their children decide to move permanently to the city.

The new patronage role of migrant relatives has resulted in both the widening and the strengthening of kinship ties among the people of Becedas. Numerous villagers now maintain close contact with migrant cousins or aunts and uncles with whom they had only tenuous ties in the village context. A symbiotic relationship has been established, through which villagers derive economic benefits and security, and migrants obtain prestige. And because every villager is nowadays perceived as a potential migrant capable of being thrust overnight into the role of patron, he is treated with the utmost caution by all his relatives, who fear alienating their possible *enchufe* ("contact") to economic and social mobility. In this sense, in Becedas, as in village Greece (Friedl 1959), kinship has become an increasingly crucial source of social cohesion within the community generally. Atomistic sentiments among relatives are less evident now than they were a generation ago.

Curiously, the extension of ties with ex-villagers has done nothing to diminish community feelings of identity and distinctiveness. One reason for this is the frequent difficulty of distinguishing migrants from villagers themselves. Family ties are so close that Becedas households and Madrid households, though physically separate, are often one and the same social entity. Pedro López, his wife, and two of his children live in a city apartment. But a third child—a teenage daughter—dislikes Madrid and prefers to live with her grandmother and widowed aunt in Becedas. Damián Málaga, his wife, and his two youngest children live in Becedas. He recently purchased an apartment in Madrid, which now houses his four eldest children, of whom two work, one attends school, and the last takes care of the domestic chores. Numerous villagers have children studying in Madrid and living with migrant aunts and uncles. Widowed parents regularly travel to live temporarily in the homes of married children in the city. In these, as in a variety of similar cases, family ties straddle two physically separate sites, making it difficult to determine whether particular individuals are or are not migrants. Becedas households have not disintegrated and divided. They have merely developed outposts in Madrid and encompass people who spend the majority of their time in one site or the other.

A second reason migration has not diminished community identity is that migrants still clearly belong to and participate in the life of the village. People who now live and work in Madrid enjoy the economic and cultural benefits of city life. But they in no way identify fully with the city; their urban social ties are still of a fleeting, tenuous, and ephemeral nature. Becedas migrants are residentially dispersed throughout Madrid, so an "urban village" has not developed among them. Nor are there any voluntary associations or special hangouts through which they might all keep in contact. Migrants are, by their own estimate, socially isolated in the city context. Their deepest, most tenacious ties lie with their families back in the village, and, for this reason, as well as for the fact that they are and will always be *"hijos de Becedas,"* they still identify strongly with it.

The combination of strong family ties and village identification means that Becedas operates as a magnet, constantly pulling migrants back to the countryside on a regular and frequent basis. Whether for life cycle rites, village festivals, property management, or just relaxation and clean air, migrants are a visible presence throughout the year. And when they re-enter the community, for however brief a visit, they confidently assume full participation in village life. Women wash clothing and dishes in the village streams, and bake cookies at the village ovens. Men work alongside their relatives in the fields or help with pasturage activities. Though migrants dress in a flamboyant, modern style and are, in that way, readily identifiable, they in no way try to establish themselves as a superior, privileged group, feigning incompetence in everyday village affairs. Brought up and maintaining their most devoted social ties within Becedas, they find it impossible to reject or scorn the community, for they know that if migration had meant complete severance from the village, they might never have left. No longer the center of economic life for migrants, Becedas is still the focus of their social existence. The sociocentrism of the *pueblo* has been maintained, despite the evident depopulation.

Because migrants so obviously maintain close contact with the community, villagers themselves have become less alienated from their situation than they otherwise might have been. To villagers, migrants embody the fulfillment of an economic dream that almost everyone in the community shares, and that dream includes leaving Becedas. Yet, precisely because villagers hold migrants in high esteem, they are flattered by the constant attentions the ex-villagers pay them and their community. Their own sense of self-worth, as well as the value of Becedas in their own eyes, become correspondingly enhanced. Though they too hope to leave, they have in no sense come to reject the community outright. In fact, migrant attitudes and behavior have shown them that the community continues to be a viable entity, despite massive migration. They are still very much a *pueblo*.

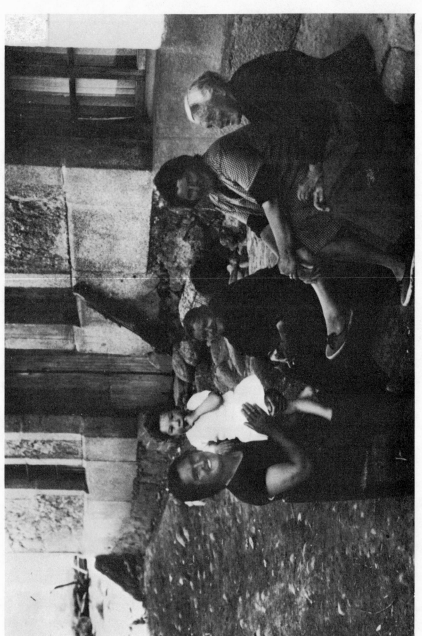

Plate 7 Neighbors.

VII

Friends and Neighbors

FRIENDSHIP AND SOCIAL STRUCTURE

In studying societies without a strong kinship organization, it is always necessary to determine other principles by which community members may be bound into relatively stable, cohesive groups. Anthropological research, for example, has always well-documented that throughout rural Latin America fictive kinship, in the form of the *compadrazgo*, operates to promote social, psychological and economic security among pairs of individuals who enter voluntarily into ongoing, ritually sanctioned relationships (Foster 1953a, Mintz and Wolf 1950). This is also true in Andalusia (Pitt-Rivers 1961: 107-108). However, the *compadrazgo*, as it is known in Latin America and southern Spain, is virtually nonexistent in the peasant communities of Castile. In Becedas at least, friendship and neighborship are the main avenues through which nonfamilial ties are expressed; they are, as it were, functional equivalents of the *compadrazgo*.

Friendship bonds have their roots in childhood. From the time a child enters school, at the age of 6, he begins to associate informally with others of his age and sex. During this early period, children are fickle about their choice of companions, and the composition of friendship groups changes radically and often. By the time children are 10 or 12 years old, however, they are already members of well-established, stable bands called cuadrillas ("groups"). Cuadrillas are divided by sex and age; they always contain members of the same sex within a 2- or 3-year age span. Usually, a cuadrilla has between four and six individuals, though larger groups are known. A famous male band of a generation ago is still referred to as *"La Cuadrilla de Los Quince"*—"The Cuadrilla of the Fifteen"—after the abnormally large size of its membership.

Residence and economic status seem to have little effect on *cuadrilla* composition. Friendships are formed primarily at school, where children come into contact with individuals from all neighborhoods in the village. Becedas is a community small enough to enable children living in diverse sections to get together easily after school hours and on Sundays. However, if two members of a *cuadrilla* happen to live near one another, it is likely that they will have greater day-to-day contact than they do with other members of their band. For economic reasons, it was common in the past for at least the poorer village girls to belong to *cuadrillas* apart from the rest. This is primarily because the poor girls could not afford to attend the private Colegio and, thus, did not associate much with those who could attend. (As mentioned earlier, virtually all boys have always attended the free government school.) Now, however, due to migration, there are so few children of any one age group that economic distinctions within *cuadrillas* have completely disappeared, and we find, for example, that Inés Hernández, a government school pupil from the poorest village household, is fast friends with Raimunda Trapero, a Colegio pupil from a prosperous family, these two forming the backbone of a band containing several other girls of their age.

The cuadrilla functions to provide psychological support for its members. On any occasion, when a young person is in the public eye, he or she feels much more at ease when accompanied by a group of friends. *Cuadrilla* members accompany one another to Sunday Mass, go strolling together along the highway on holidays, and stay huddled together at dances, whether in Becedas or in neighboring villages. They also attend the Easter and Pentecost *hornazos*, picnics of specially baked breads brought out to the threshing floors for group consumption. When a boy and girl alone pass each other casually in the street or on the highway, they avoid eye contact and rarely speak. Accompanied by their respective *cuadrillas*, however, the boys feel confident enough to make cat calls, and the girls are relaxed enough to laugh and giggle among themselves in response. The atmosphere is much less emotionally charged when everyone is surrounded by his or her special friends.

There is inevitably some feeling of rivalry among *cuadrillas* of the same age and sex. Members of different *cuadrillas* are usually on cordial terms with one another. But *cuadrilla* loyalty inherently means the creation of in-groups and out-groups, the exclusive sharing of secrets and experiences with those of one's own *cuadrilla*. Petty jealousies are aroused over which *cuadrilla* gets to dance with the prettiest girls or handsomest boys, which brings the largest or most elaborate *merienda* to the *hornazo*, and so on. Within each *cuadrilla*, there are often open discussions of sex, including boys bragging about sexual conquests. For this reason, brothers are virtually never members of the same *cuadrilla*, for they are ashamed to be in one another's presence when there are any discussions, or even innuendos, concerning sex.

However strong, *cuadrilla* loyalties and bonds begin to loosen when children reach their late teens, at which time they begin to have steady sweethearts. Emotional loyalties and confidences then switch to one's boyfriend or girlfriend and to the one or two other *cuadrilla* members and their sweethearts toward whom one feels a special affinity. Girls, in particular, begin to associate with only a few of their closest friends, usually the ones who are paired with a common group of boyfriends. Such foursomes and sixsomes help to stabilize long courtships, for members of these groups always try to patch a ruptured romance, putting pressure on the young couple to reunite.

Prior to marriage, a young man's *cuadrilla* relationship is supplemented and, toward marriage years, almost entirely supplanted by two types of formalized friendship. The first, a loose bond created among a relatively large number of boys is based on membership in the village bachelors' society, an unnamed organization with little structure but with significant social functions. Upon reaching the age of 15, all young village boys officially become *mozos*, eligible bachelors, by paying what is known as the *cuartilla* (four liters of wine, so named because they make up a quarter of a *cántaro* [a standard-sized jug]) to those who are already initiated members of the society. The *mozos* participate as a group in certain annual events, such as the *calvotá* of All Saints' Day (November 1), when they make an excursion into the surrounding mountains to build fires and roast chestnuts, or the *ronda*, the early morning songfest of the Day of Santa Teresa (August 27), when they decorate horses and carts and ride through the village streets at 4:00 A.M., waking all the inhabitants with their loud voices. Until 1965, all *mozos* contributed a small sum to pay for musicians, who played regularly on Sunday evenings at the village dance. In that year, due to rising musicians' fees and the increasing dearth of *mozos* brought on by migration, the Sunday dances were officially canceled.

Now, as traditionally, the main function of the bachelors' society is to regulate courtship. As in most parts of Old Castile, when a young, unmarried man from another village begins seriously to court a Becedas girl, he must pay for the privilege of courtship by handing over a sum of money, known as the *pijardo*, to Becedas *mozos*.[1] The *pijardo* may vary from as little as 200 pesetas (3 dollars) to as much as 1500 pesetas (over 20 dollars), depending upon the *mozos'* personal inclinations toward the outsider, their assessment of how much he can afford, and so on. Whatever the variations, all courting male outsiders must pay something, the entire amout of which is usually spent on a drinking bout in which all *mozos* and the outsider participate throughout the very night of payment. In this way the outsider becomes semi-initiated into the community of Becedas bachelors, and any tension that formerly existed between him and the others may be informally dissolved.

The custom of *pijardo* payment makes it clear that Becedas *mozos* conceive of themselves as a corporate group, with collective rights over the unmarried woman of their village. Moreover, this group includes nonresident *mozos*, Becedas bachelors who now live in Madrid or other large cities. *Pijardo* payment is usually demanded of outsiders in late August, during the feast days of Santa Teresa, when migrants have returned to the village to vacation. All *mozos*, both resident and migrant, extract *pijardo* at this time and share the benefits of such payment in common.

Usually, *mozos* will not request *pijardo* of an outsider unless he has entered his sweetheart's house at least once—the signal that he has serious intent to marry. And outsiders themselves refuse payment unless they are certain that they and their Becedas sweethearts will marry. Teófilo Martín, from nearby San Bartolomé, twice refused the demands of Becedas *mozos* that he pay *pijardo* for the privilege of courting Brígida Ovejero, a Becedas girl. Only when he was sure that he and Brígida would marry did he relinquish the requested 300 pesetas. For if he had paid and then not married her, he would have considered the money wasted.

At times, there is disagreement over just how far a courtship has proceeded, and Becedas *mozos* are provoked to extract payment by force, ganging up on the outsider if he tries to continue the romance without delivering the demanded sum. But neither party in such a dispute would

---

[1] Such payment is widespread in villages of the northern Meseta. Freeman (1970: 53) reports of the custom in the Sierra Ministra, as does Arguedas (1968: 141) in Zamora, where payment is called *la mediana*. In the province of Guadalajara, outsider *mozos* pay *la patente* (Pérez–Díaz 1966: 93). In Becedas, the *pijardo* is sometimes also called the *piso*, though the former term is much more common.

argue that the *pijardo* should be paid if a couple does not intend to marry.[2] From the perspectives of both the outsider and the *mozos* the *pijardo* is designed essentially to compensate village men for the loss of their eligible young women.[3] Though the compensation is largely symbolic, payment provides the primary focus of the Becedas *mozos'* expression of their solidarity vis-à-vis bachelors from other towns and villages. Becedas *mozos* are, thus, like a corporation that claims rights over the ultimate disposition of their primary common resource, the unmarried village women.

As already mentioned, the *mozos* are a loosely organized group that operates as a unit only under specific circumstances. Unlike other parts of Spain, where the *mozos* have a formal leader (Foster 1960: 126), Becedas bachelors get informal direction and leadership from another, smaller group of young men called the *quintos*. Strictly defined, *quinto* means "conscript,"[4] and a man is officially considered a *quinto* from the time he is 20 years old, when he must register for the draft and, along with other villagers of the same age, take his physical examination. In Becedas, *quinto* also means "age mate," someone born during the same calendar year and who will, therefore, enter the army at the same time as oneself. From their earliest years, boys become aware of who their *quintos* are, even though the relationship will not take on true importance until later in life. And long after a man has actually completed military service, he will continue to refer to an age mate as *"mi quinto Fulano"* and use the term affectionately, despite the fact that his contact with the man may have, over time, dwindled to virtually nothing.

In the years just prior to entering military service, *quintos* come to form strong emotional attachments to one another. During this period, they participate in a series of events which increases their group consciousness and solidifies their feelings for one another for life. This is the time of their de facto leadership over village *mozos*, a brief era that they will forever look back upon as the happiest in memory. During their nineteenth year, *quintos* participate in the following activities:

---

[2] Nonetheless, a *pijardo* payment, already made, is *not* returned to an outsider if, for some reason, he cannot or does not marry his intended.

[3] Fuente Arrimadas (1925) traces the custom back to pre-Christian times, when such payment was essentially like bridewealth, designed to compensate a woman's patrilocal tribe not only for the loss of her person (and, hence, her labor and reproductive powers), but also for the various material goods that she carried with her at the time of marriage (I: 259).

[4] The word originated at a time when only a fifth of all young men, hence, *la quinta parte*, chosen by lot, were required to do military service.

January 1   The entire day is spent in one another's company, drinking and merrymaking. All *quintos* have the evening meal together, each contributing an equal amount toward expenses.

Carnaval Quintos eat both the noon and evening meals together, contributing equally for the cost.

April 30   At night, all *quintos* gather to chop down a tall poplar tree for making the maypole (*mayo*), which they erect in the center of the church plaza. This is accompanied by a good deal of (community-approved) rowdiness and drinking.

May 1   *Quintos* are obliged to pay for, cook, and serve dinner to all the other village *mozos*. Sometimes, only refreshments, instead of a full meal, are provided.

May 31   *Quintos* disassemble the *mayo* and deliver and sell the poplar trunk to one of the village carpenters. With the earned money, they spend the evening together in a drinking bout.

During their twentieth year, when it is said they enter *en quinta*, *quintos* participate in these events:

January 1   At sunup, the *quintos* get together to *tocar a diana*, as it is known. "*A diana*" is the special term for *ronda*, used only on *quinto* occasions, but it also, appropriately, means "reveille," the military call used to awaken soldiers to their day's duties. The young men make two complete rounds through the village streets, singing:

A *diana que toca mañana*,	A diana announces the morning,
A *diana que toca mañana*,	A diana announces the morning,
A *diana que toca mañana*	A diana announces the morning,
Para los quintos que se van a ir,	For the quintos who are going to go,
A *diana que toca mañana*	A diana announces the morning
Para los quintos que se van a venir.	For the quintos who are going to come.

The first round of the village is made without halting; as they make the second round, however, the quintos stop in the house of each of their number for cookies and drinks.

February   During this month, a day is appointed for all *quintos* to have their physical examination (colloquially, *a tallarse*, "to be measured"). On this day, *quintos* eat the noon and evening meals together, splitting the cost equally.

Carnaval—First Day   At sunup, the *quintos* gather to *tocar a diana*, just as on January 1, but this time accompanied on horseback by their girlfriends. At night, *quintos* alone share the meal.

Carnaval—Second Day Quintos eat all three meals together. After breakfast, they ride through the village streets, they and their horses dressed in colorful costume, to *pedir el chorizo* ("beg for the sausage"), asking for donations of food and money. Virtually everyone donates something—a half dozen eggs, potatoes, a couple of pesetas, or a sausage, from whence the event's name. With the donations, the *quintos* pay for musicians (in 1970, a man with his flute [*dulzaina*], accompanied by his young son with a drum), and make Carnaval meals together.

Carnaval—Third Day (always Ash Wednesday) After breakfast, *quintos* get together to *correr las cintas*, "run the ribbons," as it is known. This is a spectacular event, attended by all villagers who can afford the time. Rolls of long ribbons, each attached to a small metal ring, are strung up across and above the road. Armed with a short pointed stick, each *quinto* is supposed to ride on horseback past the ribbons and catch his stick inside one of the metal rings, thus disengaging a ribbon with which he then may decorate himself. The feat is dangerous because it involves riding the horse at a gallop while trying to concentrate on hooking a ring.[5] This last night of Carnaval, the *quintos* once again eat together and sponsor a village dance. If there is leftover food, they will continue to get together every Sunday until it is used up.

This list of formal events should provide a good idea of why *quintos* forever feel an emotional attachment to one another. Through the constant sharing of food and experiences, they come to identify themselves as a single unit, a unit within which they have participated in the most carefree, enjoyable occasions of a lifetime. Two events in particular—the physical examination and the running of the ribbons—seem to stick most in men's memories. And this is not surprising, since both these experiences are, in their own ways, dangerous and threatening and place the individual in an exposed and vulnerable position. (Middle-class Americans, who routinely take periodic physicals, should not underestimate the psychological impact and the fear that this experience evokes in peasants.) It is the social support provided by the group of *quintos* in these anxiety situations, as well as the mere fact that the men have all "gone through it together," that binds them emotionally for life. After military

---

[5] Traditionally, the event was quite different in that chickens, rather than ribbons, were used. The object was to run past the chickens, strung up by their feet, and try to rip their heads off their bodies. This would sometimes get gruesome, as a poor beast might have half a neck attached to its body before someone would, after a number of attempts, finally disengage it. The Franco regime outlawed this type of Carnaval observance after the Civil War; the ribbons were the villagers' substitute.

service, *quintos* no longer form a cohesive social unit, but they always maintain feelings for one another, never hesitating to stop and chat or to buy each other drinks whenever the occasion arises.

Even after marriage, Becedas males retain friendship as an important type of social bond. It is recognized as normal and natural that some men get along better than others and are more likely to spend free time or engage in reciprocal work with one another than with other men. *Amigos de verdad*, "true friends," are completely comfortable in one another's company, feel no compunction about asking favors from one another— either to borrow some farm implement or to help out with an agricultural task—and play cards and drink together in the cafes on Sundays and holidays. These are the people who form the backbone of cooperative work groups and who borrow from one another in times of need. Indeed, friendship among adult men seems more an outgrowth of economic necessity than the fulfillment of a need for companionship, much of which is already provided by the man's family.

Yet, at times, two men may grow absolutely inseparable and dependent upon one another, with definite emotional (though never physically sexual) overtones of homosexuality. Such men spend every available moment in one another's company and often address one another as *compadre*, the only use of this term in the village. Porfirio Tomás was an extremely close friend of Samuel Sampedro before the tragic death of the latter in an auto accident. Of all the men at Samuel's funeral, Porfirio was the most openly grief striken, crying profusely throughout the proceedings. Such behavior is usually reserved for relatives of the deceased. A few days after the funeral, Porfirio told me that he and Samuel were so close that their wives used to joke about divorcing them for negligence, since they spent so much time together. They would often be up on weekdays until 1:00 or 2:00 in the morning, just enjoying one another's company.

To be sure, such relationships are rare. Most friendships are built around economic convenience, the habit of two people who get on well together consistently to call upon one another for reciprocal aid. Yet, in all friendships, there is a recognizable and culturally acceptable emotional attachment between two men who simply prefer to be with one another more than with others.

However, when women reach their mid and late twenties and marry, the friendship cliques to which they belonged dissolve almost entirely. There are only two exceptions to this generalization. First is the young married woman, still childless, who participates in *cuadrilla* life somewhat longer than those who are already mothers, and this is only because she can afford the time to do so. Once a child is born, there is no longer any opportunity, nor justification, for a woman to maintain her prior voluntary social bonds. Her primary realm is now the home, and her first loyalties are to her husband and children and, as we shall soon see, to those who help her maintain her home—her neighbors. Friendship, as a basis for social cohesion among married adults, is almost exclusively restricted to men.

The second exception is the woman who remains unmarried throughout adult life. Spinsters usually cannot afford as much time to devote to friends as they did in their youth, for as adults they bear a large responsibility for the upkeep of the household that they generally share with parents or siblings. Nonetheless, on Sundays and holidays, they do spend a good portion of their time with other, similarly situated women who may be thought of more as casual companions than as true friends. Unmarried women who regularly socialize with one another never seem to develop the close emotional bonds that exist between male friends, nor is economic exchange inherent in their relationship. For these reasons, as well as because unmarried women comprise a small minority of the village populace, friendship among them cannot be considered a critical feature of Becedas social organization. Spinsters, like married women, share their strongest nonfamilial bonds with neighbors.

NICKNAMES AND FRIENDSHIP

In Becedas, as in most Spanish communities, almost all individuals are endowed with a nickname (*mote*).[6] A person usually acquires a nickname during childhood, either as a response to some distinctive personality or physical characteristic or by inheritance from a parent or grandparent. The true importance of such names, however, lies not in their origin, which in most cases has been long forgotten, but rather in their service as instruments of friendship. For, as we shall see, villagers who most often employ nicknames, either as terms of reference or address, are usually those enmeshed in a friendship network, individuals who are, in various ways, able to further their voluntary ties through nickname use.

In their variety and character, nicknames are a particularly effective means for the community to identify its individual members. Just as a real name may conjure in the listener's mind images of a certain personality or physical being, descriptive and colorful nicknames evoke this response even more so. A large class of nicknames mock prominent physical features: Pinocho ("Pinochio") and Narizotas (from the word *nariz*

---

[6] Portions of this discussion are based on Brandes (1975).

—"nose") both have unusually large noses; Chiquinín ("Tiny") is almost 7 feet tall; and Barrigón ("Fatso") is quite portly. Negrín ("Little Black One") has dark skin, and Caraquemá ("Scorched Face") is badly scarred from facial burns.

Another large class of nicknames poke fun at distinctive personality traits: Changarría (from *changarro*—"cow bell") talks a lot, hence, makes a lot of noise; Huevona (from *huevos*—"eggs," the popular euphemism for testicles) is an unusually bossy and aggressive woman; and Carpanta ("Lazy") is a man who works himself to the bone, with little material reward. A number of individuals derive their nicknames from words that they mispronounced in humorous fashion as a child: Ceriñas said *ceriñas* rather than *cerillas* ("matches"); Trujo said *trujo* instead of trajo (the past tense third person singular of *traer*—"to bring"); and Relores' name stems from his mispronunciation of *relojes* ("clocks").

Informants are completely unable to explain the derivation of many other nicknames. Some of these—Canyamaque, Carrocas, Farifó, Rampuja —are semantically empty. Others—Coronel ("Colonel"), Matacocos ("Boogie-man Killer"), Capitan ("Captain"), Pantalones ("Trousers")— have meanings, but ones that no longer can be directly associated with the individuals who bear the names. In some cases, names like these have been inherited from ancestors who, if alive, could presumably explain their origin. But now, the names have a totally forgotten etymology.

Many nicknames, probably a large majority, are inherited. There seems to be no fixed rules for inheritance, though there is a tendency for boys to inherit through the paternal line and girls to inherit through the maternal line. A name may be passed down directly from grandparent to parent to child, or the child may inherit the name directly from a grandparent, skipping the middle generation. In any case, there is no way to predict absolutely how a name will be carried on in the next generation. One young man is even called Fari, after Farifó, the husband of his former wetnurse. This, and other similarly improbable cases, defy all attempts to regularize the inheritance rules.

It is also difficult to discover why some adults have inherited nicknames and others have not. My impression is that most children, say, under the age of 10 or 12, are known by the name of some relative. Later, their friends will hit upon a nickname that is appropriate to them alone, and this new name, with greater descriptive validity, will eventually supplant the old inherited family name. Children who, for whatever reasons, never acquire an individual nickname will always be known by the inherited name. At times, however, an inherited name is undeniably descriptive as well, and, in this case, the name will inevitably stick through life. Elvira Tomás, for example, is called La Gorda, "The Fat One," even though she is not particularly overweight. Originally, she inherited the name from her father, El Gordo, who *was* fat. The name has stuck with Elvira because it is appropriate in another sense of the word. The word *gorda*, in Becedas, is a euphemism for *mierda*—"shit." Since Elvira is a messy housewife, her home perennially littered and disorderly, the name Gorda suits her perfectly, aside from the coincidence that she happened to be the daughter of a portly individual.

In order to understand the social significance of nicknames, it is necessary to examine the distribution of nickname use by age and sex among the village population. In general, children of both sexes, from the time they go to school until late teens, are known by nicknames; that is, peers and elders alike use their nicknames as terms of reference and address with considerable frequency. The same holds true of adult men, virtually all of whom have "living" nicknames by which they are referred to and, under specific circumstances, addressed. The only villagers who, in general, are not known by nicknames are older girls, adult women, and elderly men. These are, with some exceptions (as may be surmised from a few of the preceding examples), classes of individuals who at one time possessed a nickname but who now are known almost invariably by their given names.

In other words, nickname use is largely restricted to those segments of the population in which friendship, as a mechanism of social cohesion, is found. Among males, as already noted, friendship ties in various forms are maintained from early childhood throughout the adult years. The one exception is, significantly, among elderly men, whose friends are mostly deceased and who rely for companionship primarily on their family. Among females, friendship characterizes relations during childhood and the teenage years but dwindles to virtually nothing in adulthood, especially after marriage. Thus, the correlation between having a viable, living nickname and being part of a friendship network is startling but unmistakable. This correlation becomes understandable only when we examine the precise circumstances under which nicknames are used. For the evidence indicates that, in Becedas, villagers draw upon and manipulate nicknames to further their relationships with friends, to increase the trust and decrease the social distance between themselves and those with whom they have a voluntary social bond.

In Becedas, as in other Spanish villages (Pitt–Rivers 1961: 163), people are hypersensitive about nicknames. In general, their use is viewed as backward and degrading. They are never used in dealings with strangers, for this would be a horrible mortification for the individuals who are identified by nicknames and, by extension, to the entire community. Within the village, however, the use of nicknames is an indicator—almost a barometer—of the degree of trust among friends. And, in Becedas, trust (or *confianza*), is the psychological basis of all friendships.

Some people dislike their nicknames intensely, either because the names are unspeakably offensive or simply because they touch a particularly sensitive area of the individual's character. These names are used among close friends in referring to the person, but they are never used to his face. When friends employ a nickname behind a person's back, they are asserting their social solidarity, their common distance from and attitudes toward that person. Two friends might, for example, consistently refer to Emilio by his hated nickname, Caganudos (an extremely derogatory term concerning a form of defecation), thus implying their common mocking condescension toward him. But they would never do so with a friend or relative of Emilio, for, given his attitude toward the name, such reference would be highly insulting and could only cause animosities.

There are numerous instances in which an individual inwardly dislikes his nickname but nonetheless permits its restricted use in his own presence. Frequently, two close friends regularly call one another by their nicknames but get angry when anyone other than a close friend uses the term in their presence. Here, friends demonstrate true *confianza* by permitting one another liberties denied to ordinary acquaintances. It is as if the friends are saying to one another, "I know that you dislike this name, but we have such a close bond that I feel entitled to use it anyway. We have enough mutual trust so that you know I do not employ the name in derision."[7]

Nickname use, then, is effectively manipulated to define personal relationships, and the degree of social affiliation or distance—that is, of *confianza*—between individuals. This is why close relatives, particularly nuclear family members, rarely address each other by nickname. Since mutual trust among such people is, at least ideally, an inherent part of their relationship, addressing one another by nickname would imply the need to overcome serious social distance, a distance which on occasion exists in reality but which is nonetheless culturally unacceptable.

Although nicknames exist throughout rural Spain, their social meaning varies with the special circumstances of each local setting. In Andalusia, where nicknames are rarely ever used in address, Pitt–Rivers (1961:168) found them to be an effective means of social control. In Becedas, how-

---

[7] For a community in the Scottish Highlands, Dorian (1970) describes the same function of nicknames, that is, the promotion of social solidarity among friends. In Tzintzuntzan, nicknames also operate as a distance-reducing device (Foster 1964a: 119–121).

ever, they seem to function mainly as a means of defining and maintaining voluntary social ties and, thus, of promoting social cohesion.

NEIGHBORSHIP

When my family and I first moved into our house in Becedas, we were almost immediately struck by the warm reception given us by our neighbors. Neighbors entered our house without hesitation, helped us unpack and get our things in order, and offered advice on how to make our stay in the village more comfortable. Typically, they introduced themselves by saying, "Hello, I am your neighbor, Fulano. I live just over there. If you need anything, you know where your (that is, the neighbor's) house is" (*"Ya sabe donde está su casa"*). Neighbors took us under their wings to such an extent that we felt as if we had been initiated into a large family. Indeed, there was a good social justification for our feelings, for several times during the course of our field trip we were told, "You know, here neighbors mean even *more* than family." Though this, in some measure, overstates the case, we did come to discover that neighborship is, along with friendship, the most important extrakinship source of social integration in Becedas.

Let us first examine the composition of the neighborhood group. The streets in Becedas are long and narrow with an unbroken row of buildings along either side, consisting of blocks of three to five contiguous houses separated from other blocks by barns. Villagers consider their neighbors to be the people who live in their particular block of houses, and the one facing them, usually from 6 to 12 households in all (see Map 3).

Neighborship cuts across economic lines: The village contains neither notably wealthy nor very poor neighborhoods, and the homes of well-to-do villagers are scattered at random throughout the settlement. In fact, the wealthiest Becedas family lives opposite the poorest, and the women of these two households have an extremely close emotional bond and continually associate with one another. Such social equality among neighbors is just one manifestation of the egalitarian ethos of the *pueblo* discussed earlier.

When asked why neighbors are so important, informants invariably answer, "Why, if you get sick, or someone in your family dies, they're the ones who have to call the doctor, and attend and take care of you." Neighbors are the social insurance that tides families over in a period of crisis. When a person falls ill, neighbors assume many of the household chores such as cooking, washing, shopping, and child care. An ill person is ne

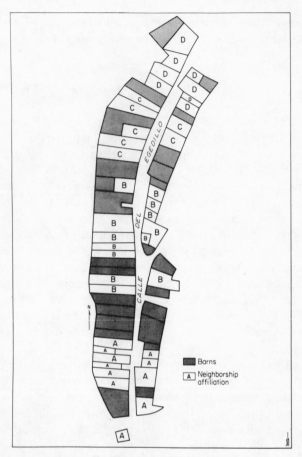

Map 3   Neighborship along the Calle de Egedillo.

left alone, for the neighbors spend as much time as possible visiting and attending the stricken home, in order to provide emotional support and reassurance.[8]

In addition, neighbors are expected to show unusual concern when one ͐ their number dies. Along with the deceased's family, they are the only ⸗morally required to attend the religious services that take place on ⸗tive mornings after a burial. They also must attend the an-

⸗inciple of social cohesion is one of the least often described ⸗ants in general. For this reason, I am struck by the almost ⸗d function of neighborship between Becedas and the ⸗él and Hofer 1969: 172–181).

niversary memorial services that occur annually for 3 years following a person's death. On occasion, all neighbors observe mourning for a full week after another neighbor's death, an unusually strong expression of solidarity and grief for the deceased and his family.

Villagers are highly critical of a person who acts inappropriately at the time of a neighbor's death. Several years ago, a group of women neighbors, including Elvira Torres, whose husband Miguel was seriously ill, were invited to attend the wedding of a non-neighbor. Out of obligation to the newlyweds, all went to the ceremony and reception except Elvira, who stayed behind to care for Miguel. Most left the reception early and returned to see how Miguel was getting on. When it became obvious that he was dying, they stayed to attend him. One neighbor, however, did not return from the reception until the next morning, despite Miguel's critical condition. People still remember and talk about how she ignored her neighborly obligations and coldly turned her back on the aggrieved family in its hour of need. Although the incident did not cause a permanent rupture of relations, it created a lasting undercurrent of resentment and hostility toward the thoughtless woman.

Neighbors of both sexes have important rights and obligations to one another where illness and death are concerned. But in the mundane affairs of everyday life, neighborship, as a principle of social cohesion, is more important to women. Because women are bound to the home, they have much greater daily contact with neighbors than do men, and the neighborhood group, to a large extent, is the focus of their social world. Female neighbors are expected to validate their relationship through the exchange of various goods and services. Food exchanges occur throughout the village but have a special importance among neighbors. The day after a saint's day, baptism, wedding, or other festive occasion, it is customary to distribute leftover food among neighbors, who then reciprocate by returning the plate on which they received the gift with some other food item. Other types of material goods are also exchanged: To provide a neighbor the coals from one's own fire, when hers is still unmade, is an especially meaningful gesture of neighborly concern and care.

Neighbors also engage in reciprocal work services, albeit on a smaller scale than friends. When women make soap or bake, they frequently receive the aid of their neighbors. Sometimes neighbors may collaborate on the completion of a sweater, one knitting the sleeves, another the back, a third piecing the whole together. Every spring, neighborhood women congregate to slice and prepare potatoes for sowing: The first day, they slice on behalf of one of their number; the second day, they perform the same task for another; and so on until each one's potatoes are ready for planting. Significantly, this task is called *a rajar las patatas*, where *rajar* has the double meaning of "to slice" and "to chatter, to jabber." This linguistic usage underscores the dual purpose of the activity: to prepare the potatoes, as well as to socialize.

Actually female neighbors are expected to spend a good deal of time together, especially during the afternoon when they gather in groups to mend, embroider, or knit.[9] When the weather permits, the village is replete with small groups of women, sitting together in the street on low chairs and benches, only occasionally retiring indoors to fetch another knitting needle, tend the fire, or perform some other small chore.

Women deeply resent a neighbor who cannot spend a suitable amount of time in their company. Marta Ortiz, for example, socializes relatively little because every afternoon she visits her invalid mother who lives in a different section of the village. On one occasion, when Marta was returning home from her mother's, her neighbors urged her to join them. She gracefully refused, saying that it was too cold and that she had a great deal of housework to finish. The women retorted with a biting comment: "And when you're sick your mother's neighbors will take care of you!" The remark was uttered as a joke, but the message was hardly disguised. If Marta refused to be neighborly, then these women might refuse assistance in her moment of need. Thus, although neighborship is primarily a form of social security in case of illness or death, the premiums must be paid daily in the form of many small gestures that assure ongoing interaction.

There is another significant aspect of this story. Marta likes her mother's neighbors better than her own, so she uses her invalid mother as an excuse to stay away. Nonetheless, her first loyalty must be to her own neighbors, whether she likes them or not. Thus, unlike friendship, the neighborship bond is ascribed and involuntary. As the saying has it:

> *Dura mas una mala vecina*   A bad neighbor lasts longer
> *Que la nieve marcelina.*   Than the March snows.

A woman cannot, without negative repercussions, avoid intense and prolonged contact with her neighbors. It is the frightening threat of abandonment in the time of greatest need that makes neighborship an important and cohesive social bond.

---

[9] Halpern (1967: 184) describes a similar institution in Serbia, so there is reason to believe that this is a social form found throughout the Mediterranean.

INTERPERSONAL RELATIONS AMONG
FRIENDS AND NEIGHBORS[10]

Of all my experiences in Becedas, one stands out most clearly as the key to understanding interpersonal relations outside the family. I was walking through the fields with Alberto Torres, when he spied a harness hidden under a bush. Farmers often hide agricultural implements in one field, while they go to work temporarily in another. Alberto stopped, pointed to the harness, and said, "If that harness didn't have a signifying marker, we'd steal it." "We would?" I queried. "Yes," he said, "we know that the owner has placed some identifying mark (*señal*) on the harness, but we don't know what it is. If we knew, we'd obliterate the mark and take the harness, just as we would take a thousand peseta note that we found lying on the ground. What difference would it make? No one would know it isn't ours."

Alberto's attitude reveals a prominent feature of the villagers' world view: their shame orientation. Unlike Japan and other parts of the world (De Vos 1960), where feelings of guilt play a major role in guiding behavior, in Spain and throughout the Mediterranean (Peristiany 1965), shame is the primary socializing emotion. This is why villagers generally do not choose between alternative courses of action on the basis of what is morally right or wrong but, rather, on the basis of what will *appear* acceptable to the community. Individuals conform to ideal or expected behavior patterns because violation of the rules evokes negative sanctions from society. There is little inner motivation to behave normally or correctly. Therefore, it never occurred to Alberto to question the legitimacy of taking someone else's harness; rather he was concerned only with whether or not he would be caught and thereby bring shame upon himself and his family.

As a consequence of this shame orientation, interpersonal relations are frequently marked by deep distrust. It is simply assumed that if a person can get away with it, he will engage in almost any activity to further his own well-being regardless of how his actions affect others. People are viewed as compulsively unlawful, driven to lying, cheating, or stealing whenever they are given the opportunity. The saints are admired for their selflessness, but, in the real world, the trusting person is at best naive, at worst a fool, particularly vulnerable to the underhanded methods of schemers who will inevitably surround and drain him. The only bastion

---

[10] The material in this section appears in a different context, in Brandes (1973a).

of reliability is the nuclear family, a protective shell that insulates its members against incursions and hostile attacks by the world outside.[11]

This sense of distrust and vulnerability is clearly revealed in responses to the standard Murray Thematic Apperception Test (Murray 1943). Murray Card #17BM, for example, simply portrays a naked man clinging to a rope. Of the 21 individuals who responded to this card, 9 interpreted the man as a burglar who has surreptitiously entered a house to take what is not his. One informant said:

> This person looks like a trapeze artist, but he is actually a burglar working in conjunction with another who is above. And this one is climbing up the rope to carry off what he can.

Another respondent stated:

> What I don't know is whether this person works for a circus or is an evildoer who climbs into houses by means of the rope in order to steal. He looks more like a burglar than a circus worker; by means of the rope he climbs into houses to steal.

In another picture (Murray Card #5) portraying a woman looking into a room from a half-open door, there is a similar concern over theft. One 40-year-old woman interpreted the card thus:

> This woman looks like she's spying on someone in the house . . . . It must be someone who is doing some bad deed in the house, and she's spying. [What is the person doing?]
>
> The person is taking something away from her, and she's looking on to see what he carries off.

Of the same picture, a 47-year-old man states:

> This is a woman who is going to steal, and she doesn't know whether or not to enter. Here's the place she's looking for, but she doesn't know whether or not to enter, to steal.

There is a similar obsession with burglary, with people sneaking around where they do not belong in order to haul off something, in the responses to a number of other Murray cards. In the context of the ethnographic

---

[11] Federico Garcia Lorca (1955) understood well the tendency of his people to withdraw, psychologically, under the protective wings of the nuclear family. In the play *Blood Wedding*, a mother gives the following advice to her daughter, who is about to be married:

> MOTHER: Do you know what it is to be married, child?
> BRIDE: *Seriously*, I do.
> MOTHER: A man, some children and a wall two yards thick for everything else.

data, these interpretations can only be construed as projections of an inner fear for the safety of one's person and possessions and of a psychological sense of vulnerability to the world at large.

The villagers' distrust extends to a variety of behavior besides theft. They are, for example, afraid of being turned in (*denunciado*) by fellow villagers to the Civil Guard for violation of national laws. When Anselmo Torres caught a rabbit off season, a violation punishable by a substantial fine, he brought the animal to his house via a circuitous, little-traveled route, hiding the animal inside his trousers as he did so. He and his family alone shared the excitement and culinary benefits of his catch, and had I not been accompanying him when he found the animal, I doubtless never would have learned of it. He seemed anxious lest any envious or vindictive villager denounce him anonymously to the authorities.

Villagers are especially skeptical about what others tell them of their business transactions, and usually interpret such testimonies as attempts to undermine their own financial security. One one occasion, Eusebio and his friend Felipe had gone to the Béjar market to sell potatoes. After several hours, it was clear that Felipe was outselling Eusebio. When Eusebio casually asked Felipe what price he was getting, the latter replied directly, "Seven pesetas." Eusebio privately told me later that his friend was undoubtedly selling at a lower price than he admitted, and that the high-price quote was given in an attempt to undercut Eusebio by encouraging him to ask an exhorbitant amount. Even friends are subject to the distrust that pervades virtually all interpersonal relations in Becedas.

There is, then, a strange paradox in interpersonal relations. On the one hand, there is a strong undercurrent of fear and distrust, and, on the other, there are stable, ongoing social bonds with friends and neighbors. However, these bonds can be successful only if people constantly prove to one another that they are trustworthy, that there is a basis for *confianza*, "trust," in their relationships. In a society in which everyone outside the nuclear family is immediately suspect, in which one is at every moment thought to be vulnerable to the underhanded attacks of others, voluntary, nonkinship ties require a constant positive assertion of trust. Reliability and *confianza*, under such circumstances, may never be taken for granted.

For this reason, culturally approved and formalized mechanisms have developed whereby fellow villagers can demonstrate their mutual trust and good intentions in daily interaction. Such demonstration is apparent, for example, in speech forms. When two people pass one another on the street, one of them is likely to call out, "¿A donde vas?"—"Where are you going?"—or "¿De donde vienes?"—"Where are you coming from?" Among close friends and neighbors, a relatively explicit answer is required:

"To help Fulano cut hay at El Regajo," or "From visiting my mother, who hasn't been feeling well lately." Among more casual acquaintances, the answer might be vaguer: "I'm going up that way," or "I'm off to get the horses." Sometimes a greeting is phrased as an interrogation: "Are you on your way to the Béjar market?" or "Bringing your cows to pasture, eh?" In any case, individuals must provide some adequate idea of where they are going or what they are up to. The answer is vague or specific depending on the intimacy of the relationship. But to maintain a posture of secrecy or privacy is taboo under any circumstances; one must always maintain the impression, however false, that he has nothing to hide and that he expects the same of others.

In reciprocity and exchange, a similar assertion of trust through speech is required. Friends and neighbors constantly order one another about. One friend says to another, "You have to come help me reap tomorrow." A neighbor states frankly to the woman next door, "I need to borrow your meat chopper on Saturday." There is never any formal request, as in our own society. To use the word "please" in asking someone a favor, or to say "thank you" upon its receipt, is unheard of. Such formalities are insulting, for the status of friend or neighbor implies the right to borrow and to ask favors, with the expectation, of course, that the service eventually will be reciprocated. Formal requests accompany only distant relationships, among individuals who have no basis for *confianza*. To phrase a request as a command is to assert one's trust in and closeness to another.

Similarly, it is considered unfriendly or unneighborly to expect immediate compensation for a favor. When a person borrows money or asks for credit at a village store, he often reminds his creditor that the debt weighs on him. Almost inevitably the creditor retorts "¡*Que prisa tienes!*"— "Don't be in such a hurry!" as if to say, "Don't worry, I trust you to make good your debt." On one occasion, a village middleman who provides villagers with seedlings sold a considerable number of young apple trees to a friend. When the friend stated that he would be unable to pay right away, the middleman said appropriately, "¡*Que prisa tienes!*" The debt dragged on for months, and, worried about getting his fair return, the middleman periodically complained to me about his friend's outstanding credit. Yet, every time the subject came up between middleman and friend, the middleman invariably stated that he should take his time to pay, thus asserting his trust and giving verbal reassurance of the maintenance of friendship.

In addition to speech forms, there are several other behavioral means of expressing trust. First is a strong requirement to be sociable and to stay within public view. Men are expected to attend the village bars on Sundays and holidays, where they spend hours playing cards and exchanging drinks. On weekdays, whenever time permits, men should properly be seen in the streets, chatting with friends and neighbors. This same cultural demand explains why women spend hours every afternoon with their neighbors. People become extremely uncomfortable unless they have some idea of what a neighbor is up to.

On one occasion, four of our neighbors were sitting in the sun quietly talking and mending, as usual, when they noticed that Florencia Calle, another neighbor who ordinarily joins them, was down the street engaged in conversation with someone who was out of their view. After 15 minutes, the women became markedly uncomfortable, and the topic of conversation became Florencia. "What a long conversation she's having," one woman said. "I wonder who she's talking to," remarked another. There were several nervous silences after which these statements, in several variations, were repeated. It was only when Florencia terminated her conversation, and the women could see that she had been talking to her sister-in-law, that the atmosphere in the neighborhood group relaxed, and normal, easy-going chatter resumed. In Becedas, only the woman who lets her neighbor know about her activities is trustworthy. Conversely, a woman who wishes to be trusted will be sure to stay within the public eye.

For this reason, too, the distinction between indoors and outdoors is blurred, in that neighbors and friends have ready access to one another's homes. During the day, outside doors usually are left slightly ajar. If a person wishes to visit, he knocks, loudly shouts "*¿Se puede?*"—"May I?"— and then, without even waiting for an answer, enters the house and finds his way to wherever people are gathered. To be a good friend or neighbor demands the tolerance of such entrance, for it assumes that the people inside have nothing to hide and may be trusted to carry on only culturally approved activities. Significantly, however, whenever a house is left unoccupied for any length of time, as when a family goes to Béjar or to Madrid, the door is securely locked in order to prevent theft and unwanted incursions of privacy. Villagers engage in trust-maintaining mechanisms only to the extent that their person and property are not endangered.

The area just outside a house often becomes spacially united with the building itself. People never hestitate to sit on the stone benches located outside their neighbors' houses. On occasion, a person sitting outside will casually intrude on a conversation that he can overhear from within. No pretense is made or care taken to assure the privacy of a home. When a bullfight or any other program of particular interest is televised, those with television sets often open their outside windows and face the set toward the street so that everyone may watch. In cold weather, the set still faces the street, while numerous onlookers, their noses pressed against the window panes, enjoy the show. By so placing a television set, a family not only fulfills the cultural requirement of sharing, but also symbolically says to outsiders, "We are not afraid of displaying our activities or possessions. You may scrutinize our home carefully. You can trust us."

As if tacit permission to view the more accessible portions of the home were not sufficient, friends, neighbors, and relatives are also periodically ushered to the second-story bedrooms. Whenever a villager purchases a new piece of bedroom furniture, paints a room, or makes any improvement whatever in his dwelling, he is expected to invite all people who might be interested, especially neighbors, to appreciate it. One of the village storekeepers and his wife were criticized severely for failing to invite anyone to see their new upstairs living quarters. For this behavior, they were labeled *"orgullosos"* ("haughty") and *"estúpidos"* ("callous"), both extremely derogatory terms that are usually reserved only for those who openly defy *pueblo* norms. Ideally, any change in a villager's material condition should be displayed openly to the community at large.

Through such behavior—speech forms and license to intrude upon quasiprivate personal space—the people of Becedas exhibit an almost pathological fear of secrecy or privacy. The quiet person, the person who keeps to himself, seldom gossips openly in the streets, refuses to join the men in the bars on Sundays, is not only antisocial, in our own vernacular sense of the term, but is also dangerous. He is, as one informant put it, like the deceptively tame bull who, without the slightest warning, will give you his horn. Much preferable is the open, aggressive *toro*, whose actions may be calculated and predicted and against whom there is at least some hope of defense.

Thus, to keep within the public arena is to prove that you can be trusted, that you are not following the natural tendency of all people to cheat, lie, and plot against the best interests of others. The individual who insists on cloistering himself or who makes no special effort to reveal his motives and goals is viewed not only as dangerous, but also as slightly crazy. If such a person is young enough, he will effectively exclude himself from the marriage market, and the state of several old spinsters and bachelors may be attributed to these personal idiosyncracies.

This analysis reveals two prominent aspects of interpersonal relations in Becedas. First, because villagers live, according to their own world view, in a hostile and threatening environment, and because their economy and living arrangements demand close association with potentially threatening people, they see security in stable friendship and neighborship relations. To maintain these social ties, however, requires the constant assertion of mutual trust through a variety of standard cultural devices. These devices are designed to demonstrate personal innocence and to prove goodwill, and, conversely, to insure the trustworthiness of others by reducing their margin of personal privacy.

Second, the evidence from Becedas suggests that these villagers are not "naturally" open, friendly, and effervescent. Rather, such behavior is a cultural requirement of these people, an essentially defensive posture that affords them the security necessary for existence in a psychologically hostile milieu. Even the much observed and beloved gesturing of Mediterranean Europeans, which is common among the people of Becedas, may also be interpreted in this light. For, to keep one's hands in constant view, to throw open one's arms spontaneously in a burst of joy, affection, or dismay, operates as a symbolic demonstration of personal innocence, of carefree exposure to the world and freedom from the fear of being observed. Here, as in his other behavior, the villager is saying, "I have nothing to hide. You can trust me."

MIGRANTS AS FRIENDS AND NEIGHBORS

As demonstrated in the last chapter, migrants maintain strong kinship affiliations with villagers and visit Becedas at regular intervals in large numbers. In many cases, too, a person is required to live part of the year in Madrid and part in the village, making it difficult, if not impossible, to state definitely whether or not he is a migrant. Such intimate, large-scale outside contact might be construed as leading to the breakdown of social cohesion within the village. After all, each individual presumably can extend his obligations just so far; maintaining close ties with urbanites would mean having to forego, or at least weaken, links with fellow villagers. Further, a large influx of urbanites with little permanent stake in the community could reasonably be expected to create an atmosphere of anonymity, in which fellow villagers concern themselves only marginally with one another's affairs and have little impact on one another's opinions and behavior. These potential consequences of urban contact, however, have not occurred in Becedas. Instead, migrants seem to adapt to and become incorporated within the existing community structure, even for their brief or intermittent periods of actual village residence.

First, let us examine migrant–village friendships. We have already seen how young migrant men reaffirm their *mozo* affiliation by participation in summer events, like extracting *pijardo* payments from outsiders. And they, like their female counterparts, join fully in the antics expected of young

people during Carnaval, the patron saint's festival, or other village occasions for which they might be present. Contrary to what we might
anticipate, there appears to be very little social distance between migrant
and village youngsters. Even highly sophisticated university students, long-
time city dwellers, show no visible condescension toward village age mates,
and resume their individual and group relationships with ease and confi-
dence whenever they arrive back in the community.

The situation is a bit different for adults. Men who leave the community for work in Madrid rarely retain the close friendships that they
may have had previously with villagers. As mentioned, Becedas friendships, though sometimes emotionally charged, always contain a strong
element of expediency and economic reciprocity. Migrants, though they
regularly become patrons to relatives, are less eager to assume this role
with former friends from whom they can expect little in return. Close
friends, in this instance, are more a liability than an asset, so migrant–
village friendships take on the character of what Yehudi Cohen (1961)
has called "casual friendship"—an amicable relationship that involves little
or no effective claims of one party on the other. To be sure, this pattern
excludes migrant men from full incorporation into Becedas society. Yet, it
operates in the long run to maintain the usual intensity of intravillage
friendships, by eliminating a potential source of competition and challenge
to those friendships. If migrant–village friendships are themselves of no
particular structural importance, they at least do nothing to detract from
the strong, extant voluntary ties within the community.

The main avenue through which migrants become integrated within the
Becedas community is (aside from kin ties) neighborship. Many migrants
own their own village homes, where they reside for the duration of their
stay; others simply move in with relatives who live permanently in Becedas.
But regardless of the arrangement, migrants automatically become members of a neighborhood group and become bound by the appropriate community role expectations. This means, above all, that migrants must keep
their homes open to the constant intrusions and scrutiny of their neighbors.
Attempts at anonymity and privacy mark migrants, as they do year-long
village residents, as targets of gossip and ostracism. If only to preserve the
good name of their village families, as well as to maintain decent community relations themselves, migrants conform to community expectations
of openness. For the same reasons, migrant women regularly spend several
hours each afternoon sitting outdoors with neighbors, or assisting them
with baking, soapmaking, child care, or other routine tasks. The rights and
obligations of migrant neighbors are virtually the same as those of full-
time village residents, and through the institution of neighborship mi-

grants become instantly incorporated within the community whenever they assume residence there.

Migrants not only conform to their proper roles as neighbors but also unknowingly act to heighten feelings of solidarity among neighborhood groups. The mere presence of urbanites stimulates what may only be called neighborhood pride, and, during the times of year when migrants are present, neighborhood groups seem to be super-sensitive about littered or otherwise unsightly streets. Women, in a joking though firm manner, place pressure on one another to clean and sweep the areas outside their houses, so that the *veraneantes* ("summer visitors") will have no reason to complain about primitive conditions. If a street remains uncared for, the entire neighborhood group responsible is criticized by other groups, and as much pressure as possible (again, in the form of lighthearted though biting remarks) is brought to bear on its uncooperative members in order to avert collective shame. Migrant women are as subject to neighborhood sanctions as are permanent village residents. And, though they participate fully in neighborhood street-cleaning projects, it is clear that the major impetus comes from permanent villagers in an attempt to impress the others. As with friendship, neighborship relations have in no way been weakened as a result of migration or migrant presence in the village.

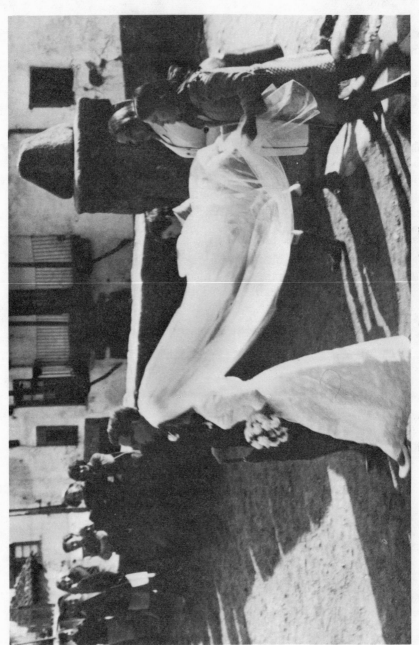

Plate 8   A migrant couple marries in the village.

VIII

Ritual and Social Structure:
The Life Cycle Rites

INTRODUCTION

In Becedas, villagers vary greatly in their religious attitudes. On the one hand, everyone, without exception, considers himself a Roman Catholic and professes belief in God, Jesus Christ, the Virgin Mary, and the saints. On the other hand, a large number—perhaps 15 to 20%—of villagers of both sexes dislike the Church as an institution and neither attend Mass nor participate in the obligatory annual confession and communion. Despite differing attitudes toward the Church and clergy, all villagers participate in the life cycle rites, the crucial sacraments of baptism, confirmation, first communion, marriage, and extreme unction. These are the most living and vibrant aspects of religion in the village today; without them, validation as a full and complete human being and, of more immediate importance, as a member of the *pueblo* would be inconceivable.

As in societies through the world, the *rites de passage* (as Van Gennep [1960] called them over a half-century ago) in Becedas mark stages—religious, moral, and social—in the development of every individual. But they also have a wider significance, for they are the events around which existing social relationships dissolve and coalesce in new forms or, alternatively, are confirmed and reinforced. In Becedas, the life cycle rites are of special interest because of their extraordinary richness and elaboration. All the participants in these rituals are forced to define precisely their relationships to one another and to assume and act out the roles appropriate to them. Further, the rituals themselves are sensitive barometers of change. Though they have largely retained their traditional forms, they have not been immune to the social and economic developments that have affected the village over recent decades. It is, then, on these aspects of the life cycle rites—their implications for social structure and change—that I propose to concentrate.

BAPTISM AND FIRST COMMUNION

According to canon law, every child must take three sacraments: baptism, confirmation, and first communion. In Becedas, only baptism and first communion are cause for celebration. Confirmation, in which a child's connection with the Church, already established by baptism, is ratified, is carried out only once every 6 or 7 years, when the Bishop of Avila (in former times, the Bishop of Plasencia) visits the village and ritually confirms all eligible children en masse. *Padrinos de confirmación*, confirmation godparents, who fulfill the Church requirement for ritual sponsorship of the children, are chosen by the village priest at random from among any villagers who are available and willing at the time of the ceremony. Thus, all children confirmed at the same time have the same sponsors, and no special social relationship is established between them and their confirmation godparents, much less between the godparents and the child's family. In fact, rarely does anyone remember who his or his children's confirmation godparents are, or even that he has such godparents.

Unlike confirmation, baptismal godparents are carefully selected and play a major role. As Anderson (1956), Foster (1953a), Mintz and Wolf (1950), and Pitt–Rivers (1958) have pointed out, Catholic law provides considerable flexibility in the choice of sponsors for ritual occasions. Such flexibility permits individuals to manipulate ritual sponsorship for the furtherance of social ends by validating existing social ties or by establishing new ones. Throughout Latin America, the godparenthood system is highly elaborated; godparents are chosen for many more occasions than are actually required by the Church (such as ear-piercing, first haircut, graduation from elementary, secondary, and normal school), and through the *compadrazgo*, or co-godparenthood relationship, individuals create formal, ceremonially sanctioned social ties with a large number of nonkinsmen. In Castile, however, ritual kinship plays a much more restricted role, tending to reinforce already existing bonds rather than create new ones.

In Becedas, the parents of the newborn choose the baptismal godparents, who are almost always a married sibling and his or her spouse. For the first child of a union, the couple's marriage godparents ideally become the *padrinos de bautizo*. Marriage godparents are usually drawn from the husband's side of the family, preferably an elder, male, married sibling or, where such kinsman is lacking, a younger male or older female sibling and his or her spouse. Thus, a first child's baptismal godparents are chosen from among his father's relatives. As a balance to the ritual ties already established with the husband's family, parents prefer to choose baptismal godparents for the second and subsequent children from among the wife's brothers and sisters. Only rarely is a non-family member chosen to be a baptismal sponsor.

Although baptismal godparenthood reinforces and validates already existing relationships, the attitudes and behavior of these relatives toward one another undergo no substantial change as a result of the fictive kinship bond. Often, grown children are not even aware who their baptismal godparents are. Parents remember who is godparent to each of their children, but the relationship between a child's parents and godparents remains basically the same as it was prior to the child's birth. Unlike Latin America, no formal *compadrazgo* bond is established in Becedas and in no sense do siblings who are co-godparents establish a relationship of distance and respect, substituting the formal *Usted* for *tu* in address.

Nonetheless, baptismal godparents have definite obligations toward godchildren and their families. Baptismal *padrinos* are required to pay the priest for the baptism (in 1970, 100 pesetas) and for funeral and burial expenses (including the casket) in case of death in the early years. At the time of baptism, godparents buy earrings or some other small gift for a female godchild or a shirt or set of underwear for a male godchild. While a godchild is young, some godparents present him with a nominal present for his saint's day celebration. Godparents do not supply the baptismal outfit, which in most cases is a family heirloom presented to an infant by one of his grandmothers.

Until about 1965, the baptismal ceremony was attended only by three women: the godmother, who carried and held the infant, another of the infant's aunts, and the midwife who attended at delivery. Because of restrictions imposed by the traditional postpartum quarantine, requiring a woman to stay in her own house for 40 days after giving birth, a mother never attended her child's baptism.

Now, urban attitudes and practices regarding baptism have filtered down to the village. Although the godmother still carries the infant to the baptism, she is accompanied by a large entourage of the infant's close relatives, who are also expected to attend. With disappearance of the 40-day quarantine, now viewed as "backward," even the infant's mother attends. Further, the godfather, formerly holding only a nominal position with little social recognition, has taken on a more distingiushed status and is considered, along with the godmother, an honored member of the proceedings. All these changes have been triggered by emulation of city mores.

As in the past, the baptismal ceremony is followed by the *roña*, during which the godmother tosses candy and coins to village children. When a baptismal party emerges from the church ceremony, they are greeted by a horde of youngsters, chanting loudly:

Roña, roña, confitura,	Tightwad, tightwad, jam and jelly,
Y si no que se muera	And if we don't get it, may the
la criatura.	infant die.

The children follow the baptismal entourage back to the infant's house, and the godparents climb to the balcony, from where they throw handfuls of small coins and candy to scrambling, eager children in the street below.[1] Once, the godmother alone was responsible for dispensing the gifts, but close adherence to such customs is considered overly traditional, and any family member may participate in the roña.

The celebration culminates with a lavish *merienda* of sausages, cheese, hot chocolate, and sponge cakes, served at the expense of the infant's parents in their own home. Only the infant's close relatives—his godparents, grandparents, aunts, uncles, and cousins—are invited, though neighbors are also expected to drop in for a small drink of cognac or anis liqueur. The formal *merienda* is a recent addition to the baptismal celebration, another example of the incorporation of a city practice into village ritual life.

As a result of city influences, too, the celebration of first communion, always an essential life cycle rite, has become more elaborate. "Now it's just like a wedding," is one common observation. City relatives flock to the village for the occasion, and celebrating families spend days in preparation, baking cookies and cakes and readying the house for guests.

---

[1] In other parts of Old Castile and in Tzintzuntzan, Mexico, the custom is known as the *bolo*. Foster (1967b: 159–160) considers the *bolo* an envy-reducing mechanism, designed to ward of potentially hostile feelings toward the newborn infant and its family.

As throughout Spain, first communion in Becedas is usually held on a Sunday in late spring. On that morning, the village is unusually festive, everyone scurrying busily in preparation for the great event. The 7-year-old children, all of whom receive the sacrament on this day, are given special attention, with all villagers openly admiring their first communion outfits. Until about 1960, first communicants were dressed in the finest homemade garments their families could afford. Now, however, the urban store-bought garment predominates, so the village is replete with little boys wearing sailors' and admirals' uniforms and little girls wearing miniature bridal gowns and veils. In fact, the lavishness of a child's outfit and the care with which a family chooses and purchases it, is an indication of the family's worldly success as well as its ties with urban relatives, whom villagers, as we shall see, constantly try to impress with signs of newfound prosperity.

On first communion day, the midmorning Mass is filled with villagers and guests. Each young celebrant is seated in a chair that is decorated with sheets and flowers and placed in front of the altar. Toward the end of the Mass, the children individually walk up to the altar, where they are joined by their parents to receive the holy sacrament. It is common now for city relatives to take photographs of their young nieces and nephews during the service as well as when they emerge from church. After Mass, a small breakfast of hot chocolate, milk, cake, and cookies is given by the priest for all first communion children and their mothers.

Early in the afternoon, celebrating families serve large dinners to groups of 10 to 30 guests. Even the most modest of dinners is, by village standards, a banquet and includes hors d'oeuvres of cheese and cold cuts, *paella*, chicken, fish, and, in well-to-do homes, a freshly killed goat or lamb. The attendance of *Madrileños* adds flair to the occasion, and there is no doubt that these guests bestow prestige on the celebrating family.

During late afternoon, each celebrating family holds an informal *convite* ("open house"), which their friends and neighbors are expected to attend. Individually, guests casually drop by to congratulate the family. Upon entering the house, a guest hands the father or mother of the first communicant 5 or 10 pesetas, says "for the child," and then stays just long enough to take some wine, beer, or cognac with cookies. The *convite* sometimes assumes an amusingly commercial air, with villagers merely poking their heads into the doorway, handing a 5-peseta piece to the communicant's parents, and disappearing as fast as they arrived, cupcake or cookies in hand. In this respect, the transaction is clearly and openly economic; guests are "purchasing" their refreshments. But the primary function of the *convite* is social, providing a means for friends and neighbors to show their appreciation to a family with which they maintain regular and close bonds.

MARRIAGE

In Becedas, marriage arrangements and festivities are without question the most elaborate of all life cycle occasions. Beyond ritually and legally sanctioning the creation of a new family, wedding proceedings have two essential functions: First, they are overtly designed to provide the new couple with the financial and material resources necessary to maintain themselves, at least for a while, as an independent social unit; second, they operate on an unconscious level to force people into a careful defining of their social relationships through material exchange, both symbolic and substantial.

The events preceding the wedding ceremony begin in Mass, three Sundays prior to the marriage date, with the first of three weekly readings of the banns. Following the first reading, parents of the future newlyweds serve a *convite*—again, a drink and cookies—to all villagers invited to the wedding. With this begins the increasingly strict definition of social relationships: Wedding guests of the groom attend the *convite* given by the parents, those of the bride attend that given by hers. On this day, too, in the afternoon, the groom holds the *Amonestación* (named after the word for "banns"), his farewell celebration at which he treats all the village *mozos* to drinks in a village bar. The costly party, which lasts all afternoon and culminates in more drinking and celebration at the homes of both the bride and the groom, is one of the few village occasions on which drunkeness is socially acceptable, indeed expected. The event marks the formal disassociation of the future groom from bachelorhood and may be viewed symbolically as compensation to his former comrades for depletion of the limited supply of unmarried village women, an interpretation supported by the extremely high rate of village endogamy (82% of all married couples having been born and raised in Becedas).

Soon after the *Amonestación*, really substantial gift exchanges begin between the bride and groom and their respective families. The groom's parents make a formal visit to the house of the bride to arrange the exact wedding date. On this occasion, when it is said that they go *a tratar de boda* ("to speak about the wedding"), the groom's parents present the bride with a gift of considerable value, such as gold earrings, a good bedspread or blanket, or money in an amount varying between 500 and 2000 pesetas. The groom's parents make a second visit to the bride's house, to *dar las vistas* ("tell the intentions"), which takes place approximately 2 weeks prior to the wedding date. The object is once again to present the bride with money, this time between 500 and 1000 pesetas, to be used toward the purchase of the new couple's furniture.

The bride's family, however, bears the large financial burden of purchasing all the furniture and other necessary household items. Though the quality of the goods varies with the financial situation of the bride's family, the list includes a double bed, a wardrobe, a kitchen buffet (always with glass doors for display items), a dining table with six chairs, four enamel plates, two enamel casseroles, a large enamel cup (from which the entire family drinks water), six forks, six spoons, and six glasses. Then, to be displayed in the buffet cabinets, parents usually present their daughters with six china plates, six china cups and saucers, and a never-to-be-used coffee set, including a pot with matching cups and saucers. With few exceptions, this list includes essentials necessary for the establishment of an independent home.

Subsidiary household items are provided through the substantial trousseaus of both the bride and the groom. In the past, the precise content of a trousseau was determined *"por categoría"* ("by economic status"), with well-to-do villagers expected to bring more to the union than those less advantaged. Now that everyone enjoys relative prosperity, however, there is a more or less standard trousseau expected of villagers from all families. A bride should contribute a dozen sheets and pillowcases, which she has through the years elaborately embroidered; a dozen large towels; two tablecloths; and two or three bedspreads. A groom contributes six sheets (embroidered by women in his immediate family), six towels, and a tablecloth. In addition, the bride and groom are expected to have a large assortment of completely new clothing, which for women traditionally includes a dozen complete sets of lightweight underwear, a dozen sets of thick winter underwear, a dozen pairs of stockings, and several changes of outer clothing, and for men a dozen sets of underwear (of whatever weight) and 16 new shirts. Again because of material prosperity, these items are not provided in as great quantity as in the past, since people are confident that they will be able to afford new clothing in the future. Despite this change, the underlying assumption behind all the parental gifts and trousseau bundles is still that the furniture, utensils, and clothing should last the new couple for a good many years, if not throughout their entire lifetime.

According to villagers, the new couple must be provided the means to start and maintain life as an independent social unit. In furtherance of this goal, a couple also accumulates a large monetary reserve by means of the *ofrecijo*, a wedding custom involving the formal presentation of money by invited guests. The *ofrecijo* is, in fact, the high point, the culmination and climax, of a series of wedding events, all of which include symbolic gift-giving and exchange. On the wedding morning, the groom escorts the marriage godparents from their house to his, where the wedding guests are gathered. Bride and groom receive the benediction from both sets of parents, and cookies and wine, consumed from a few communally used vessels, are passed around to the guests. Led by the groom, who is flanked on both sides by the godparents, the wedding party then proceeds to the bride's house, where refreshments are distributed by her family. Wedding guests consider attendance at these preliminaries a serious obligation; bride and groom must be accompanied and "supported," as it is said, during all stages of the marriage proceedings.

The wedding party and guests then file to the church for the nuptial Mass, the standard Catholic ceremony with some Hispanic variations. These variations include the groom's presentation to the bride of the *arras* and a handful of small pocket change, in Becedas considered symbolic of his willingness to support her financially, and the draping of the bridal veil around the shoulders of the new couple, representative of their union. Until as late as the mid-1960s, a shawl from one of the church images of the Virgin was draped around the couple, but since the introduction of the urban bridal costume, the long white veil has been substituted. (Prior to about 1967, brides were married in black.)[2]

Following the wedding ceremony, the newlyweds emerge from the church and stand at the portal, where all guests file by to congratulate them by kissing or shaking hands, depending on the degree of emotional attachment, and saying, "*Que sea para bien y para muchos años*"—May it [the marriage] work out well and last for many years." As he greets them, the groom hands each male guest a cigarette, a filter tip in honor of the occasion. This ritual completed, bride, groom, and guests walk the few yards from the church to the *Ayuntamiento* where, with little ceremony, they and their godparents sign the civil register. Everyone then returns to the bride's house for another round of refreshments.

The afternoon and early evening are taken up with the wedding banquet, which is held in one of the village cafes. Usually, there are between 100 and 150 guests, who are seated at long, sex- and age-segregated tables; the bride and groom, along with their parents and marriage godparents, sit apart at a dais. After dinner, guests divide, for card-playing, into small

---

[2] Variations of these Spanish customs have been adopted in Latin American wedding ceremonies as well (Brandes 1968: 35).

groups that are, in effect, a microcosm of the village social structure; married women, older bachelors, younger bachelors, mature spinsters, and young, unmarried women all play at separate tables. At each table, players put their winnings into a common kitty that is later used to buy candy, make hot chocolate, or do whatever else might be of mutual enjoyment to the persons involved. To this sum is added *los estilos*, money requested by each group of card-players of the marriage godfather.

Late in the afternoon, the high point of the wedding proceedings, the *ofrecijo* ("offering"), begins. A tray is placed on the dais in front of the godparents. The guests then gather in small groups around the table, watching and chatting as, one by one, they publicly present money to the bride and groom. The order of presentation is determined by the relationship of guests to the new couple: Marriage godparents present their gift first, then parents of bride and groom, respectively, followed by married siblings, married first and second cousins, *quintos*, other friends, and finally neighbors. There is nothing secret about the amount each individual gives. As guests make their presentations, they hold the bills high, counting aloud as they place money on the tray, "One hundred pesetas . . . two hundred pesetas . . . three hundred pesetas . . . ," and so on. If someone should chance not to hear or see the precise amount given, he has no qualms about asking others what transpired. Everything concerning the *ofrecijo* is accomplished openly, with the full knowledge of all present.[3] When the offering has ended, the godparents make a public count of the money, which they guard until the following day, when they give it to the newlyweds.

Several criteria determine the amount of money offered by each guest. First, all individuals with the same relationship to bride and groom are expected to give the same sum. Thus, all first cousins of the bride give one amount, uncles of the groom another, friends of the bride another, and so on. For this reason, everyone must know in exactly what capacity he attends a wedding. When an individual is invited, it is "as friend," or "as neighbor," and if you ask him if he plans to attend a particular marriage ceremony, he will answer, "Yes, I am invited *como primo hermano*

---

[3] Customs similar to this are described for villages throughout the Gredos-Sierra de la Peña de Francia range. In Navaluenga, in southeastern Avila, Díaz Lasa (1958: 165) speaks of *"la postura,"* in which money is presented publicly to a wedding couple by guests; and in La Alberca, in southwestern Salamanca, *"se corre la espiga"* at weddings, by "placing a tray on the table of the newlyweds, and filing in front of them, tossing on the tray 'la espiga', a monetary gift" (Marcos 1958: 172–173). Throughout portions of La Vera, in northern Caceres, the custom is called, for some unknown reason, *"la manzana,"* or "apple" (author's field notes).

de la novia "as the bride's first cousin" or "*como vecino del novio*" "as the groom's neighbor" or the like.

Second, the closer the biological and social relationship to the newly-weds, the more an individual is required to give: Siblings give more than cousins, cousins more than *quintos*, *quintos* more than other friends, and so on. The only flexibility in this rule is that friends and neighbors may offer either the same or differing amounts. In any case, every guest must calculate his relationship not only to the bride and groom, but also to other individuals present at the wedding before he knows the *ofrecijo* that is expected of him. For this reason, guests never know until the public presentation exactly what the going amounts are for the different categories of guests, and it is only as the *ofrecijo* slowly proceeds that people in the same category informally get together to decide on a precise amount. Obviously, the presentations of the newlyweds' closest relations, coming as they do prior to the others, set the financial tone of the event and establish the size of other guests' *ofrecijo*.

Finally, the kind of wedding dinner also affects the amount of the *ofrecijo*. Villagers feel that newlyweds, who pay for their own wedding, must be compensated for the cost of the meal and hopefully have a considerable remainder as well. Thus, the more expensive and elaborate the banquet, the larger the *ofrecijo*, though a couple is careful not to over-spend on their dinner lest their guests fail to give much above what the couple can afford. It is particularly because of the necessity to calculate the cost of the meal that guests rarely know the precise amount of their contribution prior to the banquet itself.

Villagers recognize that the primary function of the *ofrecijo* is capital accumulation. Guests know that with their gift money the newlyweds will be able to rent a house, buy a team of animals or a few plots of land, or do whatever else may be necessary to establish an independent nuclear family. The total amount collected varies greatly from one wedding to another, but in recent years it has become common for a couple to receive at least 50,000 or 60,000 pesetas (about 700 to 850 dollars), more than the average annual income for Becedas farmers. Although perhaps a fifth of this money goes toward paying wedding expenses, enough remains for the couple to invest as best they see fit, with the goal of establishing themselves as a separate social unit.

The *ofrecijo* provides for capital accumulation of a very planned, contractual nature. It is often referred to as *dinero presta'o*—"borrowed money"—because the newlyweds are expected to repay the money slowly, over the course of a lifetime, in the form of monetary presentations to those who have given it to them, or to their children, at numerous future weddings. It is this necessity for repayment that carefully determines wedding invitations. Husbands and wives, for example, are invited separately, according to their relationship to the couple. A man might attend as "friend of the groom," while his wife goes as "second cousin of the bride"; they would then present their gifts independently, in amounts determined by their distinct statuses vis-à-vis the newlyweds. When men and women go without their spouses to a wedding, as frequently occurs, it is invariably found that only one of the newlyweds had attended the guest's wedding, thereby presenting only one gift; to keep the exchange as equitable as possible, the guest is similarly expected to come alone, thus paying an *ofrecijo* for only himself, not for his spouse as well. The amount that any pair of individuals exchanges over the course of their lifetime in *ofrecijo* payments is rarely equal. But villagers at least attempt to equalize payments to the extent that they can, and this is accomplished through careful inviting.

Because of the *ofrecijo*, attendance at a wedding is seen more as an obligation than a right. If an individual is unable to afford the going *ofrecijo* rate, he must find the resources to pay anyway; for, to present less than this amount is not only shameful but also assures that his family will be shortchanged by puny payments at their weddings in future years. The *ofrecijo* is above all an economic act; actual attendance at a wedding is desirable but not mandatory so long as the invited guest sends along a surrogate publicly to present the gift on his behalf. Families and individuals have ongoing contracts to provide one another and their children a large capital reserve at the time of marriage. The obligatory, binding nature of the *ofrecijo* places it somewhat in the same class as the rotating credit association in other parts of the world (Anderson 1966, Bascom 1952, Geertz 1962) as a standard device for capital accumulation.

But the *ofrecijo* is also of serious social significance, for it provides one of the most concrete means by which ongoing ties between pairs of individuals may be expressed and maintained. All wedding guests are, throughout the proceedings, forced to calculate their social relationship to the newlyweds and to others and to give material meaning to that relationship. The act of presenting money not only reinforces existing ties but also establishes new ones on a firmer basis. For, at every wedding, there are always present a few *uninvited* guests, people who are not required to come and offer money but who do so anyway, in order to show their appreciation to the newlyweds for some favor they may have performed, or to create and formally recognize a social bond that may have existed previously in only tenuous fashion.

Because of the conscious definition of status inherent in the *ofrecijo*, the custom places the social structure of the village in relief and enables us to identify and define essential social units. It was only after witnessing an *ofrecijo*, several months into my field trip, that I began to realize the social importance of *quintos*, friends, and neighbors in Becedas; the precise definition of status in the gift-giving provided me the clue that eventually led to an understanding of these social units as functional equivalents of the Latin American *compadragzo*. For just as *compadres* in Mexico form and ratify their relationships through ritual and symbolic gift exchange at weddings (Brandes 1968), so friends and neighbors in Becedas solidify and reinforce their ties through *ofrecijo* payments.

This explains why the *ofrecijo* is presented ostentatiously, rather than being hidden in an envelope and handed discreetly and furtively to the newlyweds. By so offering the money, villagers openly display to their friends, neighbors, and relatives that they fulfill their obligations, that they can be trusted to make good their social, as well as economic, debts. Open presentation not only demonstrates good will and trustworthiness but also operates as a security measure. For informants insist that, if they should present the money in private, they might later be accused, by the newly-weds or others, of skimping on—or even entirely ignoring—their obliga-tions, which of course would result in reduced *ofrecijo* payments to them-selves or their families in later years. The *ofrecijo* is, as much as anything, a trust-maintaining device.

Let us now examine the way in which migration has influenced the *ofrecijo*, and vice versa. Since large-scale settlement in Madrid, relatives from the city have been attending village weddings in increasingly large numbers. Partially to demonstrate their new material success but also to fulfill a real sense of duty toward village relatives, migrants press informally for the presentation of steadily higher *ofrecijo* payments. Villagers, for their part, attempt to keep up with urban relatives by eagerly agreeing to pay what in previous years would be considered exhorbitant amounts. Though villagers frequently must offer much more than they can afford, meeting these payments satisfies their pride as well as their desire to show urbanites that they too are prospering. As a result, *ofrecijo* payments have soared since the mid-1960s, to more than double what they were around 1960; they are like a thermometer, rising with increasingly massive migra-tion to Madrid.

At the same time, the *ofrecijo* itself contributes to close village–urban ties, since migrants must frequently return to the village as wedding guests, to fulfill their financial obligation to a new couple. In addition, unmarried migrants, anxious to collect the *ofrecijo* justifiably due them, almost all return to the village to marry, whether it is the bride or groom, or both, who are from Becedas. Because the *ofrecijo* provides a monetary incentive for holding a village wedding, there have even been cases in which the bride, groom, and majority of guests all live in Madrid but return to Becedas for the wedding ceremony and reception. Hence, the *ofrecijo*, by virtue of its contractual nature and practicality, helps to maintain a close network of kin that transcends village boundaries and incorporates now-permanent city residents into village social and economic life.[4]

DEATH

In Becedas, villagers state that death is the only occasion on which they are all truly united and for which they lay aside, however temporarily, their disputes and schisms. As with birth and marriage rites, funerals require people consciously to assess their varying statuses and to act accordingly. Funerals are not only formal, standardized mechanisms for the expression of grief, as has been widely noted in anthropological literature (e.g., Firth 1963: 63, Goody 1962: 34-35), but they also provide for the definition and highlighting of social roles and, therefore, for the sharp delineation of select features of village social structure.

Death in Becedas triggers a seemingly automatic reaction in the community which is designed to provide the grieving family with emotional support and relief. As among the Basques (Douglass 1969: 213), the deceased's house is filled with his former neighbors, friends, and relatives within minutes after his death has become known. The community usually suspects death when the priest is called unexpectedly to an ill person's house; suspicions are confirmed after he delivers Extreme Unction, and the church bells toll in a characteristic, mournful rhythm. Immediately afterward, relatives in Béjar, Salamanca, Madrid, or other nearby cities are telephoned and requested to rush to the village. One Madrileña, upon hearing at 2:00 A.M. of the death of her father, called another Becedas migrant in Madrid, who is a taxi driver, and he delivered her to the village only 3 hours later. There is, in all instances, an unfailing sense of urgency on the part of the community to provide support for the family of the deceased.

Following a death, a close relative of the deceased—usually a child or sibling—dresses him in his finest garments. For men, this was traditionally their black wedding suit and tie, and for women, whatever black outfit they may have owned, but preferably the black wedding dress. A crucifix perhaps 1½ feet long is placed in the deceased's hands, which rest clasped on his breast. If the deceased's stomach begins to distend, indicating

---

[4] Portions of the preceding discussion are based on Brandes (1973b).

inflamación de las tripas ("intestinal inflammation"), a small bowl of salt is placed on his lower chest to prevent the supposedly imminent bursting of the intestines. This custom is practiced only on corpses that give "indications" of postmortem intestinal problems.

A wake is held during the day and night immediately following a death. Neighbors, close friends, and relatives of the deceased are expected to remain with the deceased's family, rendering whatever support or assistance they may. For the wake, the corpse is placed, in funeral dress, in a coffin, which is procured from one of the village carpenters, who always have several of different sizes on hand. As each visitor arrives, he is ushered directly to the coffin, where he kneels, crosses himself, and says an Our Father; women are required to kiss the corpse of a dead child on the forehead, but otherwise there is no bodily contact between the living and the deceased. After this short ritual, women are seated in the room with the body, where they remain quietly chatting, only occasionally reciting an Our Father or a Hail Mary in unison. Men retire to the kitchen and stay huddled together in alternately animated or subdued conversation. There is none of the celebration that characterizes portions of Basque funeral ritual (Douglass 1969: 47–49), but neither is there the stonefaced solemnity generally expected in other parts of the world on such events. Throughout the wake, villagers come and go to pay their respects; only those with close social bonds to the deceased and his immediate family remain for the entire duration.

The day after a death, the funeral service and burial are held. Until a generation ago, there were always three separate categories of funeral and burial in Becedas: *medios entierros* ("half funerals"), *entierros enteros* ("whole funerals"), and *entierros de trés* ("third-ranking funerals"), in order of increasing elaborateness and cost. *Medios entierros,* the humblest, only utilized one priest and included relatively little singing; *entierros enteros* also employed a single priest but included lengthy sung portions; and *entierros de trés,* the fanciest services, employed three priests (from which its name may also derive), all conducting an elaborate Mass. There were also comparable differences in the number of clergymen and the religious paraphernalia that accompanied the bereaved family in the funeral processions.

Then, about 1955, the *medio entierro* was eliminated, and 5 years later the *entierro de trés* was similarly done away with, so there remains only one standard funeral for everyone. This development is clearly a cultural reflection of the steadily increasing economic egalitarianism in the village over the past quarter century.

Precisely half an hour before the funeral service, the church bells toll solemnly, the cue for all village men to gather outside the home of the deceased. The priest, along with two choirboys holding candles, one man holding a large crucifix, and another holding the *manga* (a pole with a conically draped banner), march from the church to the deceased's home, where the village men have been waiting. (Men married during the preceding calendar year are required to take turns carrying the crucifix and *manga* at funerals.) While four pallbearers—the deceased's closest male relatives—hold the coffin over the threshold of his house, the priest recites a prayer and sprinkles holy water and incense; all then file to the church, the village men trailing the religious personnel and pallbearers. The funeral service is conducted with the coffin placed immediately in front of the altar. Aside from a few close female relatives of the deceased, everyone present is male. Women play virtually no role at funerals.

After the service, the priest, followed by the pallbearers and men, walks to the cemetery, which lies about a half kilometer outside the village; no women attend this event. As the coffin is lowered into the ground, close relatives and associates of the deceased toss handfuls of earth over it. The burial completed, the mourners march back to the village and gather once again at the deceased's home. The primary male mourners of the family stand in line at the doorway as all the village men file by to shake their hands and say, "May God accompany you in your grief," with which the formal funeral proceedings end.

Memorial services are held for three consecutive mornings after the funeral; when the church bells toll, friends, neighbors, and relatives of the grieving family meet at the deceased's house and accompany them to Mass. Unlike the funeral services, the more casual acquaintances of the deceased and his family need not participate, though on rare occasions when there is little work to be done, they may. Both men and women attend these memorial Masses, along with subsequent memorial services held on the first, second, and third anniversaries of a person's death. The third anniversary Mass marks the end of formal obligations of nonfamily or distantly related individuals in the community toward the deceased.

The meticulous care that villagers take in fulfilling this role obligation can be portrayed vividly by extending our analysis for a moment to the custom of *luto*, or mourning. As with other customs occasioned by life crisis events, the manner of holding mourning for a dead relative has changed because of increased contact with the urban world. First, following the urban pattern, mourning has become less severe than it was even as late as the late 1950s. For example, whereas formerly women in mourning were required to cover their heads with a black kerchief, now adherence to this custom is so rare that it has become the mark of only the saintliest, most self-sacrificing of villagers. Nor is it any longer considered crucial to abstain from listening to the radio during the entire mourning period.

But perhaps the greatest reflection of urban influence in recent years has been the tendency to abbreviate the period of mourning. Thus, whereas formerly one would be expected to mourn approximately 3 years for the death of a brother or sister, now a villager will remain in mourning only a half year or year. If a parent died, one would have to stay in mourning for about 4 years; now the expected period is between a half year and a year. When an uncle or cousin died, a person would have to show his grief for about 2 months; now it is a rare individual who mourns even a week for either of these categories of relatives.

Whatever the length of the mourning period, there always has been and still is a gradual process, called *aliviar el luto*, by which the degree of mourning is, by a series of steps, reduced, leading to the abandonment of mourning altogether. First, after a given length of time a woman changes from wearing black stockings to wearing sheer ones. Second, she changes from a black to gray sweater or top. Finally, she is permitted to wear a colored skirt, the overt sign that she is no longer in mourning.

As with other life cycle customs, in mourning it is crucial that villagers who all stand in the same relationship to the individual around whom the occasion is organized, in this case the deceased, act in precisely the same manner. That is, all aunts of a deceased person are expected not only to remain in mourning for the same length of time but also to *aliviar el luto* at the same rate. The same is demanded of all brothers and sisters after the death of their father or mother.

It is recognized, of course, that urban relatives are free of such restrictions because of the relative anonymity provided them in the city. It is, in fact, largely because of this freedom that the people of Becedas have been impelled to shorten the period of mourning. Not only have urban relatives conveyed to villagers the notion that long mourning periods are outmoded, but also villagers are beginning to resent the extra sacrifices demanded of them. Nonetheless, while mourning periods as a whole have been shortened, the face-to-face social environment of the community still requires strict adherence to the traditional system whereby the rate of reduction of mourning is coordinated among those of similar social status.

The fact that mourning periods are presently in flux makes such coordination particularly difficult. I am reminded of the wives of two brothers who were mourning for the wife of a third brother. About 6 months after the woman's death, one of the sisters-in-law decided that she had sacrificed long enough and would begin reducing the degree of her mourning. So one Sunday she donned sheer stockings instead of black ones. Under traditional conditions, when there was more or less agreement on the duration of mourning periods for different categories of relatives, the second sister-in-law would have followed suit. In this instance, however, she thought the first too hasty and, with more than a touch of self-righteous defiance, continued to wear black. After 2 or 3 days, the first sister-in-law, shamed by the purity of the other and afraid of the criticism that had already begun to spread within the community, reverted to black stockings. After 4 more months, both sisters-in-law coincidentally began once again to wear sheer stockings.

The case is interesting for its illustration of the cultural disorientation introduced into Becedas by the attempt to emulate urban norms. Under social conditions in the city, an individual is more or less free to determine for himself the length and the degree of his mourning. But in the face-to-face environment of Becedas, such liberty is impossible. Try as they may to be as free of antiquated rules as their city relatives, the people of Becedas are still aware that traditional village structural relations retain their basic vigor and must be ratified as strongly and as frequently as ever.

RITUAL AND STRUCTURAL CONTINUITY

It is clear from this analysis that the life cycle rites in Becedas are of great importance to the village community. Perhaps because the rites are invested with such great significance, in terms of the religious, social, and moral transformation of the major participants, they become the primary pivotal points around which villagers periodically define their relationships. The most meaningful way for a friend, relative, or neighbor to reaffirm his relationship is to participate in the culturally appropriate role at a life cycle occasion. Conversely, the surest way to cause hurt feelings and social cleavages is to ignore one's obligations during these events.

Thus, the life cycle rites provide a picture of the social structure in relief, highlighting the crucial lines of association and division that underlie village society. On some occasions, whether one is friend or neighbor becomes the important basis for ritual action; on others, one's sexual affiliation assumes similar significance. No matter what the particular rite, however, it is likely to operate toward a clear definition of the individual's status vis-à-vis diverse groups of people in his community. In this way, the life cycle rites not only aid the anthropologist by highlighting the fundamental social units of village life but also (and, of course, more importantly) benefit the villagers themselves by promoting the cohesion of these units.

For, when individuals are forced to become conscious of their social relationships and to give these relationships concrete expression through material exchange or emotional support, they simultaneously demonstrate
deep commitment to one another and thereby strengthen their mutual
bond.

Once again, we are confronted with a situation in which migration and
the extension of outside ties have in no way reduced the strength of relationships within the community. To be sure, the *content* of the life cycle
rites has been altered significantly as a result of the emulation of urban
mores; the implications of this development for the survival of a peasantry
in Becedas will be explored in the concluding chapter. Yet, the life cycle
occasions still provide a critical opportunity for people to assert rights over,
and obligations to a wide segment of the village populace. And even
though the precise nature of these claims may be in flux, they have not
become any less extensive or burdensome than they were a generation ago,
and they operate as before to promote mutual trust and sympathy among
kinsmen, friends, and neighbors.

It is crucial, too, to recognize that life cycle occasions work like a mag-
netic force, continually attracting migrants back into the community.
Whether to assert their own claims over villagers—as in the collection of
ofrecijo payments in marriage—or to express their obligations to relatives—
as in participation in wakes and funerals—migrants are regularly and conspicuously present during these special occasions. In fact, it is fair to say
that widespread migration from Becedas is recent enough that most migrants observe more life cycle rites in the village than they do in Madrid
or wherever else they have settled. Family ties, which are as important to
migrants as they are to villagers, require migrants to return to the village
and participate fully. Here, as in so many other aspects of life, the sociocentrism of the *pueblo* has been retained.

Plate 9 Consuelo Hernández preparing a *roscón* for Madrid relatives.

IX

Conclusion: Migration and the Changing Peasant Order

THE PROBLEM RESTATED

In Chapter 1, we examined a variety of models for the structure and composition of the peasant community and the relationship between that community and the outside world. At that time, we reviewed some prevalent social scientific notions on the disappearance of peasantries and showed that the changing ties between rural cultivators and the nation state of which they are a part bear primary responsibility for peasant demise. It seems appropriate now to place the developments that have occurred in Becedas over the past generation in the light of that initial discussion. This involves a recapitulation and synthesis of already familiar material, as well as the introduction of related additional information. We also wish to speculate about the immediate and long-term future of the *pueblo*.

Since the definition of peasantry encompasses a broad range of economic, cultural, and social phenomena, we may begin the discussion by asking whether Becedas—after several decades of undeniable modernization and change—is still a peasant community. Do the people of modern

Becedas conform to any of the standard notions of peasantry? This question is of interest and significance not because of the mere problem of classification, which is a sterile issue in and of itself, but because it provides a convenient starting point for analyzing processes of change and especially for identifying if and how alterations in one sphere of life affect other aspects of individual or community existence. Specifically, we want to use the Becedas experience to determine whether or not acute economic and cultural change necessarily involves a disruption of the social order, and whether or not modernization and development inevitably produce a disintegration of community structure and sentiment.

At the outset, let us remember that, even though there are potentially an enormous variety of factors that promote the restructuring of community relations with the outside world, in Becedas the primary and most immediate impetus for change has come from migration. Unlike many other parts of peasant Spain, Becedas has not experienced consistently high rates of out-migration. Unfortunately, precise population figures are unavailable for the eighteenth and nineteenth centuries, but, as mentioned in Chapter 2, all indications show that Becedas was prospering and growing throughout that period. Perhaps because of the adoption of potato cultivation in the late eighteenth century, enabling Becedas to support a greater number of inhabitants, the number of village houses, household heads, stores, and mills all show a steady increase. This, of course, does not preclude the possibility of simultaneous, heavy out-migration from the community. But, given the available evidence, such a population movement seems highly unlikely to have occurred.

Twentieth-century figures are more precise, though for the years before 1940, they exist only in the aggregate for the municipality as a whole (which includes the village of Palacios de Becedas as well as Becedas proper). Table 8 demonstrates conclusively that no single decade before 1950 even remotely reached the migration levels of the two decades since. In the period 1910–1920, there was actually a substantial (and presently unexplainable) migration into the community, and 1930–1940 shows a relatively high rate of out-migration, doubtless caused by the disruptions of the Civil War. But even this latter decade reveals only a third as great a migration rate as that found in the period since 1950. Taken as a whole, the municipality figures justify the contention that massive migration from Becedas marks a significant break with the community's traditional population pattern.

When people migrate from a small community in large numbers, the community itself is necessarily altered, as is its relationship to the outside world. In Becedas, migration has stimulated far-reaching economic and

TABLE 8
Population and Migration in the Municipality of Becedas
(Becedas and Palacios de Becedas), 1910–1970

Year	Total births previous decade	Total deaths previous decade	Natural population increase	Total population	Estimated net migration	Percentage rate of migration
1910	—	—	—	1249	—	—
1920	575	565	10	1401	+142	11.4
1930	595	393	202	1586	− 17	1.2
1940	462	286	176	1625	−137	8.6
1950	428	326	102	1659	− 68	4.2
1960	339	201	138	1415	−382	23.0
1970	154	143	11	1048	−378	26.7

cultural changes that have been substantial enough effectively to thrust its people out of the peasant category—and this despite the retention of a basically unmechanized, traditional agricultural technology. Yet, socially, the Becedas community is close-knit and cohesive and has maintained its position as a source of personal identity for its inhabitants. Becedas is still a part-society.

MIGRATION AND ECONOMIC ADAPTATION

To assess the impact of migration on the Becedas economy, we must first turn to one neatly encapsulated economic definition of peasantry and measure developments in our village against it. According to this definition, peasants are "members of households whose major activity is farming, which produce a major part of the goods and services they consume, which exercise substantial control over the land they farm, and which supply the major part of their labor requirements from their own energies" (Tilly 1974:1). Certainly, according to at least some of these criteria, the people of Becedas still may be counted as peasants, particularly to the degree that they have come to exercise increasing control over the land and to utilize household labor organization.

We may recall that, economically, the most crucial effect of migration has been a transformation of the land tenure system. Around 1950, large numbers of landless or land poor villagers derived their primary income from working for a few wealthy landholders for unsteady and uncertain daily wages. Now, all villagers own some land, and most control a good deal more through increasingly liberal sharecropping and rental agreements. To be sure, some villagers still supplement their earnings through daily wage labor; but whereas formerly these men first worked for others, cultivating their own small plot or two only if they had time, they now devote their labor first to their own fields, seeking extra employment only if they are otherwise unoccupied. The agricultural priorities of yesterday have been reversed, giving small farmers an amount of control over the land never before experienced. We are confronted now with a village of independent, self-employed rural proprietors.

At the same time, however, the people of Becedas have in effect lost control over their economic destinies through increasing involvement in the national, and even world, market system. Of course, during no time in its long history has the village ever been totally free of market involvement. Like peasant communities everywhere, this one has never been wholly self-sufficient. Yet, the past record shows both a more diversified agriculture and a greater degree of economic independence than exists now. Throughout the twentieth century and especially since the 1950s, there has been a steady tendency toward specialization and cash and crop farming. Flax and grain first gave way to irrigated fruits and vegetables, and these latter, in turn, now seem to be losing ground to fodder crops that will sustain the growing village dairy herds. Whatever the form of economic adaptation, it has always taken place with regard to the advantages and limitations of the mountain environment, on the one hand, and to the available marketing and commercial opportunities, on the other.

The switch to commercial agriculture has been stimulated, of course, by the increasing demand for cash. Becedas farmers have come to enjoy a higher standard of living than ever before. They cook on gas stoves, walk on concrete and tile floors, are entertained by privately owned radios and televisions, and have a susbtantially nutritious and varied diet, including meat or fish daily. They rely on crop and dairy sales to support these and other ever-expanding needs, including, among other things, telephones (which nearly a quarter of the households possess) and modern furnishings and clothing. The people of Becedas have virtually lost whatever self-sufficiency and economic insulation from the outside they may have had. Ironically, as they have gained in proprietorship and control over the land, they have become simultaneously subjected to and dominated by the vicissitudes of the market. More than ever, they now resemble modern commercial farmers.

MIGRATION AND CULTURAL CHANGE

Among the most profound changes resulting from migration are alterations in the definition of correct or desirable behavior, in knowledge of the outside world, and in the material aspects of life. Increasingly close contact with urbanites has provided peasants the opportunity for widespread emulation of city ways, with the consequent prestige and satisfaction that come from knowing that one is sophisticated and modern, rather than provincial and narrow. All of these changes signify a cultural revolution in the countryside, a revolution that has all but totally eliminated the distinctive, localized beliefs and customs found in peasant villages of the past.

Friedl (1964) has defined the conditions necessary for effective emulation of an elite by peasants, and these conditions, derived from her work in Greece, shed light on the current situation in Becedas. First, there must be an availability of models, individuals whose cultural patterns may be copied. Through sporadic, direct contacts with the city of Béjar, the people of Becedas have always had the opportunity to know urbanites and to observe their distinguishing manners and attitudes, but only recently have villagers really been able to have widespread, intense relations with individuals who live in Madrid and other metropolitan areas. The social network of Becedas, once so restricted by endogamy, has overnight become far-flung. In addition, social relations between villagers and city dwellers are close, characterized by frequent telephone calls, letters, and visits. These city–based relatives, who provide Becedas direct models for emulation, are, to use Wolf's (1956: 1075–1076) terminology, "brokers," mediating between the urban, nation-oriented culture, and the parochial version of that culture as manifested in the village.

Second, Friedl says, effective emulation requires an attitude on the part of both peasant and elite that they are in the same social universe. Although the people of Becedas have always had contact with potential models for emulation, until the mid-1960s, this second condition remained unfulfilled. For the most part, villagers' contact with city dwellers was restricted to shopkeepers, outside middlemen, and government officials, with whom they entered into fleeting symbiotic economic and political relationships but with whom, too, they maintained a notable social distance. Whereas identification with such people was impossible, villagers identify strongly with the migrants. Although villagers envy the material prosperity of urban relatives, they in no way consider them inherently different or superior because of it. In fact, having witnessed the rise of these ex-villagers from a situation similar to their own, they are convinced that they are equally capable of such advancement. Further, migrants, by returning to the village periodically—for the *matanza*, patronal fiestas, summer vacation, or whatever—prove their loyalty to the people of Becedas, and their continued devotion to the community. Thus, the migrants are an inherent part of the social universe of the village, and this, as much as their mere contact with the people, makes them effective as brokers.

Finally, according to Friedl (1964: 580) there must be "an increase in agricultural income" and "an expansion of the occupational structure of the total society so that upward mobility for farmers' children is feasible," conditions that permit individuals to realize their newfound desires by providing them the economic resources and occupational avenues for imitation and advancement. As already noted, the expanding Spanish economy and changing land tenure system have fulfilled these criteria in Becedas. In addition to rising incomes and opportunities for villagers, however, migration has led to substantial economic assistance from the migrants themselves. Unmarried children who work in the city invariably send a large portion of their earnings to their village families, and a constant stream of used clothing arrives by mail to help keep village women and children fashionably dressed. Urban relatives are also a reliable source of loans to village families should they need to make house improvements, pay medical bills, or make some other extraordinary expenditure. The fact that half of the 46 televisions in Becedas (as of 1970) were either gifts from city relatives or purchased with their financial help gives an idea of the large extent to which the villagers' lives have been transformed by outside assistance.

So provided with effective models and means for emulation, the people of Becedas are experiencing rapid loss of their traditional cultural values, along with the concomitant accumulation of the symbols and accoutrements of urban life. It is common for people to denigrate and ridicule openly the more "folkloric" aspects of their culture as *atrasa'o*, "backward." To adhere too closely to life cycle rituals, for example—for a woman to wear a black wedding dress, to isolate herself for 40 days after giving birth, or, if she is baptismal godmother, to insist on being the only person to toss the *roña*—such behavior is considered incomprehensible and foolish. On the other hand, to throw a large baptismal party, take a short honeymoon, or dress in modern clothing, including see-through blouses, is considered acceptable and forward-looking, desirable adoptions of a more advanced (*adelanta'o*) life style. For the same reason, long mourning periods, once rigidly observed, are becoming shorter and less standardized, following the urban pattern. It is in the myriad of small ways in which people ignore or actively reject the traditional cultural expectations that the influence of the urban world is most acutely manifested.

Moreover, adoption of city ways is becoming increasingly important to maintain a positive self-image. In health care, for example, some individuals still rely on folk *curanderos* ("healers"), but most villagers patronize not only the village physician, a general practitioner, but medical specialists as well. In fact, much boasting and prestige surrounds the person who visits a pediatrician in Béjar or an allergist in Avila, and villagers are always sure to mention that their specialist has *rayos*—Xrays—the ultimate in modernity. Prestige and self-satisfaction also accrue to the family that has installed a toilet, a symbol of civilized urban existence; people are often embarrassed to admit that theirs is not yet installed.

The adoption of urban practices and accoutrements not only helps maintain a positive self-image but also indicates a new attitude toward the display of wealth. Villagers admit that their two worst vices are envy (*envidia*) and selfishness (*egoismo*). Extreme poverty and scarcity in the *pueblos*, they say, have always instilled a general fear of revealing one's possessions, lest one be forced into sharing with others more than one can reasonably afford, or one becomes the object of envy, scorn, and theft. Speaking of an earlier generation of villagers, one man said, "They were so poor that they had nothing anyone would want, yet they always feared being robbed."

Paradoxically, now that the village has prospered and there *are* valuable family possessions, people have become less concerned about revealing them. If anything, the more a family can surround itself with the symbols of urban life—radio, television, gas heater, fashionable clothing—the greater its prestige. Villagers are no longer fearful of display because that very display justifies their continued residence in Becedas. Since so many of their close relatives have recently settled successfully in the city, those who remain behind feel defensive about their immobility. Conspicuous display is the means by which villagers can rationalize—to themselves, to their fellow villagers, and to the migrants—their continued acceptance of village life. By spending money and modernizing, villagers are, in effect, telling the world that they have *chosen*, albeit temporarily, to remain behind, rather than being forced financially or otherwise to do so.

In Becedas, then, economic change has been associated with, indeed in most respects has created and stimulated, significant cultural transformations. Such a transformation is nowhere more evident than in the following incident. One rainy Saturday afternoon, my landlord and close friend, Ignacio Alvarez, and I were seated in his parlor (whose existence is in itself an indication of tremendous change) on his plastic-covered couch, watching the news of the day on television. As he began to discuss the Swiss currency and French political scene with me in as sophisticated a fashion as I might, the news program was suddenly disturbed by heavy static. Wondering whether the static was caused by his own set or by some outside interference, Ignacio phoned his village friend Valentín

Casanueva, who was watching the same program and who assured him that there was some outside disturbance. Like their fellow villagers, these men are not peasants, sharing and expressing a clearly definable part-culture; they are full participants in the national culture of Spain with which they have become so intimately familiar.

MIGRATION AND COMMUNITY SOLIDARITY

As we saw in Chapter 1, ever since the days of Tönnies and Durkheim, social scientists have labored under the notion that cities are atomized, disorderly, and chaotic, and that, to the degree that rural towns and villages come into contact with cities, they too would come to acquire these characteristics. Robert Redfield, writing in the 1940s, applied this idea specifically to the study of contemporary peasantry, and his work has had a strong theoretical influence on community studies written since the Second World War. For Becedas, there have undoubtedly been profound economic and cultural changes resulting from migration and from increased contact with Madrid. The limted, though critical, economic and cultural autonomy that the village once enjoyed has been virtually eliminated. Have migration and urban contact also destroyed Becedas society, transforming the village into an atomistic, random collection of individuals whose loyalties and identities lie outside the territorial unit in which they happen to reside? Has Becedas become, socially, like a little Madrid?

To answer these questions, let us first examine social solidarity within Becedas and how this might have changed in degree over the past generation. Following one common sociological approach, let us take solidarity to be "the average strength of existing ties among members of the group, and . . . take 'strength' to mean the extent of effective claims any pair of individuals have on one another" (Tilly 1973: 9). Using this criterion, we can only say that solidarity has increased in Becedas despite—or more likely because of—migration and the extension of urban ties. The increase in cooperative and communal labor, documented in Chapter 5, demonstrates most dramatically this increase in solidarity, though we have also seen that relations between kinsmen and neighbors show a similar trend. Certainly, in Becedas now, people are at least as reliant on one another, and probably even more so, than they were a generation ago. To this extent, the presumed individualism of the city has not yet "infected" and destroyed community in Becedas.

At the same time, a sense of community in the village has been strengthened through the increase in economic and social homogeneity.

Economically, the ever-expanding supply of land and diminishing supply of labor, both brought on by migration, have jointly acted as a leveling mechanism. Property ownership and control no longer divide the populace. There is now a tendency for each family, regardless of actual landholdings, to cultivate as much terrain as it itself can handle—but no more.

This equality is reflected above all in marriage preferences. To be sure, there were always some marriages between those from well-to-do families and those from poor ones, but according to all evidence, property (in the form of land) was the major consideration in choosing a spouse. Families exerted tremendous pressures on their children to enter into courtship with the most landed eligible partner, so that, even if there were deviations from the pattern, the tendency was to marry one's economic equal. During the 1950s and 1960s, villagers from different economic backgrounds have entered into courtship and married without fear of reproach from their families. Now that the availability of arable land has made it possible for any young villager to acquire or control as much terrain as he himself can farm, living standards and economic prospects for all villagers have become more or less alike.

Economic equality has also altered social relations among village men, as seen, for example, in leisure-time activity. In 1950, there was only one small tavern in the village, where the 20 or so well-to-do villagers gathered on Sundays and after work on weekends to drink and play cards.[1] For the vast majority of men, who could afford neither the time nor the money to sit around a card table for hours at a stretch, there was no cultural meeting point; instead, small groups gathered occasionally in unused barns, to build a fire, to roast chestnuts and potatoes, and to drink inexpensive wine.

Now, in addition to the community-owned *Hermandad* concession, there are three large bars in Becedas, all doing a booming business, and there is no longer anyone who cannot afford the price of coffee, beer, cognac, liqueur, or a soft drink, or to treat his friends to these refreshments. Bars have become so available to villagers that, as we have seen, it is now a cultural expectation that men spend large segments of time there. It is revealing that the poorest villager spends as much time and money in the bars as anyone, and though he is criticized for irresponsibility, it is significant that he is able to afford this luxury and to mix regularly with the

---

[1] This regular meeting among well-to-do villagers (sometimes called a *tertulia*) has been described for Andalusia (Pitt–Rivers 1961: 134–135) and Italy (Verga 1964: 30). It was a common feature of Mediterranean rural life until the recent past and still persists wherever social divisions are marked.

most well-to-do villagers of Becedas. Until 1960 or so, villagers classified themselves into two social categories, *ricos* ("the rich") and *pobres* ("the poor"). Now, one rarely hears these terms used. More often it is said that *"Hoy día somos todos iguales"*—"Nowadays we're all equal."

To the extent that the village is more homogeneous than in the past, so too intravillage solidarity has increased. People are capable of identifying with and showing sympathy toward fellow community members, who share the same life situation and confront the same economic problems as themselves. Distinctions among the people of Becedas, though far from entirely eliminated, have become considerably muted, especially in the context of the extreme dependency that the community as a whole now experiences in its relationship to the outside world. Becedas farmers all worry equally when trucker middlemen begin coming, as they have recently, in fewer numbers to purchase produce. They all suffer when the government, as it did in 1970, permitted the unrestricted entry of French apples into Spain, thereby lowering fruit prices well below reasonable expectations. They are all technologically stifled. Their fate is mutually bound to the same unpredictable and powerful market forces, and this common subordination to the outside has evoked in them a cohesive sentiment that permitted and encouraged them, for example, to adopt cooperative insecticide spraying. More than ever, the people of Becedas share the same circumstances, and they know it.

Hence, even though Becedas has become significantly less autonomous in the cultural and economic realms, the heightened dependency on and intimacy with the outside world has in no way created an atomized, disorganized village society. In both structure and sentiment, the Becedas populace is at least as unified and cohesive as it has been at any time in the recent past. Of course, the people have a much higher standard of living than ever before, but this does not mean that their claims on one another have become any weaker or less effective, for available evidence shows the opposite to be true. At every level of village society, from the household to the whole community, divisions seem less important, and cooperation and unity more so, than in the past.

On the other hand, to say that solidarity and cohesion have increased is not necessarily to say that the social structure of the village has remained constant. Clearly, one crucial impact of migration has been the formation of strong and tenacious social bonds with urbanites. The social network of the villagers is not nearly as confined territorially as it was in the past. As we have seen, ties with Madrid are so continuous and intimate that migrants, as well as some villagers (like widows and widowers) who live a good part of the year in Madrid, must be considered in some respects as much a part of Becedas society as those who permanently reside in the community. People leave the village, but their identification and involvement with it remain substantial. As in the past, Becedas society has its locus in the actual territory of Becedas. Unlike a generation ago, however, Becedas has become more and more like what Tilly might call a "non-territorial community" (1973: 4), with migrants forming a dispersed and latent element of community membership; full-fledged community participation and affiliation occur instantly upon periodic resumption of residence in the home base. Largely because permanent villagers maintain close ties with migrant kinsmen, these kinsmen return frequently to Becedas, becoming incorporated automatically into the ongoing structural relations of the village and thereby affirming their identification with the community as a whole.

More and more, sociologists and others are questioning our original and still deep-seated assumption that cities are atomistic and disorganized (Hammel and Yarbrough 1973, Tilly 1973, Tilly and Brown 1973, Webber *et al.* 1964). The Becedas experience certainly belies the further assumption that modernization and increased contact with the outside world spell the end of community. Communities, we must recognize, can become less autonomous and discrete without becoming a chaotic and random assortment of unrelated and unrelating individuals. Becedas is still very much a part-society.

THE COMMUNITY UNDERMINED: SOME THOUGHTS ON THE FUTURE

At this point, we are forced to assess the long-term meaning of the continuity and change that Becedas has experienced since the mid-1950s. In particular, we want to ask whether the village community is a viable entity of the future, and if the retention of community solidarity and sentiment, in the face of acute economic and cultural change, is only a temporary and short-lived phenomenon, an ephemeral phase in Becedas' evolution. For there is strong evidence to believe that Becedas, as an ongoing community in the widest sense, will no longer exist in the near future, and that atomization and disintegration may yet overtake it.

There are at work a variety of factors that both reflect and promote the destruction of community in Becedas. First is the increasingly overt and acceptable demand for the privacy and anonymity of city life, which many villagers have themselves tasted and with which they are all familiar. It is true that, just as today one constantly hears complaints about the numerous small intrusions on everyday privacy, the emphasis on openness and demonstrativeness in village life has probably always evoked feelings of annoyance and constriction. People now, as always, object to being asked at every turn where they are going and what they are about; they resent having others walk in their homes unannounced; they decry having to sit outside with their neighbors, lest they be criticized. Though they persist in these patterns as strongly as ever, and though they still need the psychological reassurance that this behavior provides, they have begun to vocalize the frustrations it entails and openly to state their preference for a less socially communal—i.e., a more private and individualistic—way of life. And it is significant that, whenever they rationalize their opposition to this behavioral syndrome, they state, "These things aren't done in Madrid, are they? So why should we do them." They yearn for the less restricted urban milieu and envy their migrant relatives for it.

The following incident reveals changing attitudes in this regard. One summer day, an itinerant troop of circus performers came to the village to give their show. They received verbal permission from the mayor (who had to leave the village immediately afterward), erected their tent in the Plaza del Egedillo, and readied themselves for the evening event. The whole town became animated as preparations for the performance proceeded. Then, suddenly and without warning, the vice mayor, chief village executive by virtue of the mayor's absence, announced that he would refuse the performers permission to put on their act. His reason was that an old villager, who lives in a house on the Plaza, was bedridden and possibly near death. It was in deference to him and his family that the vice mayor wanted to cancel the show. Since the performers lacked written permission from the mayor; the vice mayor had final say in the matter.

As soon as word of the cancellation was out, a large segment of the community protested vigorously among themselves and to the Civil Guards in the village. Something like this could never happen in Madrid or Salamanca, they said; only in the *pueblos* would anyone dream of infringing on the rights of people to enjoy themselves because of an old man's illness. The vice mayor came under severe attack, and, after a full hour of bickering, the matter was finally settled. The performers were allowed to give the show but were restricted from playing music or engaging in loud antics.

The case is interesting because, as recently as the mid-1950s, it is highly unlikely anyone would have *openly* protested cancellation of the show, though they might very well have felt resentment underneath. In 1970, however, the protest was vehement, and rested essentially and explicitly on the value of urban anonymity. Increasingly aware of another, more sophisticated way of life, the people feel psychologically as well as economically cramped by life in their small community. For this, as well as other reasons, they are unable to find complete satisfaction within the village context and must reconcile themselves to seeking it elsewhere. Villagers will no longer submit to the informal—yet often tyrannical—public control which is both indicative of and necessary for community cohesion.

Just as the open craving for privacy shows a tendency toward social atomism, so too economic values seem to be expressing an increasingly individualistic theme. The marked change in the economic situation of the village has stimulated people to readjust the way they view their control over the future. Traditionally, and to some extent still, villagers have been imbued with what may be termed a fatalistic attitude, a posture of resignation that is evident in a number of the more common village sayings, such as:

> *Casamiento y mortaja* Marriage and shroud
> *Del cielo baja.* Are handed down from above.

and,

> *El hombre propone* Man proposes
> *Y Dios dispone.* And God disposes.

In other words, man has little control over his universe, God is the ultimate source of authority over action and events, and an individual cannot assume personal responsibility for the direction of his own life. This is why villagers rarely speak about the future without adding, *"Si Dios quiere"*—"If God wishes," and why a salutation such as *"Buenos días"*—"Good day"—is usually countered with a *"Nos dé Dios"*—"May God give us," as if we should not count our chickens. After all, it is presumptuous to say *"Buenos días"* early in the morning if one really does not know definitely if the day will unfold favorably. God's will must be invoked to help assure a favorable outcome.

This attitude has been expressed in the belief that one could not, through conscious, directed effort, improve one's economic situation. It was thought, in many respects rightly so, that the material pie was finite, that wealth (consisting, in the peasant's universe, primarily of land) had been distributed once and forever, and that this distribution could, under no foreseeable circumstances, be altered. In other words, villagers held something akin to what Foster has described as the "Image of Limited Good" (Foster 1965). As an expression of this outlook, sudden financial success was almost always explained as the result of luck, usually in the form of lottery winnings. Rarely, if ever, would villagers attribute success to the personal qualities or efforts of the fortunate individual.[2]

Today, a few villagers, among them the elderly or those who have for some reason or another been blocked from financial success, still cling to the old explanations. Why does one person rise materially and another not? Says Consuelo Hernández, "One person's orchard bears a lot of fruit, his neighbor's none." Why has Teodoro Máquez suddenly acquired a large number of cows? Arturo Torres attributes the success to a wealthy widow friend of Teodoro's family who reputedly provides him with large, interest-free loans. Why has Margarita and Ignacio's store experienced such rapid expansion? Says a long-term acquaintance of theirs, "They secretly won the lottery but won't tell a soul about it." This type of story even extends to the success of migrants. To María Ovejero, any ex-villager who works at the American air base (at Torrejón, just outside Madrid) and becomes well-to-do must have achieved that status through theft, not regular earnings. Theft, the lottery, personal connections—they are all the same type of explanation because they assume that wealth is infused from the outside; that is, they assume a situation of limited goods.

Recently, however, new explanations for success have gained wide appeal, especially, as might be expected, among those who have benefited most from the new conditions. As opposed to the old explanations, which rely on the roles of luck or infusions of wealth from the outside, the new explanations view financial success as the result of certain personality traits: hard work, thrift, or talent. As Margarita Trapero says, "Give one man a nickel (*duro*) and he'll squander it; give it to another and he'll convert it into a dime." Similarly, Teodoro Márquez attributes his own good fortune at cattle raising to an inborn talent for being able to distinguish a good cow from a bad one. He compares himself to Valeriano Casa, who owns many more cows but whose enterprise never expands, simply because "he's bad at cattle raising." Here we see expressions of a new mentality, one that asserts that the individual has at least some control over his economic future. And the new outlook in turn reflects the changed socioeconomic conditions. As a result of migration, village resources, especially land, are more available than ever. From the ordinary villager's standpoint, material goods no longer exist in finite supply, and the latitude

---

[2] Similar explanations for financial success have been described for other peasant communities characterized by an "Image of Limited Good," the classic case being that of treasure tales as an explanation for material achievement in Tzintzuntzan, Mexico (Foster 1964b). The role of luck in accounting for success is also reported in south Italy by Banfield (1958) and Colclough (1971).

for his establishing at least some control over his future is actually greater than ever before.

The new individualistic sentiments strike a blow to the sense of community in Becedas, in that they introduce an element of moral discrimination among men that did not exist in the past. When fate was the explanation for socioeconomic status, no one could be blamed for his station in life. Everyone was equally subject to the same capricious and inexplicable forces. For this reason, a man could feel honorable and proud and could conduct his life in an admirable way, even if he had considerably less than another. New explanations of success or failure, based on personal demeanor and attributes, pave the way for a condemnation of those with less, on the grounds that they possess serious personal defects. The resulting condescension of the successful—which has already begun to emerge in Becedas—and feelings of inadequacy on the part of the others—which have not emerged—could eventually destroy whatever sense of community might otherwise exist in the village. We are already aware of the divisiveness that these attitudes have wrought in the United States (Sennett and Cobb 1972).

Another serious threat to community originates in the religious realm. Ever since the publication of Durkheim's (1961) *Elementary Forms of the Religious Life*, social scientists have recognized the interdependence between religion and society, the former at once expressing and bolstering the latter. For Iberia itself, several studies have sought to show specifically how common participation in religious ritual both reflects and supports communal and community sentiment (Freeman 1968, Riegelhaupt 1973).

Located in a deeply conservative and religious region, Becedas has always enjoyed wide public participation in religious celebrations. Until the late 1950s, the village ritual calendar was dotted with numerous sacred events, the most important of which were 14 annual processions. Everyone, regardless of age, sex, or degree of anti-clericalism, attended these processions. They operated not only to give religious expression to communal feelings, but also to promote and reinforce those feelings. If only by providing all villagers the opportunity to congregate together and pay homage to a particular saint, on whom they believed their collective well-being depended, each procession aroused sentiments of community identity and cohesion.

During the 1960s, a large number of these processions were gradually discontinued, so that only five were performed during 1972, and it likely that several others have been eliminated since. Given the background of increasing modernization and urban contact in Becedas, our immediate tendency would be to attribute this abandonment of processions to an overall process of secularization. After all, many social scientists, following Redfield (1941, 1947), have assumed that urbanites are more secular than rural peoples, and have taken declining ceremonial and ritual life among peasants to be the result of increasing contact with the city. Other scholars consider particular religious tenets and practices to be incongruent with the needs and goals of modernization and development, and believe that religious activities necessarily disappear in the wake of economic change (e.g., Moore 1965). From the vantage point of these theorists, the decline of processions in Becedas would be perfectly understandable as results of other socioeconomic changes that have deeply affected the village.

There are, however, at least two problems in applying these theories to our case. First, it has been clearly demonstrated, at least for Spain, that there is no necessary correlation between degree of religiosity and level of urbanization (Linz and Cazorla 1968–1969). Urban contact does not, therefore, automatically imply the diffusion of secular ideas to the country-side. Second, the causal link from this village seems to be the reverse of what these theories predict. In Becedas, the elimination of processions has preceded, rather than followed upon, either secularization or the destruction of community. Processions are being abandoned *in the face of* community solidarity and sentiment and, as a matter of fact, against the wishes of the majority of village inhabitants.

Let us see why. In 1966, Don Sagrario became the new parish priest of Becedas, replacing the old and much loved and revered village curate, Don Eusebio. Don Sagrario is a young, dynamic, modern priest who brought to the parish an entirely different outlook from the one the people had known before. With complete candor, he admits to his goal of religious purification. He wishes to cleanse Becedas religion of what he regards as superstitions, and trim it down to the bare legal necessity as defined by Rome. Above all, he wants villagers to act on the basis of faith, not blind adherence to custom. "I don't care if only five people attend my Mass," he says, "as long as those five truly believe." This attitude represents an individualization of the religious spirit, along the lines of what we have generally come to associate with early Protestantism. And it is in this reformist context that Don Sagrario has, by his own admission and design, gradually reduced the number of village processions, his eventual goal being the retention of only two—those of Corpus Cristi and of the village patron saint.

Does the elimination of processions, when they are actively desired by the populace, pose a threat to community solidarity? Will the absence of this important bolster to community identity destroy that identity? Obviously, in and of itself, the discontinuation of processions is not going to have this effect. But, operating in conjunction with other forces tending toward community atomization, the elimination of common ritual might very well work in that direction. If people can no longer express community sentiment through religion, neither will religion act in support of that sentiment.

The most critical threats to community in Becedas, however, are revealed by demographic and economic trends. For any true community to exist, it must at least replace its old and deceased inhabitants through marriage and reproduction. Village marriage records show the celebration of fewer and fewer weddings in the village; in fact, since 1970, the only people to be married in the Becedas church have been migrants or people who married migrants and moved from the village immediately afterward. Modern Becedas parents care little about prospective ownership and control over property. Rather, they prefer that their children marry a person who is likely to settle in a city or, better still, one who is already so settled. Marriage now is viewed as a vehicle of escape from the harsh, parochial conditions of village life, and, therefore, many young women are reluctant to enter into courtship with *any* village man, hoping instead to win the heart of some ex-villager with an apartment and a job in Madrid. In fact, the serious depletion in the numbers of village youths has virtually forced women, in particular, to look outside the community for a husband. Of the relatively few eligible bachelors left in Becedas, most are, by comparison with the young women (who have less opportunity to leave the village on their own), either dull or in some way psychologically or physically handicapped. For most village women, the pickings are poor, so instead of "burying themselves," as they say, women prefer to seek their husbands elsewhere. This desire has already drastically altered the endogamous marriage pattern so prevalent in the past. More important, the reduction in village marriages, along with the concomitant declining number of village births (documented in Chapter 3), suggest that villagers are not replenishing their old and consistently more depleted populace. Without a firmer commitment on the part of its young people to stay put—a commitment that does not seem to be forthcoming—Becedas cannot survive, except perhaps as a geriatric and vacation colony.

What is more, the economic prospects for the young seem bleaker than ever, despite vastly increased living standards, and this further reduces hopes that the young will stay on and resist migration. Migration and the consequent redistribution of property and influx of material assistance from outside the community have permitted the people of Becedas to survive, and even prosper, in spite of technological stagnation. But, as the villagers themselves realize, such prosperity can be only temporary. Already the effects of land consolidation and mechanization throughout large areas of Spain are felt in Becedas. In 1970, the fruit and potato sales were poor; prices were unusually low, and virtually all families were left with large portions of their crops unsold. The excess produce, which lay rotting for months in barns and lofts, bore grave witness to the fact that Becedas could no longer compete under modern market conditions.

Further, villagers know that their position can only worsen, for the harsh, rugged terrain in which they have for centuries eked out a living is a hopeless impediment to significant modernization. To be sure, there have been technological innovations, such as insecticide spraying and mechanical reaping, but what is really needed is large-scale production, facilitated by land consolidation and the use of tractors. Where the terrain is broken into numerous small terraces and where orchards and treeless parcels lie side by side in a checkerboard pattern, these changes can never come to pass.

All around them, the people of Becedas see agricultural transformations of enormous scale. Only a few kilometers away, on the wide, rolling hills of Salamanca, a huge reservoir and irrigation project enabled farmers to introduce crops traditionally confined to well-watered areas like that of Becedas; at the same time, because of favorable topography, these farmers have introduced a high degree of mechanization. The people of Becedas purchase the old, worn carts and farm implements from these transformed villages at ridiculously low prices; and although they brag about the bargains, they know, beneath it all, that the sales represent their own technological stagnation and eventual demise.

It is for this reason that all but the oldest and most tradition-bound of villagers desire eventually to leave Becedas for the city. Those who cannot make this change on their own are waiting for their children to mature and lead the way for them, a trend already manifested by the extremely low number of young people in the village. Whenever I asked informants about courting customs, they always replied, with a look of resignation, "What can we tell you. Now there are no youth in the village, so there is no courtship. Everyone is escaping." This statement is no exaggeration; it reflects the overriding sense of doom, a feeling of impending decline, that inevitably casts a shadow over the undeniable prosperity of recent years.

At the same time, however, we may speculate that Becedas will not become permanently depopulated and abandoned, as has happened and continues to happen to so many villagers of Castile. For just as the village's natural setting will be ultimately responsible for the death of a viable agriculture, it may assure Becedas's survival by another means—summer tourism, a trend that is already well apparent. While agricultural land is now considered virtually worthless and is sold for a penny, property values within the village nucleus have soared, making it practically impossible for villagers to purchase or permanently rent a house or house lot. Migrants retain their houses, improving them and rebuilding them, in the hopes of establishing favorable quarters to which they can periodically retire from the noise, traffic, and summer heat of Madrid. And this is the dream of all villagers who plan to settle in the cities of Spain.

In addition to migrants, other *Madrileños* are beginning to spend their summers in Becedas. The summer of 1972 marked a real turning point in the social character of the village, for it was the first time in anyone's memory that strangers—people who could not be readily identified by the community at large—were evident in large numbers. No longer were only ex-villagers returning for vacation, but along with them came their neighbors from Madrid apartment houses, the families of men with whom they work in the city, and others who had somehow heard of Becedas and had chosen it as their vacation spot for the year. In preparation for the continuing influx of outsiders, several villagers have begun to plan and construct additions to their homes that will be used for summer rental.

But more than just natural advantages are on the side of Becedas's survival. In mid-1971, Becedas was declared by the State to be a *Centro Comarcal*, or Regional Center, one of hundreds of such centers being established throughout Spain as part of a plan to concentrate rural populations and services. Though, under this plan, Becedas will not extend political jurisdiction over the surrounding villages, it will be the seat of certain services not available in those villages and will benefit immeasurably from substantial governmental assistance to public works projects. As of 1972, the projects underway included:

1. Construction of a Health Center with quarters for lodging medical personnel, as well as medical service rooms which will eventually house X-ray machines and facilities for minor operations.
2. Pavement of three main village streets, with eventual extension of the project to include the whole village.
3. Installation of a sewage and running water system to include all homes.
4. Installation of modern public lighting, a project virtually completed by September 1972.

All of these developments are designed as incentives to deter the people of Becedas from migrating to the city.

Will the plan work? Obviously, in and of themselves, these physical improvements can do nothing to restrain people from leaving, for the cities are already well-endowed with these services and much more. Only if the villagers find a viable economic base will the new improvements make a difference and persuade people that conditions warrant their remaining. It is difficult to predict whether such a base can be found and adopted, but an inroad has already been made in the extension of pasturage activities. While Becedas's terrain is unsuitable for mechanized agriculture, it is excellent for cattle raising. The perpetually well-watered slopes of Peña Negra provide fine pasturage, and much of the presently cultivated farmland could readily be converted into meadow. If credit can be awarded toward the purchase of cows, and the marketing of milk can be further facilitated along the lines already established, Becedas could become a major dairy producer.

Under favorable circumstances, Becedas's economy might then become not too difficult from that of many Swiss communities, in which tourism and pasturage activities have become wedded. Blessed with an abundance of creeks and streams, situated in a valley of trees and deep green meadows, refreshed by cool mountain breezes in summertime, and located within easy access of the urban centers of Castile, Becedas may well survive, albeit in much altered form, the demographic and economic upheavals it presently endures.

References

Arensberg, Conrad
  1959 *The Irish countryman: An anthropological study.* Gloucester, Mass.: Peter Smith.
Arensberg, Conrad, and Solon Kimball
  1968 *Family and Community Ireland.* 2nd ed. Cambridge, Mass.: Harvard Univ. Press.
Anderson, Barbara Gallatin
  1956 A survey of Italian godparenthood. *Papers of the Kroeber Anthropological Society* 15: 1–110.
Anderson, Robert T.
  1966 Rotating credit associations in India. *Economic Development and Cultural Change* 14: 334–339.
Anderson, Robert T., and Barbara G. Anderson
  1964 *The vanishing village: A Danish maritime community.* Seattle: Univ. of Washington Press.
  1966 *Bus stop for Paris: The transformation of a French village.* Garden City, N.Y.: Doubleday (Anchor Books).
Arguedas, José María
  1968 *Las comunidades de España y del Peru.* Lima: Universidad Nacional de San Marcos.

Bailey, F. G.
1971 Gifts and poison. *In Gifts and poison: The politics of reputation*, edited by F. G. Bailey. New York: Schocken Books. Pp. 1–25.
Banfield, Edward C.
1958 *The moral basis of a backward society*. New York: Free Press.
Bascom, William
1952 The esusu: A credit institution of the Yoruba. *Journal of the Royal Anthropological Institute* 82: 63–70.
Benítez Cano, Fernando
1967 La emigración en la comarca extremeña conocida con el nombre de "La Siberia." *Estudios Geográficos* 28(108): 357–377.
Bloch, Marc
1966 *French rural history: An essay on its basic characteristics*. Berkeley and Los Angeles: Univ. of California Press.
Brandes, Judith B.
n.d. Sonzay: Village in transition. Unpublished Manuscript.
Brandes, Stanley H.
1968 Tzintzuntzan wedding: A study in cultural complexity. *Papers of the Kroeber Anthropological Society* 39: 30–53.
1973a Social structure and interpersonal relations in Navanogal (Spain). *American Anthropologist* 75(3): 750–765.
1973b Wedding ritual and social structure in a Castilian peasant village. *Anthropological Quarterly* 46(2): 65–74.
1975 The structural and demographic implications of nicknames in Navanogal, Spain. *American Ethnologist* 2(1). Forthcoming.
Campbell, J. K.
1964 *Honour, family and patronage: A study of institutions and moral values in a Greek mountain community*. Oxford: Univ. of Oxford Press (Clarendon).
Caro Baroja, Julio
1949 Los arados españoles: Sus tipos y repartición. *Revista de Dialectología y Tradiciones Populares* 5(1): 3–96.
1957 El sociocentrismo de los pueblos españoles. *In Razas, pueblos, linajes*. Madrid: Revista de Occidente.
1963 The city and the country: Reflexions on some ancient commonplaces. *In Mediterranean countrymen*, edited by Julian Pitt-Rivers. Paris and The Hague: Mouton. Pp. 27–40.
Chayanov, A. V.
1966 *The theory of peasant economy*. Translated by Organizatsiia Krestianskogo Khoziaistva. Homewood, Ill.: Irwin.
Cohen, Yehudi
1961 Patterns of friendship. *In Social structure and personality: A casebook*, edited by Yehudi Cohen. New York: Holt. Pp. 351–386.
Colclough, N. T.
1971 Social mobility and social control in a southern Italian village. *In Gifts and poison: The politics of reputation*, edited by F. G. Bailey. New York: Schocken Books. Pp. 212–230.
Costa y Martínez, Joaquín
1915 *Colectivismo agrario en España*. Madrid: Biblioteca Costa.

Dalton, George
1974 How exactly are peasants 'exploited'? *American Anthropologist* 76(3): 553–561.
De Vos, George
1960 The relation of guilt toward parents to achievement and arranged marriage among the Japanese. *Psychiatry* 23: 287–301.
Deane, Shirley
1965 *In a Corsican village.* New York: Vanguard Press.
Del Campo Urbano, Salustiano
1972 Composición, dinámica y distribución de la población española. In *La España de los años 70: La sociedad*, edited by M. Fraga Iribarne, J. Velarde Fuertes, and S. del Campo Urbano. Vol. 1. Madrid: Editorial Moneda y Crédito. Pp. 15–145.
Dias, Jorge
1948 *Vilarinho da Furna: Uma alderia comunitaria.* Porto: Instituto de Alta Cultura.
1953 *Rio de Onor: Comunitarismo agro–pastoril.* Porto: Instituto de Alta Cultura.
Díaz, May N.
1966 *Tonalá: Conservatism, responsibility, and authority in a Mexican town.* Berkeley and Los Angeles: Univ. of California Press.
Díaz Lasa, María Carmen
1958 Costumbres de boda en Navaluenga (Avila). *Revista de Dialectología y Tradiciones Populares* 14(1–2): 164–169.
Díez Nicolás, Juan
1972 La urbanización el urbanismo en la década de los 70. In *La España de los años 70: La sociedad*, edited by M. Fraga Iribarne, J. Velarde Fuertes, and S. del Campo Urbano. Vol. 1. Madrid: Editorial Moneda y Crédito. Pp. 147–218.
Dorian, Nancy C.
1970 A substitute name system in the Scottish Highlands. *American Anthropologist* 72: 303–319.
Douglass, William A.
1969 *Death in Murélaga: Funerary ritual in a Spanish Basque village.* Seattle: Univ. of Washington Press.
Durkheim, Emile
1961 *The elementary forms of the religious life.* [1893] Translated by Joseph Ward Swain. New York: Collier Books.
1964 *The division of labor in society.* [1893] Translated by George Simpson. Glencoe, Ill.: Free Press.
Embree, John F.
1939 *Suye Mura: A Japanese village.* Chicago: Univ. of Chicago Press.
Ensenada, Marqués de la
1751 *Catastro, Becedas.* 5 vols. Avila: Archives of the Casa de la Cultura.
Erasmus, Charles
1956 Culture structure and process: The occurrence and disappearance of reciprocal farm labor. *Southwestern Journal of Anthropology* 12: 444–469.
Esteban Sánchez, Wenceslao
1957 Becedas. *Diccionario geográfico de España* 4: 252–253. Madrid.

Fél, Edit, and Tamas Hofer
    1969   Proper peasants: Traditional life in a Hungarian village. Chicago: Aldine.
Firth, Raymond
    1963   Elements of social organization. Boston: Beacon Press.
Flores, Xavier
    1969   Estructura socioeconómica de la agricultura española. Barcelona: Ediciones
           Peninsular.
Foster, George M.
    1953a Cofradía and compradrazgo in Spain and Spanish America. Southwestern
           Journal of Anthropology 9:1–28.
    1953b What is folk culture? American Anthropologist 55: 159–173.
    1960   Culture and conquest: America's Spanish heritage. New York: Wenner–
           Gren Foundation, Viking Fund Publications in Anthropology, No.
           27.
    1961a The dyadic contract: A model for the social structure of a Mexican peasant
           village. American Anthropologist 63: 1173–1192.
    1961b Interpersonal relations in peasant society. Human Organization 19: 174–178.
    1963   The dyadic contract. II Patron–client relationship. American Anthropologist
           65: 1280–1294.
    1964a Speech forms and perception of social distance in a Spanish-speaking Mexi-
           can village. Southwestern Journal of Anthropology 20: 107–122.
    1964b Treasure tales, and the image of the static economy in a Mexican peasant
           community. Journal of American Folklore 77: 39–44.
    1965   Peasant society and the image of limited good. American Anthropologist 67:
           293–315.
    1967a Introduction: What is a peasant? In Peasant society: A reader, edited by
           Jack M. Potter, May N. Díaz, and George M. Foster. Boston: Little, Brown.
           Pp. 2–14.
    1967b Tzintzuntzan: Mexican peasants in a changing world. Boston: Little, Brown.
    1973   Traditional societies and technological change. 2nd ed. New York, Evan-
           ston, and London: Harper.
Frankenberg, Ronald
    1966   Communities in Britain. Middlesex and Baltimore: Penguin Books.
Franklin, S. H.
    1969   The European peasantry: The final phase. London: Methuen.
Freeman, Susan Tax
    1968   Religious aspects of the social organization of a Castilian village. American
           Anthropologist 70: 34–49.
    1970   Neighbors: The social contract in a Castilian hamlet. Chicago: Univ. of
           Chicago Press.
Friedl, Ernestine
    1959   The role of kinship in the transmission of national culture to rural villages
           in mainland Greece. American Anthropologist 61: 30–38.
    1964   Lagging emulation in post-peasant society. American Anthropologist 66:
           569–586.
Fromm, Erich, and Michael Maccoby
    1970   Social character in a Mexican village: A sociopsychoanalytic study. Engle-
           wood Cliffs, N. J.: Prentice–Hall.
Fuente Arrimadas, Nicolás de la
    1925   Fisiografía e historia del Barco de Avila. 2 vols. Avila.

Galeskie, Boguslaw
  1971 Social organization and rural social change. In *Peasants and peasant societies*, edited by Teodor Shanin. Middlesex and Baltimore: Penguin Books.
García Fernández, Jesús
  1964 El movimiento migratorio de trabajadores en España. *Estudios Geográficos* 25(95): 139–174.
Geertz, Clifford
  1962 The rotating credit association: A "middle rung" in economic development. *Economic Development and Social Change* 10: 241–263.
Gómez–Tabanera, J. M. *et. al.*
  1967 *Migración y sociedad en la Galicia contemporánea.* Madrid: Ediciones Guadarrama.
González–Rothvoss, Mariano
  1953 Influencia de la emigración en el crecimiento de la población española en los ultimos cien anos (1850–1950). *Revista Internacional de Sociología* 41: 61–84.
Goody, Jack
  1962 *Death, property, and the ancestors.* Palo Alto: Stanford Univ. Press.
Hajnal, John
  1964 European marriage patterns in perspective. In *Population in history*, edited by D. V. Glass and D. E. C. Eversley. London: Arnold Press. Pp. 101–143.
Halpern, Joel M.
  1967a *The changing village community.* Englewood Cliffs, N.J.: Prentice-Hall.
  1967b *The Serbian village: Social and cultural change in a Yugoslav community.* New York, Evanston, and London: Harper.
Hammel, Eugene A., and Charles Yarbrough
  1973 Social mobility and the durability of family ties. *Journal of Anthropological Research* 29(3): 145–163.
Instituto Nacional de Estadística
  1972 *España: Anuario estadístico.* Madrid.
Kenny, Michael
  1966 *A Spanish tapestry: Town and country in Castile.* New York, Evanston, and London: Harper.
  1972 The return of the Spanish emigrant. *Nord Nytt* 2: 101–129.
Klein, Julius
  1920 *The Mesta: A study in Spanish economic history.* Cambridge, Mass.: Harvard Economic Studies, Vol. 20.
Kroeber, Alfred
  1948 *Anthropology.* New York: Harcourt.
Linz, Juan J., and Jose Cazorla
  1968–1969 Religiosidad y estructura social en Andalucía: La practica religiosa. *Anales de Sociología* 4(4–5): 75–96.
Lisón Tolosana, Carmelo
  1966 *Belmonte de los Caballeros: A sociological study of a Spanish town.* Oxford: Oxford Univ. Press (Clarendon).
Lopreato, Joseph
  1967 *Peasants no more: Social class and social change in an underdeveloped society.* San Francisco: Chandler.
Lorca, Federico García
  1955 *Three tragedies: Blood wedding, Yerma, Bernarda Alba.* Translated by

James Graham–Lujan Richard and L. O'Connell. New York: New Directions.

Madoz, Pascual
1845–1850 *Diccionario geográfico–estadístico–histórico de España y sus posesiones ultra-mar.* 16 vols. Madrid.

Mahr, August C.
1965 Origin and significance of Pennsylvania Dutch barn symbols. In *The study of folklore,* edited by Alan Dundes. Englewood Cliffs, N.J.: Prentice–Hall. Pp. 373–399.

Maine, Henry
1861 *Ancient Law.* London: J. Murray.

Marcos de Sande, Moisés
1958 Costumbres de boda en La Alberca (Salamanca). *Revista de Dialectología y Tradiciones Populares* 14(1–2): 169–173.

Marriott, McKim
1969 Little communities in an indigneous civilization. In *Village India,* edited by McKim Marriott. Chicago: Univ. of Chicago Press. Pp. 171–222.

Martín Angulo, Evaristo
1963 Becedas. In *Ofrenda a la Santísima Virgen del Castañar.* Vol. 2. Béjar. Pp. 531–533.

Martínez Marí, José María
1966 La inmigración en el área de Barcelona. *Estudios Geográficos* 27(105): 541–546.

Mellado, Francisco de Paula
1845 *España geográfica, histórica, esadística y pintoresca.* Madrid.

Mendras, Henri
1970 *The vanishing peasant: Innovation and change in French agriculture.* Translated by Jean Lerner. Cambridge, Mass.: MIT Press.

Miñano, Sebastián de
1826–1829 *Diccionario geográfico de España y Portugal.* 11 vols. Madrid.

Ministerio de Hacienda de Avila
1965 Catastro de la riqueza rústica. Provincia de Avila, Partido Judicial de Barco de Avila, Término Municipal de Becedas.

Mintz, Sidney W., and Eric R. Wolf
1950 An analysis of ritual co-parenthood (compadrazgo). *Southwestern Journal of Anthropology* 6: 341–368.

Moore, Wilbert E.
1965 *The impact of industry.* Englewood Cliffs, N.J.: Prentice–Hall.

Murray, Henry A.
1943 *Thematic apperception test.* Cambridge, Mass.: Harvard Univ. Press.

Parsons, Talcott, and Robert F. Bales
1955 *Family socialization and interaction process.* Glencoe, Ill.: Free Press.

Pérez–Díaz, Víctor M.
1969 *Emigración y sociedad en la Tierra de Campos: Estudio de un proceso migratorio y un proceso de cambio social.* Madrid: Estudios del Instituto de Desarrollo Económico.

1971 *Emigración y cambio social.* Barcelona: Ediciones Ariel.

1972 *Estructura social del campo y éxodo rural: Estudio de un pueblo de Castilla.* Rev. ed. Madrid: Editorial Tecnos.

Peristiany, J. G. (Editor)
1965 *Honour and shame: The values of Mediterranean society.* London: Weidenfeld and Nicolson.

Pitt–Rivers, Julian A.
1958 Ritual kinship in Spain. *Transactions of the New York Academy of Sciences, Series II* 20: 424–431.
1961 *People of the sierra.* Chicago: Univ. of Chicago Press.

Radcliffe–Brown, A. R.
1965 *Structure and function in primitive society.* New York: Free Press.

Redfield, Robert
1941 *The folk culture of Yucatan.* Chicago: Univ. of Chicago Press.
1947 The folk society. *American Journal of Sociology* 52: 293–308.
1956 *Peasant society and culture.* Chicago: Univ. of Chicago Press.

Redfield, Robert, and Milton Singer
1954 The cultural role of cities. *Economic Development and Cultural Change* 3: 53–73.

Riegelhaupt, Joyce F.
1967 Prognosticative calendar systems II. *American Anthropologist* 69: 82–83.
1973 Festas and Padres: The organization of religious action in a Portuguese parish. *American Anthropologist* 75(3): 835–852.

Saul, John S., and Roger Woods
1971 African peasantries. In *Peasants and peasant societies*, edited by Teodor Shanin. Middlesex and Baltimore: Penguin Books. Pp. 103–114.

Sennett, Richard, and Jonathan Cobb
1972 *The hidden injuries of class.* New York: Vantage Books.

Shanin, Teodor
1971 Peasantry as a political factor. In *Peasants and peasant societies*, edited by Teodor Shanin. Middlesex and Baltimore: Penguin Books. Pp. 238–263.

Siguán Soler, Miguel
1966 Las raíces de la emigración campesina. *Estudios Geográficos* 27 (105): 533–540.

Simic, Andrei
1973 *The peasant urbanites: A study of rural–urban mobility in Serbia.* New York and London: Seminar Press.

Taboada, Jesús
1969 La matanza del cerdo en Galicia. *Revista de Dialectología y Tradiciones Populares* 25(1–2): 89–106.

Teresa de Avila, Saint
1957 *The life of Saint Teresa of Avila by herself.* Translated by J. M. Cohen. Middlesex and Baltimore: Penguin Books.

Tilly, Charles
1973 Do communities act? Ann Arbor: Center for Research on Social Organization Working Paper #92. Mimeo.
1974 Rural collective action in modern Europe. Ann Arbor: Center for Research on Social Organization Working Paper #96. Mimeo.

Tilly, Charles, and C. Harold Brown
1974 On uprooting, kinship, and the auspices of migration. In *An urban world*, edited by Charles Tilly. Boston: Little, Brown. Pp. 108–133.

Tönnies, Ferdinand
  1963 *Community and society.* [1877] Translated by Charles P. Loomis. New
          York, Evanston, and London: Harper.
Unamuno, Miguel de
  1968 Andanzas y visiones españolas. Madrid: Espasa-Calpe Colección Austral,
          no. 160.
Van Gennep, Arnold
  1960 *The rites of passage.* Translated by Monika B. Vizedom and Gabrielle L.
          Caffee. Chicago: Univ. of Chicago Press.
Verga, Giovanni
  1964 *The house by the medlar tree.* Translated by Raymond Rosenthal. New
          York: Signet Classics.
Webber, Melvin *et al.*
  1964 *Explorations into urban structure.* Philadelphia: Univ. of Pennsylvania
          Press.
Weber, Max
  1958 Capitalism and rural society in Germany. In *From Max Weber: Essays in
          sociology,* edited by H. H. Gerth and C. Wright Mills. New York: Oxford
          Univ. Press. Pp. 363–385.
Wolf, Eric R.
  1955 Types of Latin American peasantry: A preliminary discussion. *American
          Anthropologist* 57: 452–471.
  1956 Aspects of group relations in a complex society: Mexico. *American Anthro-
          pologist* 58: 1065–1078.
  1957 Closed corporate peasant communities in Mesoamerica and Central Java.
          Southwestern Journal of Anthropology 13(1): 1–18.
  1966 *Peasants.* Englewood Cliffs, N.J.: Prentice–Hall.

Glossary of Spanish Terms

adelanta'o: advanced, progressive; contraction of *adelantado*
adra: rotation of communal labor responsibilities by household (Sierra Ministra)
aguacil: variant of standard Spanish *alguacil*; bailiff
aguador: community irrigation officer; literally, "water man"
alcalde: mayor
aliviar el luto: gradually to reduce mourning restrictions
almuerzo: morning meal
ambiente: ambiance, liveliness and activity
a medias: by halves, sharecropped
amigo de verdad: true friend
amonestación: marriage banns; man's farewell celebration to village bachelors, in honor of his impending wedding
arado: plow
aricar: to harrow
arras: small coins presented to the bride by the groom during their wedding ceremony
atrasa'o: backwards, behind the times; contraction of *atrasado*

ayuntamiento: municipal government; town hall
barrio: quarter, neighborhood
bautizo: baptism
brasero: brasier
burro: donkey; tall ladder used for harvesting fruit
cabañuelas: weather prognostication
cabrero: goatherd
calvotá: annual *mozo* excursion and chestnut roast on All Saints' Day
cañada: cattle path
cantero: one of the two types of irrigation furrow pattern used on level land
carro: animal-drawn cart
catastro: property register used for purposes of taxation
cena: evening meal
centro comarcal: regional center
cerillas: matches
cerrao: land devoted to rye cultivation
changarro: cow bell
cocido: stew made usually with meat, sausages, potatoes, and chick peas
cocina bilbaina: cast iron, wood-burning stove; literally, "Bilbao stove"
comida: midday meal
comisiones: commercial contracts made between village middlemen and outside buyers
comisionistas: village middlemen
compadrazgo: the fictive kinship system operating through co-godparenthood
compadre: a person to whom one is bound through the compadrazgo; literally, "co-parent"; in Becedas, close friend
confianza: trust
confirmación: confirmation
convite: party, open house
corito: hired reaper, literally "timid one"
correo: mail; bus
correr las cintas: literally, "running the ribbons"; annual *quinto* Carnaval event in which the young men, on horseback, attempt to spike small rings
cosecha: harvest, harvest time; (Becedas) bean and potato harvest
cuadra: small barn attached to house
cuadrilla: clique of unmarried youths
curandero(a): folk medical practitioner
cursillo: literally, "little course"; weekend-long, Church-sponsored religious retreat
dar entre parra y parra: to hoe; literally, "to strike between grapevine and grapevine"

dar las vistas: literally, "to tell the intentions"; (for the groom's parents) to visit the bride two weeks prior to the wedding

dar tierra: literally, "to strike earth"; to weed and till the ground with a plow, after sowing

dehesa: meadow

dental: wooden foundation for the iron plowshare

denunciado: denounced; anonymously turned in to civil authorities

dinero presta'o: borrowed money; used to describe *ofrecijo* payments

domicilio: house

dulzaina: traditional flute-like wind instrument

duro: five-peseta coin

egoismo: selfishness

enchufe: contact; influential person; literally, "electrical plug"

entierro de trés: third or highest-ranking funeral; funeral conducted by three priests

entierro entero: full-scale funeral; second-ranking of the three traditional funeral types

envidia: envy

eras: threshing floor

estilos: money requested by wedding guests of the marriage godfather

estúpido: stupid, callous

fanega: traditional unit of land measurement, varying regionally; in Becedas, the amount of land on which 100 kilos of potato tubers can be sown

forastero: stranger, outsider; one not of the *pueblo*

gordo(a): fat; (m.) the highest state lottery prize

guadaña: scythe

hacer las presas: repairing the irrigation canals; literally, "building the dams"

Hermandad: literally, "brotherhood"; state-organized syndicalist union of *pueblo* farmers; building in which the union is housed

hijo(a) del pueblo: literally, "son (daughter) of the *pueblo*"; one born in the *pueblo*, native to a particular *pueblo*

horca: wooden forked prop for tree branches

hornazo: traditional Easter cake; village-wide picnic outing on Easter Sunday

huerta: irrigated orchard

huerto: small garden located within confines of the village settlement

huevos: eggs, testicles

inflamación de las tripas: intestinal inflammation, an unpleasant bodily disorder manifested by a corpse

jornalero: day laborer

labrador: farmer; small-scale independent peasant proprietor

leche mingá: bread soaked in milk; literally, "soft-breaded milk," after the standard Spanish *leche migada*

limpiar: to winnow; to clean

linar: any irrigated, treeless land parcel; literally, "flax field"

lote: lot, share

luto: mourning; period of mourning

madrina: godmother

manga: conical religious banner carried in processions; sleeve

marica: sissy

mata: parcel of woodland

matanza: pig slaughter; family celebration surrounding the annual pig slaughter

mayo: May; maypole

medio entierro: simplest and lowest ranking of the three traditional funeral types; literally, "half funeral"

merienda: late afternoon snack

Mesta: once powerful Spanish sheep-owners guild

mierda: dirt; shit

mísere: downtrodden; stingy

mote: nickname

mozo(a): young unmarried man (woman); (m.) member of the village bachelor's society

municipio: municipality; lowest level discrete political-administrative entity in Spain

naríz: nose

novio (a): sweetheart; fiancé(e); groom (bride)

ofrecijo: monetary wedding gift; event at which such gift is publicly presented

orejera: wooden dowels on the plow used to regulate the depth and width of furrows

orgulloso: haughty, condescending

oveja: sheep

ovejero: one who deals in or cares for sheep

padrino: godfather

paella: a rice entree, native to Valencia, served at feasts; usually prepared with vegetables and any combination of chicken, pork, sausage, and shellfish

palaera: the simpler, though less productive, of the two types of irrigation furrow pattern used on level land

partido judicial: judicial district

pastos: pastures; (Becedas) communally owned pastures

patria chica: literally, "small country"; town, village, or hamlet of one's birth

pedir el chorizo: literally, "to beg for the sausage"; Carnaval event in which *quintos* ask villagers for donations of food and money

peonada: the area of grassland that one man, using a scythe, can reap in a day

pico: peak

pijardo: payment forced by village *mozos* upon outsider suitors for the privilege of courting village girls

pipos blancos: navy beans

pobres: the poor, a traditional segment of the Becedas populace

porquero: pigherd

practicante: trained and licensed medical practitioner, who might be classified somewhere between our categories of nurse and doctor

pregón: public announcement

primo(a) hermano(a): first cousin

promesa: religious vow usually made to a saint in return for some favor

pueblo: town, village; people of a town or village

quinto(a): age-mate; (m.) military conscript

rajar: to chatter; to slice

ramos: branches; (Becedas) Spanish broom

rayos: X-rays

recogerse: to take refuge, as from some undesirable fate

recolección: fruit harvest

regadera: irrigation canal

regadío: irrigated terrain

regadores públicos: public irrigators (Pyrenees)

reja: plowshare

reloj: clock, watch

ricos: the rich, a traditional social category of Becedas

roña: tightwad; baptismal event in which the godmother tosses candy and coins to the village children

ronda: early morning songfest of village youths

secano: dry land, unirrigated land

señorío: dominion of a lord

sentido: understanding or reason

sierra: mountain range; (Becedas) dry scrubland where Spanish broom is found

siesta: afternoon nap; colloq., 24-hour period

sopas: garlic-flavored broth in which bread is soaked

sueldo: salary

tablero: a type of irrigation furrow pattern used on slopes

término: town or village boundaries; that territory subject to the authority of an *ayuntamiento*.

tertulia: regular social gathering of a small group

tierra: land; (Becedas) unirrigated parcel planted with wheat or barley

tocar a diana: literally, "to play reveille"; *quinto* merrymaking on New Year's morning

toro: bull

trapero: dealer in or maker of cloth or rags

trapo: cloth, rag

trillo: wooden spike-toothed threshing sledge of ancient Roman design

tú: second-person singular pronoun, an intimate and informal mode of address

Usted: third-person singular pronoun, a respectful and distance-creating mode of address

vaca de trabajo: work cow

vaca suiza: Swiss cow, primarily kept for milk and calves

vaquero: cowherd

vecino(a): neighbor; *pueblo* resident; (m.) household head

vega: fertile plain

ventas ambulantes: movable salesstands

vereneante(a): summer visitor

vigilante: head *aguador*, and chief irrigation coordinator for the village.

Index